To: Sterling

From: The Alexanders

Congratulations on your baptism

POPSICLES
BLACK HOLES
& BURNT TOAST

Other books by Kay D. Rizzo:

Chloe Celeste Chronicles
Chloe May Chronicles
Face to Face With Forgiveness
For His Honor
Go for the Gold!
I Will Die Free
More Than Mountains
On Wings of Praise
Praise a la Carte
Secret Dreams of Dolly Spencer
She Said No

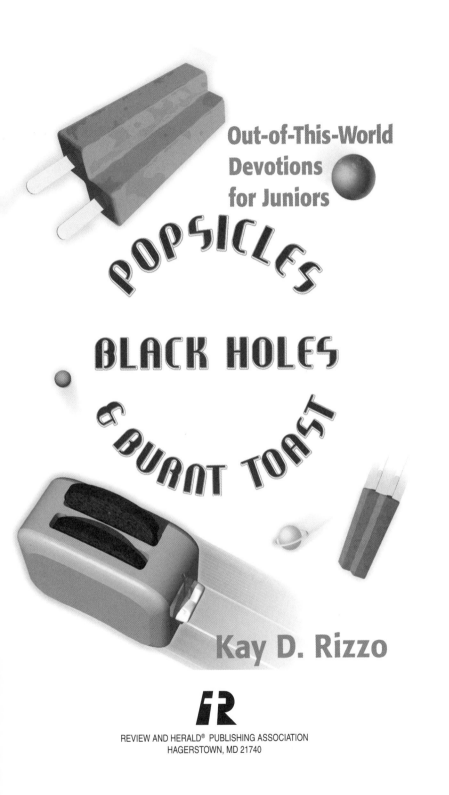

Out-of-This-World
Devotions
for Juniors

POPSICLES

BLACK HOLES

& BURNT TOAST

Kay D. Rizzo

ℛ

REVIEW AND HERALD® PUBLISHING ASSOCIATION
HAGERSTOWN, MD 21740

This book was
Edited by Andy Nash
Copyedited by Jocelyn Fay and Lori Halvorsen
Designed by Mark O'Connor
Cover art by Terrill Thomas
Electronic makeup by Shirley M. Bolivar
Typeset: 11.5/14 Cheltenham

PRINTED IN U.S.A.

06 05 04 03 02   5 4 3 2 1

R&H Cataloging Service
Rizzo, Kay Darlene, 1945-
    Popsicles, black holes, and burnt toast

    1. Teenagers—Prayerbooks and devotions—English.   2. Devotional
calendars—Juvenile literature.   I. Title.

242.6

ISBN 0-8280-1574-0

DEDICATION

To Jarod, my continual source of joy and wonder . . .
Love, Grandma

ACKNOWLEDGMENTS

A special thank-you
to Van Quine and Judith Wood, reference desk librarians
at the Visalia, California, branch of the Tulare County Library,
for helping me track down interesting trivia
and historical anecdotes for this book.

DEAR READER.

What does "out of this world" mean to you? To me, it means expanding my thinking into the universe of the incredible! It means going beyond my physical limitations—doing, seeing, and tasting the unbelievable!

Sure sounds like heaven, doesn't it?

God says, "No eye has seen, no ear has heard, no mind has conceived what God has prepared for those who love him" (1 Corinthians 2:9, NIV). "Let your imaginations go wild," God urges, "and even then you will not have even a *glimpse* of how wonderful heaven will be!"

So that's what we're going to do! This year you and I will travel through time and space. Together, we'll expand our minds into a universe overflowing with God's love and His unimaginable possibilities. Fasten your seatbelt! We're in for an incredible journey that's *out of this world!*

Your friend,
Kay Rizzo

Out of This World

What no one ever saw or heard, what no one ever thought could happen, is the very thing God prepared for those who love him. 1 Corinthians 2:9, TEV.

Ya gotta see it! It's out of this world!" What was my friend talking about? A pink-and-white 1958 Plymouth with rocket ship fins.

In 2003 a 1958 Plymouth is ancient history, like a Model A or a Hudson. Not too many around in working order. Most have been crushed and recycled into newer cars also described as "out of this world!"

What's out of this world to me? A PC that translates my thoughts into hard copy? A cellular phone that replicates dinner? Here's a list of five ideas that would be out of this world to me.

1. A slice of chocolate cheese cake with hot fudge pecan sauce—sugar-free, calorie-free, and packed with Vitamin C.

2. Swimming with dolphins.

3. Being guest pianist for the London Philharmonic Orchestra.

4. Snowboarding down Mount McKinley.

5. Playing hopscotch on the moon.

What would you include in your out-of-this-world list? According to today's text, no matter how crazy our ideas are, we haven't seen, heard, or imagined how wild God's plans are for us. His ideas are totally out of this world.

2 January

A Missile in the Laundry Basket

You will be able to extinguish all the flaming arrows of the evil one. Ephesians 6:16, NASB.

Myra, a foreign exchange student, returned to Kosovo the week war broke out between the Serbs and the Kosovars. Having given her heart to Jesus while in the United States, the high school junior was eager to share her new faith with her family.

Her opportunity came when the Serbian army fired on a Kosovar neighborhood near Myra's home. At the first sound of gunfire Myra and her family ran into their windowless laundry room and crouched beside the washing machine.

While Myra prayed for protection a Serb missile shot through their parlor window and skittered down the hall to the washroom, landing in a basket of clean clothes. Myra squealed with joy. "See, Dad? My God did protect us."

"It was a dud," her father scoffed.

When the attack ended, he tossed the unexploded bomb into the street. Later the town militia retrieved the missile and tossed it onto a scrap heap at the edge of town, where the "dud" exploded, sending fragments and debris in all directions.

No one can convince Myra that God's incredible promises are out of this world. Even her parents are wondering if their daughter might be right.

Oops, Goofed Again

The Lord our God is merciful and forgiving even though we have rebelled against him. Daniel 9:9, NIV.

I bought a blouse with tiny pleats down the front. After wearing it once, I washed it. Poof! The pleats disappeared in the machine. I hadn't noticed that the tag on the blouse said, "Dry-clean only." Oops! I goofed.

I tried to boil an egg in my microwave. *Baboom!* The door flew open and peppered my kitchen counters, floor, and ceiling with egg fragments. The microwave's guidebook said *not* to boil eggs. Oops! I goofed.

One night I accidentally brushed my teeth with Cortaid, an anti-itch cream. Oops! Goofed again.

Researchers say one out of every six choices we make will be wrong. So what does a perfect God do with imperfect children? He forgives, that's what. Even when I don't follow the advice He gave in His "manual," He forgives.

Best of all, I don't need to sleep on a bed of nails or walk on sizzling hot coals or wear itchy underwear to earn His forgiveness. All I do is ask, and my goofs are forgotten. Zip! Just like that. Only an out-of-this-world God could love His kids that much. Only an out-of-this-world God could so graciously forgive.

Did It Hurt?

If we confess our sins, he is faithful and just and will forgive us our sins. 1 John 1:9, NIV.

The parents of 3-year-old Erin give Christian concerts around the world. Before one concert Erin's mother took the girl for a walk to occupy her attention. In the church's entryway Erin spotted a full-sized, carved, wooden statue of Jesus hanging on the cross.

"That's Jesus, isn't it, Mommy?" she asked.

"Yes, honey."

Barely coming to the statue's knees, tiny Erin asked to be lifted for a better view. Her mother obliged. Gently Erin touched the carved fingers and hands. Her fingers touched the nails protruding from His hands. "That hurt Jesus, didn't it, Mommy?"

"Yes, it did, honey."

The child studied the nails and hands. "Jesus hurt for me, didn't He? He loves me that much!"

Out of the mouth of a baby. Why did Jesus allow the demons of hell to put Him on a cross? Love. He loves us so much that He'd rather die than lose us.

Can I understand that love? Can you? You and I will spend all of eternity and still not uncover the mystery of God's love. And yet even a 3-year-old can understand enough to accept God's love and His sacrifice.

Just Call Me Grace

It is through the grace of our Lord Jesus that we are saved. Acts 15:11, NIV.

Do you ever feel you can't do anything right? I do.

When I'm around footstools, puppies, and crawling babies, beware! If it's trippable, I trip over it. If it's spillable, I spill it. And if it's breakable, hide it when I come to visit.

Perhaps I'm exaggerating, but some days I feel that way.

I certainly did the day I was running late and rushed to the front of the crowded meeting hall only to catch my shoe on the tangle of microphone cords atop the small stage.

I felt myself falling but couldn't stop. I fell flat on my face before my stunned audience.

Several men leaped to my aid. When I regained my footing and my composure, I assured the audience I was fine. "Only my dignity is bruised," I said. "Just call me grace."

Everyone laughed. I called myself grace, meaning graceful—which I definitely was not. God's grace has little to do with my clumsiness and everything to do with His forgiveness and His generosity. He doesn't have to forgive me; He just wants to. And when He doles out His goodness, He doesn't use a teaspoon. He pours out His grace onto us from thousand-gallon barrels. Why? He can't help Himself. He loves us that much.

Why Me?

This is how much God loved the world: He gave his Son, his one and only Son. And this is why: so that no one need be destroyed; by believing in him, anyone can have whole and lasting life. John 3:16, Message.

Andrew Parker sat with his head buried in his hands. "The forgiveness you talk about may forgive little kids for stealing cookies or pickpockets for lifting wallets, but God's grace can't include me."

"Of course it does," the pastor replied. "The text says, 'All who believe.' That includes everyone."

"You don't know what I did." The 60-year-old man's voice broke with emotion. "During the Vietnam War I became separated from my unit and came upon a chapel in the jungle. A dozen or so old men, women, and children were inside praying."

The man hesitated. "A few days earlier my best friend had died from a hand grenade thrown into a crowded bus. When I saw those Vietnamese praying, I flew into a rage and opened fire, mowing them down in less than a minute. Can your God forgive that?"

The preacher nodded. "All means all, Andrew. If God can't forgive your sin, He can't forgive anyone's. He's done His part; now it's up to you."

I'm glad God's grace includes Andrew. And I'm so very thankful He forgives me, too. How about you?

Have I Got a Deal for You!

The wall was jasper, the color of Glory, and the City was pure gold. . . . The main street of the City was pure gold, translucent as glass. Revelation 20:18-21, Message.

Recently more than 600 people in Italy paid $10,000 apiece for the first tourist flight to Mars. According to the Italian police, the would-be space travelers were told they would spend their next vacation on Mars, amid the splendors of ruined temples and painted deserts.

"Ride Martian camels from oasis to oasis. Explore mysterious canals and enjoy marvelous Martian sunsets. Trips to the moon are also available." Authorities believed the con artists made more than $6 million before they were caught. Wow! What a deal—at least for the con artists.

Did you know that God has a deal for you, too? And it is literally out of this world. But if you don't know Him, you might think it's too fantastic to believe too, like the one in Italy. But once you become acquainted with Jesus Christ, once you let Him into your heart and believe how much He loves you, you will know that His plan is real. And there's no $10,000 price tag attached. It's absolutely free to those who love Him. Now, that's a deal you can't refuse. And it's way out of this world.

Earthquake!

Find out for yourself how good the Lord is. Happy are those who find safety with him. Psalm 34:8, TEV.

One morning before dawn friends of mine awoke to find their bed shaking, walls weaving, and dishes, windows, and furniture crashing throughout the house. Terrified, John's first thought was *Run for cover!* When he tried to, he found himself trapped.

His frightened wife's first thought was *John! I need John!* She gripped his arm for all she was worth.

As their world tumbled down around them, my friends wrestled with each other, she clinging to his arm and he struggling to escape the house. Until the earthquake hit, Janice and John had no idea they'd react in opposition to each other.

Both were right, and both were wrong. Leaping out of bed in bare feet, John could have cut his feet on broken glass. But if they had stayed in bed instead of fleeing for cover, the bedroom ceiling might have come crashing down on their heads.

Their first instincts might have been bad, but their second wasn't. And that was to pray. God was there for them. They survived the earthquake with only a few broken dishes and a broken water line. God kept them safe.

Morning Prayer

I am with you; that is all you need. My power shows up best in weak people. 2 Corinthians 12:9, TLB.

Dear Lord,
      So far today, God, I've done all right.
      I haven't gossiped, haven't lost my temper,
      Haven't been greedy, grumpy, nasty, or selfish.
      I'm really happy about that.
      But in a few minutes, God,
      I'm going to get out of bed, and from then on,
      I'm going to need a lot more help.
                          —Anonymous

This prayer off the Internet speaks to me. How about you? From the minute you wake up in the morning, no matter how hard you try to do what you know is right, why do you do the very thing you shouldn't? I've felt that way lots of times too. So did the great New Testament preacher Paul.

In today's text he tells spiritual wimps like me how to build supernatural muscles. All we need to do is admit we can't fight our pesky battles alone, then ask for God's out-of-this-world power. And it's ours—just for the asking! God's mighty power sends those dastardly little demons scurrying back to where they came from; back to where they belong!

Lessons from Noah's Ark

When the bow is in the cloud, . . . I will . . . remember the ever-lasting covenant between God and every living creature . . . on the earth. Genesis 9:16, NASB.

The story of Noah and his incredible boat is full of lessons about God and about life. Here's 10 to think about:

1. When God tells you to do something, do it. It wasn't raining when Noah built the ark.

2. God will give you what you need to do the job. Remember, the ark was built by amateurs, while the *Titanic* was built by professionals.

3. Noah began providing for his children 20 years before they were born. The choices you make today will affect the safety of your kids, too.

4. Don't listen to critics—just do what needs to be done.

5. Always build on high ground.

6. Remember that we're all in the same boat.

7. Speed isn't always an advantage. Both the cheetahs and the snails were on board the ark when the rains started.

8. Don't miss the boat. When God shuts the door on this world for the last time, choose to be on the right side.

9. No matter how dark things look, there is a rainbow on the other side.

10. God the Creator *always* keeps His promises, in His appointed time.

The IRS and the Broken Garage Door

I will answer them before they even call to me. While they are still talking to me about their needs, I will go ahead and answer their prayers! Isaiah 65:24, TLB.

Two days after an unexpected tax refund from the Internal Revenue Service arrived in the mail, the giant spring on our automatic garage door opener snapped, and the door wouldn't open. It was 2:00 p.m. on Friday of Easter weekend. Our only car was trapped inside the garage. Try as we might, Richard and I couldn't lift the 350-pound door.

While Richard sputtered and puttered with the door, I called the garage door repair shops listed in the yellow pages. All except one were closed for the long weekend. If I'd called 10 minutes later, he would have been gone too. I explained what had happened, and he graciously agreed to repair our door before leaving for his vacation.

When the repairman handed Richard the bill, my husband handed me the statement. "Look at this."

We looked at each other and laughed. The tax refund was for the exact amount of the bill. Can you imagine? Two days before we needed it, God had supplied our need. Before we asked, He took care of our problem—just as He promised.

12 January

Only the Best

You can be sure that God will take care of everything you need, his generosity exceeding even yours in the glory that pours from Jesus. Philippians 4:19, Message.

Would you spend $100 for a glass of water? Some of the pioneers heading for California in 1850 did. In the middle of the Mojave Desert, thirsty people would do anything for a cup of lukewarm water.

Along the trail other necessities were often outrageously priced as well. At the beginning of their journey, a traveler could buy flour for $4 a barrel, but if they ran out while crossing the desert, the price rose to $1 a pint. A pint would make a batch of bread or two batches of pancakes—maybe.

The basic laws of supply and demand run on greed still today. I remember being caught in a surprise downpour in Albuquerque, New Mexico. Umbrellas marked $5 were suddenly being sold for $25. The same thing happens with the price of gasoline during vacation time or heating oil during a cold spell. Increasing the need increases the greed.

This is the exact opposite of God's law of love. When He promises to supply all our needs, He doesn't use a teaspoon for a measure, but a dump truck full and running over. I imagine He chuckles a little at the surprise and pleasure on our faces when we thank Him.

Cha-cha and Corky

He calls his own sheep by name. . . . And the sheep follow him because they know his voice. John 10:3, 4, NASB.

Two things Cha-cha the parrot loved more than anything else in the world: sitting on the back porch in the sun and playing pranks on Corky, the collie who slept at the foot of the steps.

Cha-cha listened to his master's voice when the farmer ordered the collie to fetch the cows each evening and to later return them to the field. Cha-cha, being a bird too smart for his feathers, discovered that he could imitate the farmer's voice and Corky would obey.

Throughout the hot, summer days the parrot would tell the dog to bring in the cows, then a short time later order him to return them to the field. After a week or two poor Corky was exhausted. So were the cows. Their milk production dropped from all the exercise, and Corky hardly had enough energy left to crawl to his bowl for his supper.

Cha-cha's fun stopped when the farmer discovered what the bird was doing and moved Cha-cha's perch to the porch on the other side of the house.

Parrots and collies, shepherds and sheep—the difference is that we can be smarter than Corky. By knowing God's Word, we will recognize the difference between His voice and that of precocious parrots or deceitful demons.

The Unfair A–

Good people will receive blessings. Proverbs 10:6, TEV.

After the students in a college philosophy class finished their exams, the instructor told them to write on the back of their test the grade they thought they deserved.

Grade myself? I certainly wanted an A. And I needed an A to balance out my C– in French. I'd worked hard, but hard enough to deserve an A? I wasn't sure.

The quotes the teacher assigned us to memorize and the outside reading—I'd done most, but not all. Reluctantly I wrote an A– on my exam. Later I learned my friend, the class clown, had given himself an A.

"But you didn't do the work."

"So?"

When the tests came back, I got my A– and my friend received his A. No fair! In time my A– didn't matter, but the lesson of honesty I learned did.

Life isn't fair! Get used to it. Evil flourishes and sometimes goes unrewarded on this earth. Praise God, the same is not true in God's world. Someday if you have learned the lesson of honesty, God will say, when He hands out your grades, "Well done, you good and faithful servant. . . . Come on in and share my happiness" (Matt. 25:21, TEV).

And that day will be way, way out of this world!

It's in the Genes

The kingdom of heaven is like a merchant looking for fine pearls. When he found one of great value, he went away and sold everything he had and bought it. Matthew 13:45, 46, NIV.

Years ago scientists reported that the chemicals and tissues of a human body was worth $1.98. Pretty cheap, huh? Today, in the age of transplant surgery, the price for human body parts has skyrocketed. Wealthy patients pay millions to receive healthy eyes, a donor heart, a kidney. And when the researchers produce human clones, as they are trying to do, who knows what your genes may be worth?

No scientific discovery, past, present, or future, can equal the price tag God puts on His kids. Remember the story of the merchant selling everything he had for the perfect pearl? We think of Jesus as that pearl and we're the merchant. But turn the story around and make Jesus the merchant and you, the priceless pearl that He sold everything for. What does it do to your value?

That's what He did, you know, when He died on the cross. Let the scientists try to put a price tag on His life, on His sacrifice. Only an eternal God could afford to love so much, to pay so much.

16 January

I Remember Jackie

Thank you for hiding the truth from those who think themselves so wise, and for revealing it to little children. Matthew 11:25, TLB.

I met Jackie at the Hamburg State Hospital for Retarded Children, where her parents had dropped her off in the middle of the night when she was 5 years old. The child's muscular dystrophy was too inconvenient, or so they told the authorities.

When our church decided to conduct weekly story hours at the hospital, Jackie was one of those allowed to attend. To us, the girl looked and acted like several of the other patients.

Imagine our surprise when we learned that each week Jackie conducted her own story hour for the children on her ward who hadn't been allowed to attend the meeting. She did this word for word.

When Jackie asked me how to give her heart to Jesus, I told her as simply as I could, to which she replied, "I've done that. I just wanted to be sure I did it right so I could tell my friends."

Whenever intelligent people try to complicate Jesus' message of love for me, I remember Jackie. Abandoned by her parents, raised where disturbed children banged their heads against walls or curled up in corners and wailed all day, she understood, gave her heart to her Savior, and immediately wanted to share what she had learned.

Why. God. Why?

The love of Christ constraineth us. 2 Corinthians 5:14.

The story that rises out of the ashes of the Columbine tragedy was of a 16-year-old girl named Cassie. After shooting students in the school library, the killer turned to Cassie and asked, "Do you believe in God?"

Knowing her fate, Cassie answered, "Yes."

The next minute she was dead.

Why? Why didn't God stop that killer? Why didn't He jam the rifle? Why didn't He strike the boy dead, instead of allowing His faithful child to die?

From the martyrs in ancient Rome to the Spanish Inquisition, to Hitler's ovens, and to Pol Pot's killing fields, these questions have challenged theologians and grieving families alike for centuries. How can a loving God allow bad things to happen to good people?

The answer that makes sense to me is based on today's text. The word *constraineth* means to hold fast, to secure. While our actions must be constrained by Christ's love, so God's actions are constrained by the same eternal law of love.

God loved Cassie, but He also loved the killer. When He gives us the gift of choice, His love won't allow Him to take it back when we make bad choices. So even the worst of crimes demonstrate God's incredible love for His kids. But that's only half the story.

(to be continued)

18 January

The Other Half of the Story

Be sure of this—that I am with you always, even to the end of the world. Matthew 28:20, TLB.

The morning of the Columbine High School shooting was no different than any other. As Cassie dressed for school, she never could have guessed that she would, that day, face and pass the biggest test of her life, that she would watch a crazed gunman kill her friend, then shove a rifle in her face and ask, "Do you believe in God?"

Without hesitation she answered, "Yes!"

Cassie's testimony went round the world; her memorial service had the largest television audience in the history of CNN. Today her legacy of faith is greater than 10 lifetimes.

But where was Cassie's God? What was He doing that morning? Did the horrid event come as a surprise to the King of the universe?

Absolutely not. From the moment baby Cassie gasped her first breath, the Father of light was right beside her, preparing her for the test He knew was coming. When the gunman pulled the trigger, God held Cassie in His arms, giving her the strength and comfort she needed.

Cassie's God is no different from yours and mine. He knows every detail of our futures and supplies us with everything we need to come through our trials as winners. Be sure of this: when God says, "I am with you always," He means it!

No Fair!

For he makes his sun to shine on bad and good people alike, and gives rain to those who do good and to those who do evil. Matthew 5:45, TEV.

So much for life's big questions, but what about the little things that happen and really bug you?

Andy, a C student in English, writes an essay on rock climbing, a sport he loves. When the teacher reads his paper, she accuses him of cheating. She says someone helped him write it. He denies it, but she gives him an F anyway. No amount of arguing changes the teacher's mind. Bad break.

During the championship soccer game, the umpire unfairly benches Shawna, the team's star player, causing them to lose the regional title. No fair!

Benji has juvenile diabetes. He gives himself shots every day. He catches colds easier than his friends. At parties Benji watches while the other kids eat cake and ice cream. Lousy luck!

AmericaOne crosses the line first at the 1999 New Zealand sailing finals, but takes second place because the crew fails to complete a penalty maneuver first. Bad news!

Paul Cuyard, captain of the *AmericaOne*, tells reporters after the race, "You've got to sail the wind that you're given."

So the rain falls on the good and the bad. God sees you through the good times and the bad. It's your attitude that makes the difference.

29

A Pot of Beans

Clay doesn't talk back to the fingers that mold it, saying, "Why did you shape me like this?" Isn't it obvious that a potter has a perfect right to shape one lump of clay into a vase for holding flowers and another into a pot for cooking beans? Romans 9:20, 21, Message.

Petite, pretty, with sparkling blue eyes and dimples in her honey-brown cheeks! Huh! To make matters worse, Kari's smart, funny, and sings like Mariah Carey.

"It would take a perm, a nose job, and major liposuction to improve me!" Anya glowers at herself in the mirror. "God, why did You make me like this?"

Anya hasn't read today's text about the potter and the clay. God, the potter, shapes the clay—us—into the form that is right for each of us. Whether we hold flowers or beans, what is important is that we allow God to carry out His plan for us.

Since I'm more of a bean pot than a vase, today's message encourages me. God says, "I'll call nobodies and make them somebodies; I'll call the unloved and make them be loved. In the place where they yelled out, 'You're nobody!' they're calling you 'God's living children'" (Romans 9:25, 26, Message).

Whether or not you consider yourself a nobody, God promises to make you into somebody—His living child—if you're willing. What a makeover!

God's Cracked Pots

For you were once darkness, but now you are light in the Lord. Live as children of light. Ephesians 5:8, NIV.

I love to throw pots. Not against the wall; I make clay pottery on a potter's wheel. Each pot I make is special to me. During a recent move I was unpacking my favorite pot, and it slipped from my hands, crashing to the floor. Tearfully I picked up the shards and carried them to the table. Because I loved my pot too much to throw it away, I carefully glued the pieces back together. And even though I did the best I could, I could see the broken places when I finished. That's when God taught me a valuable lesson.

You and I are God's cracked pots. We've been broken by sin. And as me with my pot, God still loves us. He won't give up on us, but puts us back together again. When He's finished, sometimes our broken places still show. But when His fills us with His light, it shines through the cracks.

Aren't you glad God uses our mistakes and our disabilities as places where His light shines to others who are hurting? You and I may be cracked pots, but we're God's cracked pots, and that makes all the difference.

22 January

The TP Scare

Do not worry about your life, what you will eat or drink; or about your body, what you will wear. . . . Seek first his kingdom and his righteousness, and all these things will be given to you. Matthew 6:25-33, NIV.

Factoid of the day: In 1857 Joseph C. Gayetty of New York City invented toilet paper. Decades passed before the new product replaced the "Monkey Wards" catalog.

Long before the 1970s toilet paper had become such a necessity that when two Pennsylvania State University students spread a rumor that there was a toilet paper shortage, Pennsylvania housewives stripped the grocery shelves bare of toilet tissue before noon.

In 1999, when the Y2K scare hit, the same thing happened, except this time it was panic worldwide. People stockpiled food, water, oil, wood, and yes, toilet paper. Some moved to the wilderness and fortified their property with barbed wire and automatic rifles.

Jesus said, "Don't be afraid." Seek first His kingdom and all these things will be given you. Whether or not toilet paper will be supplied along with the promised bread and water, I don't know. But I do know that through God's grace I will have everything I need. And I'll have angels, not 100 rounds of bullets, to protect me.

Barbie, Bunnies, 'n' Us

How great is the love the Father has lavished on us, that we should be called children of God! And that is what we are! 1 John 3:1, NIV.

Kelli loved her Barbie dolls. She loved to dress them in their fancy clothes and take them to pretend parties. She and her friend Jolene would play on the lawn for hours with their Barbies. Kelli's Barbies had nicer clothes, drove snazzier cars, traveled to more exciting places, and lived in fancier townhouses than could be imagined—well, almost.

One day Kelli packed her Barbies and all their clothes and furniture into cardboard boxes, labeled the boxes with a felt-tip pen as "Kelli's Barbies," and stored them in the basement. She'd outgrown playing Barbies.

God's love isn't like that with us. I am so thankful that He never outgrows us, never gets tired of us, never packs us away in some dark corner of the universe to create something newer and more beautiful. His love is literally out of this world. Beyond the Energizer bunny's ability to keep going and going and going, our heavenly Father's love for His kids will keep going and going and going through all eternity.

Whether Weather

For the wages of sin is death, but the free gift of God is eternal life in Christ Jesus, our Lord. Romans 6:23, NASB.

Hurricanes, droughts, or tornadoes, rain or shine, we can't do much about the weather. Neither can television's weather forecasters. They talk about it. They predict weather changes—remember El Niño—but they couldn't stop it, speed it up, or slow it down. The same was true with La Niña or Hurricane Mitch. Weather is beyond humans' control.

What is weather? If you wrote a formula for weather, it might look like this:

Air + water + sun = weather. So simple, right? But try to change it.

Something else I can't change is sin. I can see it. I can feel it. I can predict it. But try as hard as I can, I can't change it—alone. If I were to make a formula for sin, it might look like this: human + temptation + action = sin.

However, the God who created the winds of the hurricane and fury of the fire designed a formula for sin that is simple and easy to understand. Best yet, it works. It goes like this: "The wages of sin is death, but the free gift of God is eternal life in Christ Jesus."

34

Muscle-bound

Wisdom is better than strength. Ecclesiastes 9:16.

While a snowstorm raged outside his bedroom window, 12-year-old Jeffrey pored over his mom's gardening catalog, dreaming of giant pumpkins, crookneck squash, and thousands of beefsteak tomatoes he would grow in his garden come spring. When he told Dad about his dream, Dad asked if he'd like any help. The boy said, "I'd rather do it myself."

The day came when the sun was shining, the air was warm, and the ground had thawed enough to clear the field behind the house for Jeffrey's garden. First he scythed down the weeds. It was hard work, but he kept at it.

Plowing up the rocks embedded in the ground proved to be more difficult, one stone in particular. When Jeffrey broke for lunch, he told his dad about the rock. "I don't know what to do," he said. "It won't budge."

"Are you using all your strength?" Dad asked.

"Yes."

"No, you're not," his father replied. "You haven't asked me to help."

Jeffrey's dad was there ready to help. All the boy needed to do was to ask. It's the same when it comes to God the Father. He's our source of strength. All we need is to be wise enough to ask.

Talk About the Pits!

Praise the Lord, O my soul, . . . who redeems your life from the pit and crowns you with love and compassion. Psalm 103:2-4, NIV.

Greg awoke with a jolt to find himself upside down and being squeezed by what—he didn't know. He shouted for help. The driver of the 21-ton garbage truck heard someone shouting, but when he looked around and saw no one, he restarted the trash compactor.

Desperate, Greg pounded on the walls of his prison. The driver heard the banging. Thinking something was mechanically wrong with his truck, he stopped the compactor and heard a voice say, "Let me out of here!" The homeless Greg had been sleeping in a trash bin.

Do you ever feel worthless? As if you're garbage and you belong in a trash bin? Or, as King David puts it, in the pits? Do you have too much to do and not enough time to do it? Do you sometimes find your world upside down? As if you're being crushed?

King David's solution was the same as ours and Greg's. When we cry out for help, God promises to redeem our lives from the pit. He rescues us, just as the garbage truck driver rescued Greg from the compactor. When we're feeling our lowest, God promises to lift us lovingly out of our despair and crown us with love and compassion.

Why?

But grow in the grace and knowledge of our Lord and Savior Jesus Christ. 2 Peter 3:18, NIV.

hy do ice cubes float in a glass of water? Which is heavier, a bucket of ice or a bucket of water? Aren't solids heavier than liquids? In most cases, yes, but not with water. As water freezes it becomes lighter.

This is important, especially if you're a fish. If the pond froze from the bottom to the top instead of the other way around, the water plants would die. The fish would have shallower and shallower water in which to swim as the level of ice rose. This would cause the fish to freeze on the surface.

Instead, God designed that the surface water would freeze first, forming ice that floats. This protects all the living things beneath the surface. Just a tiny detail in a humongous world of living creatures.

Isn't it great knowing that our Creator took into account even the tiniest details, such as floating ice to protect His creatures? Do you think He would do any less for you and me, His kids?

Learning about God through His creation helps us to remember how far His grace will go for you and me, creatures He made in His image.

Dumb and Dumber

Your sins have been your downfall! Hosea 14:1, NIV.

A robbery suspect in Los Angeles was put in a lineup for identification. When the detective asked each man to say, "Give me your money or I'll shoot," the thief shouted, "That's not what I said!" Oops!

A bank robber in Virginia Beach, Virginia, learned too late that the money he stole contained a dye pack, which exploded inside his Fruit of the Looms as he ran out the door. Police kept his charred jeans as evidence. Ouch!

In Modesto, California, a man tried to hold up a Bank of America with his thumb and finger in his pocket as a weapon, except he forgot to keep his hand in his pocket. Yikes!

Then there was the Illinois man who, pretending to have a gun, kidnapped a motorist and forced him to drive to two different automated teller machines. Might have worked, except the kidnapper withdrew money from his own bank account by accident. How stupid can you get?

Stupid or smart, the way of sinners is hard. While they might not do something quite as dumb as what I've described, sooner or later they will stand before the Judge of the universe to account for their sins.

If they knew of God's plan of forgiveness and turned it down, won't they feel dumb then!

The Massacre at Ant Hill

A thousand may fall at your side, ten thousand at your right hand, but it will not come near you. I will be with [you] in trouble, I will deliver [you] and honor [you]. Psalm 91:7, 15, NIV.

The lines were drawn; a giant shadow hung over the camp, blocking out any hope of victory. The queen's faithful soldiers fought valiantly against the monstrous enemy, defending the hill.

I watched in horror as my monster cousin and his rubber band defeated a colony of black ants in my backyard.

The author of Proverbs says to go to the ant and consider its ways. But I don't think that he meant to kill the poor things. Ant or not, the fatal sting of the rubber band must hurt. And I don't like to see any of God's creatures suffer, do you? Neither does God. If He's concerned for ants, imagine how He cares for His kids, those made in His image?

His love is why God made today's promise, not to the ants or to crocodiles, but to you and me. And it's only one of hundreds of promises in His Word. Use your Bible concordance to find others. Memorize them. Use them as bullets and hand grenades against the enemy, Satan. Add them to your arsenal of grace.

30 January

Mummy Dearest

What's the price of two or three pet canaries? Some loose change, right? But God never overlooks a single one. . . . He pays even greater attention to you, down to the last detail—even numbering the hairs of your head! So don't be intimidated. . . . You're worth more than a million canaries. Luke 12:6, 7, Message.

Ants, canaries, rabbits, and children of God—what three things do they all have in common?

Number 1. God made them.

Number 2. God cares for them.

Number 3. God keeps a perfect count, right down to the number of hairs (or feathers) on their heads! And for those of you fighting a battle with chemotherapy, He tallies your hair loss too. He can't help it. He loves you.

He loved Ta-bes too, a 30-year-old singer and the wife of a barber who lived 3,000 years ago—so the inscription on her coffin reads.

The scientists say that poor Ta-bes had a bad back and died from a tiny tumor in her skull. Also, she had a large, dented nose, many cavities in her teeth, and didn't look anything like the beautiful woman painted on the outside of her coffin.

If scientists can tell so much about a woman who lived 3,000 years ago, it's easy to see how God keeps track of His kids, right down to the number of, or lack of, hairs on their head.

God's Sheep

I will judge between you strong sheep and the weak sheep. You pushed the sick ones aside and butted them away from the flock. I will rescue my sheep and not let them be mistreated any more. Ezekiel 34:20, 21, TEV.

I like being one of God's little lambs. I picture myself as a pure white, wooly, loveable, and cuddly lamb, nestled in the crook of the Shepherd's arm. I never imagine myself acting as one of those stupid, mangy creatures with mud-caked wool I see in the fields.

One day I watched a flock of sheep follow their shepherd, single file, along a barbed-wire fence. Suddenly a lamb stumbled and fell. Instead of pausing to give the animal time to get to his feet, or stepping around him, the other sheep trampled over the top of him, never stopping, never apologizing, never missing a beat.

When I read today's verse, I thought of those thoughtless sheep. When God pours His grace on me, do I let that grace spill onto others? Or do I trample on anyone getting in my way? The nerd is left out of the game; the butt of the jokes gets butted again. The girl who weighs too much or who wears dumpy clothes gets harassed again. Do I defend them, God's precious lambs? Do you?

ΙΠαⱤ on ΕαⱤlh

You do not belong to the world, but I have chosen you out of the world. John 15:19, NIV.

Adrift of snow and an eerie twilight lend an out-of-this-world glow to the one spot on earth that most resembles the planet Mars. It's the Haughton Crater on Canada's Devon Island in the Arctic Circle. A flag planted in the middle of the crater says, "Next Stop, Mars!"

NASA scientists hope that by studying Haughton Crater, they will make discoveries about what to expect on the red planet. Dry, cold, barren, the crater is a great stand-in for everything from core samples, robotic mapping, and ground-penetrating radar as well as learning how to work together as a team.

The biting-cold Arctic wasteland is made of volcanic rock produced by a meteor. Why would anyone want to spend their summer in such a place? Water. People, including astronauts, need water. If NASA can find water beneath the crater's surface, maybe water exists beneath Mars' surface too.

I'll probably never be an astronaut to the Arctic's Haughton Crater or to Mars, but I'm in training for a mission flight that will take me, in comfort, far beyond the moon, Mars, or the sun. Heaven, my destination—it's truly out of this world.

Just Imagine

The hearing ear, and the seeing eye, the Lord hath made even both of them. Proverbs 20:12.

Did you know U.S. scientists are currently testing red contact lenses on 100,000 chickens because the lenses prevent the birds from seeing red and pecking each other to death?

Do you know why Campbell's Soup cans are red and white? At a football game the owner decided that the colors give the illusion of the can advancing toward customers.

Did you know red quickens the heartbeat, which releases adrenaline in many animal species, including people? Males like reds with yellow mixed in, while females prefer blue-based reds.

Did you know some shades of pink make you less hungry, while orange makes you more? Did you know a yellow marigold looks blue to a bee?

Do you know why cheddar cheese in the Midwest is a yellow-orange, while cheddar farther east is more often a light yellow? Cheesemakers color their cheeses to please their customers.

Most plants and animals get their color from pigment, except for the *Morpho rhetenor* butterfly's colorless wings, which look blue because of the light reflected by microscopic texture variations on its wings.

What a human eye sees is but a wee fraction of the Creator's giant mural. Imagine what colors and secrets He wants to show us, here and in heaven. Just imagine.

3 February

Granny Perez's Unshakable Praise

Those who trust in the Lord are like Mount Zion, which cannot be shaken but endures forever. Psalm 125:1, NIV.

Granny Perez loved to praise God. And she didn't care who knew it. Every morning she stepped out onto her small balcony, lifted her hands toward the heavens, and shouted, "Praise God. Thank You, Lord, for a brand-new day."

Every morning Granny's neighbor, a grouchy old gentleman named Mr. Evans, whose balcony was next to hers, listened for the woman's declaration of praise, then shouted, "God had nothing to do with it."

Try as she might, Granny Perez couldn't convince the old man that God was the source of all good things and deserved his praise.

One morning Mr. Evans tried to outsmart the old lady by placing a grocery store bag of food by her door. When Granny stepped onto the balcony, she found the food. Straightening, she lifted her hands and shouted, "Praise God. Thank You, Lord, for this food."

From next door Mr. Evans replied, "God had nothing to do with it!"

Granny chuckled, then shouted, "And thank You, Lord, for making the devil pay for it!"

Laughing at her witty reply, Mr. Evans couldn't resist a tidal wave like Granny Perez. Maybe she knew something or Someone he didn't.

"I Can't See You, Daddy"

I will guide thee with mine eye. Psalm 32:8.

At 2:00 in the morning 4-year-old Jason awoke to the smell of smoke in the house. Terrified, he shouted for his daddy. An instant later the boy's bedroom door flew open, and his father burst into the room.

Scooping Jason's 2-year-old brother up in one arm, the father grabbed the older boy with his free hand and dragged him from the bedroom and down the stairs.

At the foot of the stairs Jason suddenly remembered that he had left Patches, his favorite stuffed animal, upstairs on his bed. The child wrenched free from his father's grasp and dashed up the stairs.

The father shouted after Jason, but the boy continued to run. He couldn't risk the life of his 2-year-old by running back into the house. He looked up and saw his son standing in front of his open bedroom window.

The frantic man shouted to his son, "Jump, Jason, jump!"

The boy cried, "I can't."

"Don't worry; I'll catch you."

"But I can't see you, Daddy," the 4-year-old wailed.

"But I can see you."

Sometimes when we're afraid and can't see God, we need to remember that what counts is not that we can see Him, but that He sees us and He's strong enough to catch us.

A Song in My Heart

I will sing with my spirit, but I will also sing with my mind.
1 Corinthians 14:15, NIV.

I love to sing new songs, old songs; quiet songs, loud songs; fast songs, slow songs. I can sing anytime, anywhere, out loud or, as today's text says, in my mind—such as the time I was grocery shopping. No one was around when one of my mind songs broke free without my realizing it.

There I was in the cereal aisle, searching for my favorite Cheerios yellow box, singing "This is the day that the Lord has made," when two teenage boys popped out from the end of the aisle. Oops! They'd heard me.

One snickered while the other placed his hand on his chest and bellowed one loud note, as a male opera singer might do.

If anyone were with me, I might have been embarrassed. Instead I laughed and said, "Honey, you should be so happy!"

Suddenly the boys were embarrassed and disappeared around the corner. While I didn't set out to make them uncomfortable, I meant what I said. I wish every kid, every grown-up, could be as happy as I am when I'm worshiping my God. In a grocery store, at the beach, or in the privacy of one's own bedroom music can bubble forth from a grateful heart. It happens to me all the time.

A Look in the Mirror

[Your beauty] should be . . . the unfading beauty of a gentle and quiet spirit, which is of great worth in God's sight. 1 Peter 3:4, NIV.

A t age 3 a girl sees a princess in the mirror.

At 8 she sees herself as a queen.

At 15 she sees pimples, hair too straight/too curly.

At 20, 30, and 40 she sees too fat/too thin, too short/too tall.

At 50 she sees wrinkles and laugh lines and says, "I am what I am. Take me or leave me, world."

At 60 she sees wisdom and knowledge. She is at peace with herself.

At 70 she gives thanks when she recalls that there are people in the world who can't even see.

At 80 she ignores the mirror, dons her flowered straw hat, and goes out to enjoy the world.

Little girl or grown woman, young boy or grandpa—it doesn't matter. When we let His beauty shine through us, God sees us as handsome princes or beautiful princesses regardless of our age, our complexion, or the size of our ears. It's a lesson we can learn at any age.

Seven Crazy Definitions

*My commandment is this: love one another, just as I love you.
John 15:12, TEV.*

Words can be confusing and difficult to understand. They can have many meanings. Here are a few crazy definitions of words you thought you knew:

Full name: what parents call you when you're in trouble.

Grandparents: people who think you are wonderful no matter what you do.

Showoff: the kid in school who's smarter than you.

Puddle: a small body of water your 2-year-old brother's shoes find on Sabbath morning.

Dumbwaiter: one who asks kids if they care to order dessert.

Feedback: what you get when you feed your baby sister strained carrots.

Whodunit: nobody in your house.

The word "love" doesn't mean the same all the time either. For instance, I love oranges, I love my model sailing ship, and I love my cat. But as much as I love Kiki, or my favorite ship, it's nothing like my love for my husband, Richard.

My love for God is a special kind of love too. He tells me, "I love you. And if you love Me, you will show it by loving one another. This is My will for you."

God's love makes me want to love others, including the good, the bad, and the nasty.

Chapels, Churches, and Cathedrals

Don't you realize that . . . you . . . are the house of God?
1 Corinthians 3:16, TLB .

Oneida, a small city in central New York, claims to have the world's smallest church. It is 3.5' x 6'. Wow! That's pretty small, don't you think?

When I visited England, I toured the impressive Westminster Abbey and the "Jerusalem Chamber" where the King James Bible was compiled. On the same day I visited a small chapel at the Tower of London where a teenage queen prayed before being beheaded.

Through the years people have worshiped God from lofty cathedrals to filthy prison cells to mountain caves. And God was there for His people because we are His temples—not buildings of stone or wood, but of human flesh.

Maybe you're a tiny chapel like the one in Onieda and you feel unimportant, or a white clapboard church with a tall steeple pointing to God, or a red brick house of prayer in Pennsylvania, or a little brown church in southern Alabama. Whether you're a country chapel or a city cathedral, regardless of your size, beauty, or talent, God inhabits you through your praise and worship. Like your fingerprints or your DNA, you are a unique temple because nobody can praise your heavenly Father as you can—nobody. And He loves the way you praise Him.

What Are the Chances?

The eyes of the Lord are on the righteous and his ears are attentive to their prayer. 1 Peter 3:12, NIV.

Eight-year-old Tracy sat in front of her new home in Boise, Idaho, feeling very sorry for herself. She'd recently moved 2,000 miles away from her friends. To make matters worse, her grandpa had died. She missed him so much. Nothing could make her happy, not even the bouquet of helium-filled balloons her father brought home to her.

Hoping a kid in the neighborhood would find it, she wrote a note and tied it to one of the balloons. In the note she told how lonely she was and how much she missed her grandfather, then signed her first name and her new phone number.

When school started, Tracy made new friends. She forgot about the balloon and her note. Five months later the phone rang. Someone in St. Louis, Missouri, was calling to speak with Tracy. Sixteen hundred miles away from where Tracy launched her balloon, 60-year-old Len Johnson found it. Tracy writes to her new friend and her new grandpa every week.

Incredible. What are the chances of such a thing happening?

Some people wonder, *What are the chances God hears my prayers?* I tell them, "Excellent, since He promised He would be listening, and He keeps His promises."

Grace in the Rearview Mirror

My grace is sufficient for you, for my power is made perfect in weakness. 2 Corinthians 12:9, NIV.

Donna, a music teacher, drives a white Miata convertible to school with the top down and parks it in the school lot. In the middle of a piano lesson she heard a crash and looked out her studio door to find two boys practicing their golf swings on the lawn.

A few minutes later a nervous, shamefaced 13-year-old boy knocked on her door. "Mrs. Wareham? I'm sorry. I'm the one who broke your mirror."

"My mirror?"

"The rearview mirror on your car," he explained.

"You broke it?"

"Yeah. I'm sorry. I'll pay for it."

Donna had no idea how much it would cost to replace the mirror. "Josh, do you know what grace is?"

"No." He'd heard the word in Bible class, but didn't know what it meant.

"It's a gift you don't deserve. I'll pay for the broken mirror."

The boy blinked in surprise. "But I broke it."

"I know," she said. "That's grace."

Josh sighed in relief. "Thanks. I-I-I'll do it for someone else," he promised.

Donna's mirror cost $14.95, but the greatest example of grace was God's priceless gift on the cross. How can we help wanting to worship Him?

Exercising Prayers

I . . . come that you might have life—life in all its fullness. John 10:10, TEV.

When you feel groggy and lazy after lunch, medical researchers say, "Take a walk." That's right. A brisk walk will not only wake you up; it will aid digestion, rev up your memory, sharpen your judgment, and make you smarter. Even in rats, working out increases the number of brain cells in the hippocampus, the part of the brain that regulates learning and memory. Isn't that neat?

I confess I don't really enjoy exercising, even though I know it's good for me. I'd rather play games on my computer or read a book or chat with friends. So to make exercising more fun, I pray while I walk. That's right, pray.

On the first block I praise my heavenly Father. I talk to Him as I would my dad. On the second block I thank my brother Jesus for walking beside me. During the third block I listen for the voice of the Holy Spirit in the breeze, in the warmth of the sun, and in the air I breathe.

During the rest of the blocks I pray for those I love and for those I dislike. I hold each one up to God for a special blessing. Before I know it, my walk is finished, and so is my morning prayer list. And I feel great.

Sacrifice of Gladiators

Here on earth you will have many trials and sorrows; but cheer up, for I have overcome the world. John 16:33, TLB.

In ancient Rome, Nero is said to have killed 10,000 gladiators and Christians, along with 8,000 animals, in a 100-day period.

Beneath the floor of the Roman Colosseum were cells and cages to hold the wild animals and the people to be sacrificed for the pleasure of the nearly 1 million Roman citizens. Trapdoors raised the participants of the next event to the arena. Beyond the Colosseum was an underground disposal pit for the dead carcasses—animal and human alike.

But remember, a lot of living and praising was going on in those dank cells by Christians who were to be burned at the stake or ravaged by lions. God's faithful proclaimed the name of Jesus to slaves and gladiators alike. Hearts were being softened and lives changed even as the crowds above their heads cheered their brothers' and sisters' deaths. These children of God weren't afraid, because they trusted their Savior.

Troubles will come. Jesus said so, but He also said He overcame those troubles for us. And He promises a new life forever and ever and ever in His perfect world. Pretty good exchange, huh?

13 February

The Wallet

Trust in the Lord and do good. Psalm 37:3, NIV.

If you ever wonder if God loves and cares for His children, this story's for you.

In 1998 Jack found a brown leather wallet on the street. Inside were three dollars and a letter dated 1924.

"Dear Michael," it began. The writer said her parents forbade her from seeing him again. "But I'll always love you," signed Hannah.

Jack wanted to find the owner of the love letter. He called information for a phone listing for the address on the envelope. After hearing Jack's story, the operator said that as a courtesy, she would call the number and ask if they wanted to talk with him.

After a few minutes a woman came on the line and told Jack that 30 years ago she had bought the house from a family whose daughter was named Hannah.

She gave Jack the number of the nursing home where Hannah had placed her mother. Jack called the nursing home to learn that Hannah's mother had died years before. "But I have the number of the nursing home Hannah is now in," the attendant volunteered.

Jack hung up the phone. *Why am I doing this? For the three lousy bucks?* But he couldn't stop looking. If he'd lost a wallet with such a letter, he'd want it back.

(to be continued)

A Love Story

To every thing there is a season, and a time to every purpose under the heaven. Ecclesiastes 3:1.

Even though it was late at night, Jack went to the nursing home, found the woman identified as Hannah, and showed her the letter.

Upon seeing the powder-blue envelope, she gasped, "This is the last contact I had with Michael. Michael Goldstein was a wonderful person. If you find him, tell him that I think of him often . . ." She bit her lip. ". . . that I still love him. I never did marry, you know."

Jack said goodbye and took the elevator to the first floor, the wallet still clutched in his hand. At the door the night guard glanced at the wallet in Jack's hand. "Hey, that wallet belongs to Mike Goldstein on the eighth floor. I recognize it by the red lacing. He's always losing his wallet."

Jack's heart raced with excitement as he rushed to the eighth floor and handed Mr. Goldstein the wallet. "Sir," Jack confessed, "I read your letter, and I know where Hannah is."

Three weeks later Jack got a call inviting him to a wedding. A 70-year-old romance rekindled, all in God's time. A little surprise from a loving God.

four factoids About the father of Light

Every good gift and every perfect gift . . . cometh down from the Father of lights. James 1:17.

When I switch on a light, the darkness disappears instantly. Where does it go?

Factoid 1: Light travels 186,282 miles (or seven and a half times around the world) per second. To our eyes it's *poof*—and the room is filled with light. And the darkness must leave.

The same thing happens with God, the Father of lights, and Satan, the father of darkness. God's light in your heart makes darkness flee.

Factoid 2: Sunlight is the combination of seven colors, like a rainbow. The Bible calls seven the perfect number, or "complete." God makes us complete if we ask Him.

Factoid 3: There are two kinds of light: direct, as from the sun, or reflected, as the moon. When God's light shines on us, we become as the moon, a reflected light that allows others to see God in us.

Factoid 4: We could not live without sunlight. No food to eat! No plants to produce oxygen to breathe! God's sunlight shines on the young and the old, the rich and the poor, the good and the bad. He can't help it. He loves the creatures He made so-o-o-o much.

Unconditional Surrender

Love the Lord your God with all your heart and with all your soul and with all your mind. Matthew 22: 37, NIV.

On February 16, 1862, during the American Civil War, 14,000 Confederate soldiers surrendered at Fort Donelson, Tennessee, to Union general Ulysses S. Grant. This victory earned Grant the nickname "Unconditional Surrender Grant."

The 14,000 Confederate soldiers surrendered their weapons and their bodies, but I doubt they surrendered their souls and their minds. Outside they may have had their hands raised in surrender, but in their hearts they were still "sons of the South."

Every battle has its prisoners of war, and very few enemy prisoners give over their hearts to the opposition.

The greatest war ever fought isn't only for your body, but for your heart and soul. For Satan it's a war for territory, power, and riches. For God it's a war of love and allegiance. And when it seemed God's side was losing, Jesus won the war by choosing to die on the cross for each of us.

Jesus is the only victor who gives prisoners of war a choice. He will never force you to love Him or serve Him. That's up to you. And it's up to me. Maybe it's His incredible love that makes unconditional surrender—heart, mind, and soul—to Him so easy.

A World Full of Rainbows

I do set my bow in the cloud, and it shall be for a token of a covenant between me and the earth. Genesis 9:13.

Promises! Yeah, right! That's how Jackie felt about her dad's promises. When he and Jackie's mother divorced, Dad made all sorts of promises about "being there for his little girl" and "spending quality time together." It never happened—none of it. His visits became fewer and fewer, until the child felt lucky if he saw her on her birthday or Christmas.

So when Jackie's Sabbath school teacher talked about rainbows and her heavenly Father's promise never to flood the entire earth again, she was skeptical. "How do you know? How can you be sure?" she asked.

The teacher blinked in surprise. "Because God is the perfect Father. And when He makes a promise, He keeps it."

Jackie gave her heart and life to Jesus and was baptized. Now she says, "My dad may let me down a thousand times, but my heavenly Father never does. In everything I've learned to trust my heavenly Father's word."

On rainy days Jackie searches the sky for rainbows of promise. On sunny days she turns on the garden hose, stands with her back to the sun, and in the spray enjoys God's rainbow promise.

Sorry, I Know Nothing!

Be still, and know that I am God: I will be exalted among the heathen, I will be exalted in the earth. Psalm 46:10.

On February 1, 1856, a group of Americans met in Philadelphia, Pennsylvania, to nominate a presidential candidate. They called themselves the Know-Nothing Party. That's right, the Know-Nothings.

These men banded together out of fear of the "foreigners" from Europe invading "their" country. Their country? Who's calling whom "foreigner"? There wasn't a Native American among 'em.

The movement died out when their candidate, former president Millard Fillmore, captured the vote of only one state—Maryland. But while the movement might have died, many "know-nothings" are still around today.

I know people who fear and distrust anyone who is not of their color, be it Black, White, Yellow, or Red. And there are people who live in the city who make fun of people who live in the country and vice versa. Then there are those who harass overweight kids or kids with other physical disabilities. They laugh at those who wear uncool clothes or wear their hair "wrong." Sounds like a bunch of "know-nothings" to me.

Today's text has the answer for "know-nothings" of every era. Once we "know" God, we will see others like He does. And that's "no" laughing matter.

19 February

Excuse Me?

The Lord has heard my cry for mercy; the Lord accepts my prayer. Psalm 6:9, NIV.

Jury Favors Shooting Victims in Lawsuit Against Gunmakers," said a headline in the Knoxville *News-Sentinel*. So how many victims does the jury plan to shoot? I love bloopers, whether written or spoken.

Here's one written on airline instruction cards: "If you are seated in an emergency aisle and can't read this card, please ask an attendant to reseat you." Excuse me? If the passenger can't read, how will they know to ask to be reseated?

And what about having Braille on drive-up ATM machines? Excuse me? How many blind automobile drivers do you know who might need it?

Silly mistakes—we all make them. At one time or another we say the wrong thing, or say the right thing in the wrong way. That's part of being human.

Aren't you glad that when you pray to God, you don't have to be afraid of saying something "wrong"? Aren't you thankful for the Holy Spirit, who translates your messed-up messages into clear and beautiful prayers to your Father? And all you have to do is tell Him what's on your heart.

Can you see an eager heavenly Dad leaning forward, not wanting to miss one clumsy word uttered from His child's heart?

A Noisy Sparrow

Are not five sparrows sold for two cents? Yet not one of them is forgotten before God. . . . You are of more value than many sparrows. Luke 12:6, 7, NASB.

In February 1688 the first American antislavery protest was lodged by White abolitionists. The Religious Society of Friends in Germantown, Pennsylvania, also called Quakers, protested the "traffic of men-body."

John Woolman, an antislavery Quaker, traveled through the American colonies, preaching against slave labor. One person at a time, he convinced many Quaker communities to publicly renounce the practice of slavery against Black people.

Traveling alone from place to place, through rainstorms and blizzards, Mr. Woolman must have felt like a nobody, nothing more than a noisy sparrow in the wood patch, a big zero. But he believed his cause was right. The brave man died never knowing the good he did. Two hundred years later a war against enslaving human beings was fought, and the practice of slavery was abolished.

Do you feel all alone, as if no one really cares about you or about what you think? If you're not a plumed peacock but just a sparrow with something you want to say, remember Mr. Woolman and become a noisy sparrow. Make a difference in your world, one person at a time.

Cure for the Common Cuss

These are the words of my mouth; these are what I chew on and pray. Accept them when I place them on the morning altar, O God, my Altar-Rock, God, Priest-of-My-Altar. Psalm 19:14, Message.

A preacher was trying to get his briefcase in the overhead compartment above his airline seat, but the case wouldn't fit. Frustrated, he muttered, louder than he intended, "Oh, Buddha!"

When people around him snickered, he said, "You didn't think I'd take the name of my best Friend in vain, did you?" Come to think of it, I've never heard anyone swear by using the name of Buddha, Muhammad, Confucius, or any other so-called god.

Besides being a sin against the one true God, swearing can mess up your life.

"Swearing is so commonplace . . . that many people think it's acceptable, but it's only tolerated," says James V. O'Connor, the founder of Cuss Control Academy, a school in Chicago for executives who need to retrain their tongues. That's right, retrain their tongues. The school's founder adds, "Swearing reduces the respect people have for you . . . doesn't get you hired, promoted, or romantically connected."

If you've never started cussing, don't. If you have a problem, O'Connor suggests you "think positively, be patient, stop complaining, and think before you speak." I would add, "Get to know Jesus so well that you wouldn't *want* to use His name as a cussword."

A Million Dollars and More

My God shall supply all your need according to his riches in glory by Christ Jesus. Philippians 4:19.

Imagine if you had a million dollars! Imagine a million million! A million billion trillion! Would it make you happy? I don't know about you, but I can barely imagine money much beyond a hundred dollars, let alone the numbers here. Even the richest man in America—Bill Gates—doesn't have that much in the bank.

I was 5 when my dad started his own business. There was no money for any extras. Being only 5, I didn't know much about money. I just knew my folks were unhappy.

At that time there was a program on TV called *The Millionaire.* When I went to bed at night, I prayed that "the millionaire" would come to my house and make my parents happy by giving them a million dollars.

No one came to my house with a check for $1 million. So did God answer my prayer? Did He supply my need as He promised? Yes. God knew my 5-year-old heart. He knew what I needed was to feel safe again, not a bunch of green paper. He answered by relieving my dad's financial worries and making his new business prosper.

God supplies our real, deep-down needs, the important ones we don't always see or understand. He keeps His promises.

Who Wants to Be a Millionaire?

Be concerned with everything that comes from the Kingdom of God and what he requires of you, and he will provide you with all these other things. Matthew 6:33, TEV.

Have you ever dreamed of what it would be like to win a million dollars? I have, or I should say I did until I met a woman who had won a state lottery. When I asked her what it was like, she said, "I wish I'd never heard of the state lottery!"

She went on to say, "After I won the money, my marriage fell apart. My family members got mad when I didn't give them as much money as they thought I should. And my friends thought I'd become 'too highfalutin' for them."

Too much money makes people act squirrelly. As my grandma used to say: "It's dangerous to have too many dollars and not enough sense."

Maybe that's why Jesus had so much to say about wealth. He knew our hearts, that it's easy to forget we need Him. Our hearts and our bank accounts should be out of this world.

Ask Bill Gates, the founder of Microsoft. I don't know if his bank account and his focus is on God's kingdom, but the man is discovering that greater joy comes not from hoarding money, but from giving it away.

Giants in the Land

*Sing God a brand-new song! Earth and everyone in it, sing! . . .
Shout the news of his victory from sea to sea, take the news of
his glory to the lost, news of his wonders to one and all! Psalm
96:1-3, Message.*

Scotsman John Muir captured the imagination of readers
and politicians with his eloquent descriptions of
California "giants."

"Every tree . . . seemed perfect in beauty and strength . . .
like a range of bossy up-swelling cumulus clouds on a calm
sky." He wrote 300 articles and 10 books about his travels
throughout the West. He couldn't keep quiet about the magnificent world he'd discovered.

John Muir's legacy lives on in Yosemite, Sequoia, and
Kings Canyon national parks, where you can see sequoia trees
as tall as a 26-story building. Their diameters exceed the width
of most city streets. (Two sequoias, named General Sherman
and General Grant, were more than 200 years old when Jesus
was born.)

Talk about wonders! I feel a hush come over me when I
walk through a grove of these giants, as if I'm in a grand cathedral, as if my God is walking beside me.

I thank God for people such as John Muir, who proclaimed
to America the mighty and marvelous wonders of God that he
found. I am glad that one person can make a difference when
they praise their Creator.

More Than a Name

Rejoice, because your names are written in heaven. Luke 11:20.

Did you ever wonder how things get their names? From the Bible we know that animals were named by Adam and Eve. What about other things? For instance, yo-yos or Frisbees?

Yo-yo was once a trademark. In 1929 toy maker Thomas Duncan saw Filipino boys playing with a similar toy and shouting "Yo-yo," which means "Come-come." Actually, the toy we call yo-yo can be traced back to the ancient Greeks.

The beginning of Frisbees was equally as simple. Soon after World War II a toymaker saw a group of students hurling tin pie plates at one another on a university lawn. The students were using the pie plates from a local bakery, Frisbie Bakery. Whenever someone would step in the path of one of the whirling missiles, the thrower would shout "Frisbie" as a warning. And the rest is history.

Like the yo-yo and the Frisbee, I think we grow into our names. As a child, I didn't like my name—Kay Darlene Hancock. Today I do.

Whether or not I like my name isn't what's important. That it is written in God's book of life is why I can praise Him today and every day. How about you?

The Voice of an Angel

All together now—applause for God! Sing songs to the tune of his glory, set glory to the rhythms of his praise. Say of God, "We've never seen anything like him!" When your enemies see you in action, they slink off like scolded dogs. The whole earth falls to its knees—it worships you, sings to you, can't stop enjoying your name and fame. Psalm 66:1-4, Message.

Marian Anderson was born February 27, 1897, in the poorest section of Philadelphia. She began to sing at a young age. Prejudice because of her skin color forced her to study in Europe, where she quickly became renowned for her incredible voice.

In 1939, when Marian was asked to sing at Constitution Hall in Washington, D.C., an organization called the Daughters of the American Revolution objected. The resulting publicity landed her hundreds of invitations across the country, including an invitation from the president of the United States to sing on Easter Sunday, April 9, on the steps of the Lincoln Memorial. Seventy-five thousand people attended. And her musical career in America was made.

In 1993 Marian Anderson died. But in all her years of fame she never forgot to sing her praises to her Creator for turning the devil's negatives into heavenly positives.

A Jar of Vanishing Cream

Charm is deceptive and beauty disappears, but a woman who honors the Lord should be praised. Proverbs 31:30, TEV.

Melissa hated her freckles. Whenever she looked in the mirror at herself, she didn't see her sparkling blue eyes or her saucy grin. She just saw spots! Ugly brown spots splashed across her nose. Even her fiery red hair didn't bother her as much as those horrid "angel kisses," as her dad called them.

One day Melissa read an ad in a magazine about a "magical vanishing cream." "Remove ugly flaws from your skin in seven days! Allow for three weeks delivery."

Wow, thought the girl as she mailed in her order. *I could be beautiful by my birthday.*

When the bottle of face cream arrived, Melissa opened the package and rubbed the magic potion on her face. Within two hours, the girl's face became puffy and blotchy, then itchy. Two days later, when her skin returned to normal, the freckles were still there.

Melissa learned to thank God for her freckles, especially after she grew up and met and married a man who adored her "angel kisses," every one. But better yet, this wise young man loved his wife's kind and loving spirit even more, along with the fact that she loves her heavenly Father most of all.

Muscles in a Bottle

Let not the mighty man boast of his might, . . . but let him who boasts boast of this, that he understands and knows Me, that I am the Lord. Jeremiah 9:23, NASB.

Yesterday I kind of picked on girls, so today it's your turn, guys. Just as Melissa wanted to make herself "more lovely" by removing her freckles, a lot of guys want to change their bodies to look like their favorite "action hero" figures.

Too many teenage guys take steroids to make this happen. They take drugs that can cause heart disease, cancer, liver damage, depression, and sterility to build larger muscles. And you thought Melissa's vanishing cream was dumb!

Sons of God do not need to abuse their bodies in order to be confident. Daughters of God do not need creams and lotions to be treasured by Him. They do not find their beauty and their strength in a bottle of pills or a hypodermic needle. They know that God is their one true and healthy source of strength. Any artificial shortcuts can cut short a person's life.

Thank God. He has a plan for each of His sons' and daughters' lives—a plan that's so unique and out of this world that you won't even want to mess with the artificial.

A Place of Silence

Be silent, everyone, in the presence of the Lord. Zechariah 2:13, TEV.

My two favorite places in the entire world to walk are by the ocean and in the redwood forest. Waves crashing against rocks or wind whistling through towering tree branches makes me stop and listen, as if in the waves or the breeze I can hear God speaking directly to me.

Even in total silence God speaks to me. Medical scientists say that the high sound I hear is my nervous system; the low sound is blood rushing through my veins.

Being silent is difficult for a chatterbox like me. In grade school not only could I not keep quiet, I talked fast as well—a painful combination. I lost more recesses than I can count.

My prayers are sometimes like that too. You know, talk—talk—talk—amen. I wonder if God gets frustrated, waiting for His turn to speak. He has so many exciting things to tell me, but I jabber on, oblivious to the really important stuff He knows that I don't.

However, when I stop to listen, by the ocean, the redwoods, or in the silence of my daily worship, God rewards me with new thoughts about His love for me and His purpose for my life.

All About George

Keep your eye on me; hide me under your cool wing feathers from the wicked who are out to get me, from mortal enemies closing in. Psalm 17:8, 9, Message.

George, an engineer, lived in what used to be the U.S.S.R., where he met a Texan who inspired him to dream of moving to the United States. After the U.S.S.R. broke up, George contacted the woman, and she arranged for his passage to America.

However, there were important people in Russia who didn't want George to leave the country. First they tried to talk him out of going. Then they arranged for a hit-and-run accident and stuffed him into an abandoned refrigerator for three days. And last, a bullet to his head couldn't dissuade George from emigrating.

Today George lives in Texas with his wife and four children. He says that he loves the Constitution, every inch. George thanks God every day for the series of miracles that spared his life and for the freedom of his adopted homeland.

So tell me, when was the last time you thanked God for the United States Constitution and the freedom it brings, and for life's everyday miracles straight from the arsenal of God?

A Shepherd Named Grizzly

He will give His angels charge concerning you, to guard you in all your ways. Psalm 91:11, NASB.

Seven-year-old Jeremy Crawford and his German shepherd, Grizzly, were inseparable until the little boy died from cancer. The day he died, Grizzly ran out the front door of the house and under the wheels of a passing truck.

Surprisingly, the dog lived. Jeremy's mother, Lonnie, locked the dog in the fenced-in yard, where the dog dug a hole and crawled in, refusing to eat.

After several days Jeremy's mother was surprised to find the dog clawing at the back door. She let him inside the house, where he stuck close to her side wherever she went. Depressed, Lonnie spent most of her days in bed, with Grizzly lying on the floor nearby.

One day Lonnie tried to take pills to end her life. As she filled her hands with the pills, Grizzly knocked them out of her hands to the floor. The dog barked until she flushed them down the toilet.

Then Grizzly brought Lonnie her sneakers, dumped them at her feet, and barked until the woman took him for a walk. Every day he demanded they walk until Lonnie was strong again.

Today Lonnie and Grizzly visit hospitals encouraging kids who are sick, who want to give up. Isn't God good for putting His love in the hearts of animals like Grizzly?

Imponderables

Take the glory! The honor! The power! You created it all; it was created because you wanted it. Revelation 4:11, Message.

Have you ever wondered if penguins have knees? Why do fish float upside down when they die? Why are the oceans salty? Why do we have earlobes? Silly questions, perhaps, but except for the last one, there are reasonable answers.

First, penguins, as do other birds, have knees; they just have very short legs. Two, when a dead fish begins to decompose, gases build up in the fish's stomach and bladder, which makes them go "belly up."

Oceans are salty for several reasons. The greatest amount of salt comes from rivers, which take the salt out of rocks and carry it to the sea. Add a volcano or two and fresh basalt flowing up from a giant rift that runs through all the oceans' basins, and you have salty oceans.

As to why we have earlobes, that's a question you'll have to save for Jesus. Because as far as scientists know, earlobes don't appear to have any bodily function at all.

Solomon, the wisest man who ever lived, spent time watching the ways of ants, of all things. Imagine a king or president taking time out of his busy day to study bugs. Incredible, pondering the imponderable.

Ponder this: The more we learn about God's creation, the more we know about Him. The more we know about Him, the more we love Him.

Leaping to Conclusions

The Lord sees what happens everywhere; he is watching us, whether we do good or evil. Proverbs 15:3, TEV.

O n February 29, 1704, John Whitfield was hunting turkey on the hill behind the little town of Deerfield, Massachusetts, when suddenly the air was filled with whoops and screeches. Smoke billowed up from the village. Terrified for his wife and children, the man bounded through the forest toward his log home.

By the time he reached the edge of the town, the buildings were burned and 47 of his neighbors were dead. His family, along with 117 others, had been captured by a gang of Frenchmen and Indians from Canada.

Months later John learned that the bell the Deerfield townspeople had bought for their church steeple had been ordered originally from Europe by an Indian tribe in Canada for their chapel. A pirate had stolen the bell and then sold it to the people of Deerfield. When the Indians discovered the whereabouts of their bell, they attacked the town and stole it back. The bell still hangs in the Indian chapel in Canada.

Christians fighting Christians. Doesn't seem right, does it? Yet I confess that I jump to conclusions sometimes, thinking that someone snubbed me or was mean, when, if I knew the whole story . . .

God knows the whole story. He sees everything. The world would be a kinder place if everyone asked God to help them see things as He sees.

I Wonder

I look up at your macro-skies, dark and enormous, your hand-made sky-jewelry, moon and stars mounted in their settings. Then I look at my micro-self and wonder, Why do you bother with us? Why take a second look our way? Psalm 8:3, 4, Message.

Macro-skies," dark and enormous. "Sky-jewelry." I can see a whole lot more through a modern-day telescope than David, the shepherd boy, saw, sitting on a grassy hillside. I wonder if David wondered, as I do, what it might be like to fly among the stars. The magic of the night sky has fascinated such scientists as Copernicus and Galileo, and the not-so-scientific space buffs like me. The air is so clear on the New Mexican desert that it seems I could catch a star in my hands like a lightning bug, perhaps put it in a jar to study later.

Of course, I know that many stars, planets, and suns are bigger than our earth. And while astronauts may fly to distant planets, I, like David, will have to be content to enjoy them from a distance.

And like David, I marvel at their magnitude and wonder why God takes the time to care for one gray-haired granny on Planet Earth. He loves me; that's why, just as He loves you. His love stretches beyond the farthest outback of the universe to Calvary.

Forgiving Others

Forgive as quickly and completely as the Master forgave you. And regardless of what else you put on, wear love. It's your basic all-purpose garment. Never be without it. Colossians 3:13, 14, Message.

A car accident; a family of four killed; only 15-year-old Jason lived—forever a quadriplegic. The drunken driver walked away from the accident uninjured.

Since it was the man's third driving-under-the-influence charge, the courts sentenced him to 10 years in prison. During his prison term the man found Jesus. When his heart was changed, the driver wanted to apologize to the boy for his actions.

A prison chaplain contacted Jason and asked him if he'd like to meet with the man. Jason, then 21, didn't know how he'd feel facing the man who'd robbed him of his family and his life, but he agreed to see him.

When Jason faced the object of his nightmares, he was surprised at the prisoner's small stature. In his dreams the driver had been a monster. Through tears the prisoner told of finding Jesus and asked forgiveness.

Jason tried to harden his heart, but tears filled his eyes, for his heart belonged to Jesus too. Because of the friendship that grew between the two men, Jason found a new life sharing his story with prisoners who need the cleansing forgiveness of Jesus Christ.

Whee! Be free!

Love your enemies! Pray for those who persecute you! In that way you will be acting as true sons of your Father in heaven. Matthew 5:44, 45, TLB.

Have you ever played "crack the whip" on skates? What a blast! When you are the last person in the whip, your muscles ache as the other skaters pull you across the ice. Then suddenly you let go. What fun! It's as if you can fly!

Forgiveness is like that. Resentment drags you around and around the same circle until you forgive. Then you're free!

"But," you say, "Jason hurt me. Why should I forgive him? He doesn't deserve it. He makes me sick!"

That's truer than you may realize. Holding grudges against someone will make you sick, really sick. So what if the other person doesn't deserve to be forgiven? Don't you deserve to forgive?

People who forgive are happier and healthier. When you forgive, you replace feelings of anger and stress with positive emotions, such as love, joy, and peace. It takes courage to forgive, but you'll feel a lot better.

Negative feelings, such as anger, hate, and sadness, weaken the immune system and can bring on colds, stomachaches, and much more serious diseases, too.

Sometimes you need to forgive yourself. Ever do something stupid and feel like kicking yourself into next week? Ask forgiveness, then let it go! You can be free to fly as a true son or daughter of God.

Merry Hearts and Smiley Faces

When people are happy, they smile, but when they are sad, they look depressed. . . . Happy people always enjoy life. Proverbs 15:13-15, TEV.

When you see a glass with milk in it, is it half full or half empty? If you see the glass half full, you are an optimist. If you see it as half empty, you might be a pessimist. Optimists look for the good in life, while pessimists look for the bad. And their faces show it. A frown or a smile reveals what is happening inside, not the circumstances outside.

A wise man once said, "Pessimists may often be right, but optimists are more often happy."

After a fun day at Disneyland Annie complained about the long line at Space Mountain, forgetting the great time she had shared with her family riding Mr. Toad's Wild Ride and the Jungle Cruise.

How about you? Are you a pessimist or an optimist? It's easy to be a pessimist. Nothing's perfect on this earth. Like Annie, you can always find something wrong. And as with Annie, what's happening in your heart shows on your face and in your words.

Can you imagine a grumpy Jesus? Of course not. Jesus was the greatest optimist the world has ever seen because He trusted His heavenly Dad. And you know what? We can trust Him too.

Guerrilla Kindness

I led them with cords of human kindness, with ties of love. Hosea 11:4, NIV.

I have a project for you—a campaign of guerrilla kindness. That's right, guerrilla kindness. You've all heard of guerrilla warfare, in which camouflaged soldiers hide in the jungle and shoot their unsuspecting enemies. Well, guerrilla kindness is where the "soldiers"—you and your friends—shoot unexpected acts of kindness at others.

This idea isn't original with me. Seventeen-year-old Rachel Scott, one of the Christian students killed in the Columbine High School shootings in April of 1999, wrote in her diary about her dream of starting a positive chain reaction of individual acts of kindness in her school: to reach those with disabilities and those picked on, standing up for those who are bullied.

Wouldn't it be too cool if you, I, and thousands of other kids and adults around the world made Rachel's dream a reality? What fabulous stories we would one day share with Rachel in God's kingdom. Can you see the tears of happiness she would shed to learn that her words changed so many people's lives? What do you think? Today let's defeat Satan's guerrilla warfare with God's guerrilla kindness in our homes, schools, and neighborhoods.

A Little Surprise

*Would you give your son a stone when he asks for bread? . . .
You know how to give good things to your children. How much
more, then, will your Father in heaven give good things to those
who ask him! Matthew 7:9-11, TEV.*

Happy Birthday, Valerie! Today is my little sister Valerie's birthday. I remember when I first met the blond-haired blue-eyed baby of a year and a half.

I was disgusted! I had asked God for a "magic skin" doll and got a little sister! How could my parents do such a thing to me—bring into our home a little sister? Having an older sister to boss me around all the time was enough for one kid to bear without having to share my home, my parents, and my toys with another.

Mom said that Valerie would be living with us while her mother attended college in another state. When Valerie arrived, my worst fears became a reality. The little girl charmed the heart out of my dad, my mom, and yes, even me.

I didn't know I needed a little sister, and I didn't know she would grow to be one of my best friends, but God knew. So happy birthday, Valerie. You definitely are a precious gift from a very wise God.

No Fear

The Lord is my Helper and I am not afraid of anything that mere man can do to me. Hebrews 13:6, TLB.

A slogan on cars and trucks, T-shirts, jeans, and baseball caps reads "No Fear!"

Timmy understood fear. He was terrified of Joe, the bully on his block. When the bully wrenched Timmy's new red bicycle from him, Timmy ran home and sobbed into his pillow. At dinner Timmy's dad asked how he was enjoying his new bike. Embarrassed, the boy admitted that the block bully had stolen it from him.

"Can you get it back for me?" Timmy asked.

"No; that's something you need to do tonight!" his father replied.

Face Joe? But Dad was adamant. After dinner Timmy dragged himself down the street to the bully's house and rang the doorbell. Joe opened the door. "What do you want?" he snarled.

Timmy gulped. "I want my bike back."

Suddenly Joe's eyes widened with fear. "It-it-it's right here."

Timmy couldn't believe his ears, nor the look of terror on Joe's face, until he turned and saw his frowning six-foot-five-inch father standing behind him. Somehow Joe didn't seem so big and threatening anymore.

What fears do you face? A bully named Joe? A physical disability? A scary disease? Just like Timmy, your heavenly Dad is with you, ready to cut your enemies down to size.

A Perfect Mint-ten

The Lord will perfect that which concerneth me. Psalm 138:8.

When my husband was a boy he collected baseball cards. He had every player's card from the forties and fifties—Mickey Mantle, Joe DiMaggio, Hank Aaron— all the baseball greats stored in a shoebox under his bed. When Richard returned home from college, imagine his horror to discover that his mother had cleaned out his room, throwing away the entire collection! Poor Mom Rizzo would never have thrown them out if she had known that one day the cards would be worth millions of dollars.

In the world of baseball cards, there is a class of cards called a "pristine" card. This card is absolutely perfect, not one flaw, not one wrinkle, not one smudge. If a pristine card is worth $2,500, one slightly creased corner drops its value to $25. Two creased corners drop it to $10 or less. It can never be perfect again.

Now take a newly minted, pristine $10 bill. If you bend a corner, how much is it worth? $10, right? If you crumple it? $10. If you wad it up and stomp it into the dirt? $10. God's kids are more like $10 bills than baseball cards. No matter how badly you mess up, become scarred or smudged with sin, your value to God never changes.

Nasty Little Secrets

The good man out of the good treasure of his heart brings forth what is good; and the evil man out of the evil treasure brings forth what is evil; for his mouth speaks from that which fills his heart. Luke 6:45, NASB.

A policeman pulled over a car and told the driver that because he was wearing his seat belt, he had won $5,000 from the state safety commission.

"What are you going to do with the money?" the policeman asked.

"I guess I'll get a driver's license," the man replied.

"Don't listen to him," his passenger yelled. "He's a smart aleck when he's drunk."

This awakened a man in the back seat who took one look at the cop and groaned, "I knew we wouldn't get far in a stolen car."

If you think, *How stupid! He should have kept his mouth shut,* I have news for you. Sooner or later, a man's words will reveal the secrets of his heart. The same is true for a woman, a boy, or a girl. A person might get away with evil for a while, but sooner or later, when he or she least expects it—whamo! Just like the guy in the story.

Likewise, good thoughts stored in the heart will sooner or later become evident to those around you as well.

Imagine That

This is how much God loved you: He gave Jesus, His one and only Son. Do you know why? So that you will not destroy yourself. That's why. By believing on Him, you can have a life that is whole and everlasting. John 3:16, Rizzo paraphrase.

Did you know:

☞ Heinz 57 got its name because there are 57 ingredients in the ketchup?

☞ a rat can last longer without water than a camel?

☞ an elephant can smell water 3 miles away?

☞ your stomach must produce a new layer of mucus every two weeks or it will digest itself?

☞ some insects can live up to a year without their heads?

☞ if you sprinkled salt on a dry tongue, you wouldn't taste it?

☞ a giraffe can clean its ears with its 21-inch tongue?

You could happily live your whole life without knowing these facts, but that's not true about today's promise. All joy, love, peace, and hope come from knowing and believing the words of John 3:16. God loves you so much that He'd rather die than live without you. That's the most important fact you can ever learn, and it's a fact to live by!

Meet a few Greats

Whenever you did one of these things to someone overlooked or ignored, that was me—you did it to me. Matthew 25:40, Message.

Meet Steven the Great: 10-year-old Steve returned his Nintendo birthday gift to buy a warm coat for a homeless boy at school.

Twelve-year-old Melissa the Great organizes block yard sales to raise money to send homeless kids to summer camp.

Eleven-year-old Josh and his buddies spend their summers collecting money for backpacks and school supplies for kids who wouldn't otherwise be able to afford them.

In 1996, when Betsy and Danny learned that some people wouldn't have a turkey for Thanksgiving, they raised enough money to buy turkeys for 36 hungry families. In 1997 they collected enough for 360; in 1998, 1,000; in 1999, 1,800.

Instead of balloons and birthday cakes, 6-year-old Ashley asked for a different kind of birthday party—one held at animal rescue mission. Instead of gifts, her friends brought donations for the care of the animals. Instead of games, they played with the kittens and puppies.

On her seventh birthday she raised money for the aquarium; on her eighth, a retirement home; on her ninth, a children's hospital; on her tenth, a soup kitchen; and on her eleventh, she staged a "hike" for muscular dystrophy research.

Got any great ideas on how to become one of God's greats?

17 March

Sleepless No More

He ordered his angels to guard you wherever you go. If you stumble, they'll catch you; their job is to keep you from falling. Psalm 91:11, 12, Messsage.

Jeff had cancer. The pain from the disease and the nausea from the treatment made it impossible to sleep at night. He tried drugs and pain killers—they didn't work. And the less he slept, the weaker he became; the weaker he became, the stronger his disease grew within his body.

One night in desperation he recited a prayer his mother had taught him years earlier.

"Five little angels around my bed;
One at the foot and one at my head;
One on the left and one on the right;
And one to hold me oh, so tight."

He felt silly praying the words of a child's prayer, but he continued. The first night he slept through the night after praying the prayer 35 times. The next night he slept after repeating the child's prayer 10 times. Every night he prayed the prayer, and every night he managed to sleep soundly regardless of the pain.

Jeff beat the cancer, and to this day, the 35-year-old father prays the prayer of faith to remind himself that God keeps His promises.

God's Alphabet Soup

Taste and see that the Lord is good. Psalm 34:8.

On rainy spring days I love the aroma of homemade alphabet soup bubbling in my kitchen. And when it comes to the eating—yummy!

God has a delightfully delicious soup for you to taste and enjoy. You can find it in His Word. While I don't use a recipe to make mine, God gave us His recipe, and it's incredibly satisfying. Use a King James Bible and savor the flavor of God's love. Hint: Go creative on X.

A—Romans 8:15	N—Revelation 14:1
B—Proverbs 10:22	O—Psalm 45:7
C—Lamentations 3:22	P—Isaiah 26:3
D—Psalm 32:7	Q—Ecclesiastes 9:17
E—James 1:12	R—Matthew 5:6
F—Hebrews 11:1	S—Psalm 62:2
G—2 Corinthians 12:9	T—Philippians 4:6
H—Psalm 51:10	U—Proverbs 23:23
I—Hebrews 9:15	V—1 John 5:4
J—Nehemiah 8:10	W—Colossians 1:9
K—Matthew 6:33	X—1 Peter 5:6
L—Psalm 5:11	Y—Matthew 11:29
M—Hebrews 4:16	Z—Isaiah 9:7

Jesus Christ is all this and so much more. Taste Him for yourself.

Unbelievable Love

Christ our passover is sacrificed for us. 1 Corinthians 5:7.

A father, a son, and the son's friend got caught in a sudden storm while sailing on the Pacific. A high wave swept both boys into the ocean." The preacher glanced at two boys slumped down in the third pew.

"Grabbing a rescue line, the father had to decide to which boy he would throw the lifeline. The man knew that his son knew Jesus and the other boy didn't. Shouting, 'I love you, son,' above the torrent, the father threw the lifeline to the other boy. By the time he pulled the friend into the boat, his son had disappeared beneath the waves; his body was never found."

"The father knew," the old man continued, "his son was safe in Jesus, while the friend was not. He saved the boy's life, hoping he would find salvation in Jesus too."

After the service one of the boys who'd been listening said to the preacher, "That was a nice story, but not very realistic for a father to allow his son to die so the other boy could find Christ."

"You have a point there," said the preacher, a smile filling his face. "I told the story to illustrate God's love for you. You see . . . I was the son's friend."

An SFGTD Box

You'll do best by filling your minds and meditating on things true, noble, reputable, authentic, compelling, gracious—the best, not the worst; the beautiful, not the ugly; things to praise, not things to curse. Philippians 4:8, Message.

Everyone needs a SFGTD (something for God to do) box. When you come up against something you can't handle, you can put it in the box. He will take care of it in His time.

If you have a bad hair day, think about cancer patients having a no hair day, and put it in the box.

If Mom fixed oatmeal again and you hate oatmeal, think of the kids who haven't a mom to fix oatmeal or any other breakfast for them. Put that in the box.

If Dad's car breaks down on the way to school, think about the millions of people for whom a car is an unheard-of luxury. If your sister or brother scribbles on your favorite baseball glove, think of the kids who have no family, who are all alone in the world with no one to love. Put those in the box.

If you miss the school bus home and must walk, think of the paraplegic who would love to be in your shoes.

If your worst enemy tells lies about you, things could be worse—you could be him or her.

Remember, all these problems fit neatly in your SFGTD box.

21 March

A New Song

He taught me how to sing the latest God-song, a praise-song to our God. Psalm 40:3, Message.

Nineteen-year-old Geron Davis loved to write songs. He'd been writing songs since he was 9 or 10 years old. So it was natural for Geron's pastor father to ask his teenage son to write a song for the opening of the brand-new church the congregation had finished building—three months before the scheduled service. Geron, being a busy teen, didn't sweat it. He had plenty of time.

A month before the service Geron's father asked him how the song was coming. "Fine, Dad," the boy replied, knowing he'd not written anything yet.

Nothing had changed two weeks before the event when his father asked him again. Every night the week before the celebration service, everyone, including Geron, worked late to finish in time. This left the young man with no time to write music until midnight the evening before the song would be sung.

Alone in the silence of the empty sanctuary, he sat at the new grand piano and bowed his head to pray. His fingers began to wander over the keys. Fifteen minutes later the words and music to "We Are Standing on Holy Ground" were born. Through Geron's song millions have discovered that holy ground is wherever God comes to dwell in His people.

Ministering Spirits

Are not all angels ministering spirits sent to serve those who will inherit salvation? Hebrews 1:14, NIV.

The ground came up to meet the young pilot at an incredible speed. Grant knew the plane was about to crash. "Oh, dear God, help me," he muttered as he wrestled with the controls of his blue-and-white Cessna.

Grant and several of his pilot friends were rehearsing stunts for an air show to benefit a local charity. His dream was to fly mission runs into the South American jungles. But until God opened the opportunity for him to go, he would fly when and wherever needed.

As the windshield of the plane shattered into a ball of fire, Grant saw a giant Being standing in front of him. The Being breathed into the pilot's mouth. Fresh pure oxygen filled Grant's lungs just before he lost consciousness.

Later, as he mended from a broken left leg and shattered right ankle, Grant learned that the mechanic who hauled him from the wreckage almost died from the toxic fumes in his lungs, while Grant's lungs were totally clear.

A couple watching the crash and expecting the pilot to die prayed he would experience no pain. Grant felt no pain from his injuries. Don't tell Grant God doesn't answer prayer. He knows better.

The Contact Lens

Bear ye one another's burdens, and so fulfil the law of Christ. Galatians 6:2.

Brenda clung to the side of the granite cliff, terrified to death. This was her first time rock climbing, and she was certain she'd tumble off the mountain to her death. As she made it to a ledge, with hundreds of feet below her and hundreds of feet above her, her safety rope snapped against her eye and sent her contact lens flying.

She frantically searched for the lens, praying as she looked. "Lord, You know every pebble and leaf on this mountain. Please help me." But Brenda had no success, and had to stumble down the mountain with her blurred vision.

At base camp she met a climber starting up the mountain.

"Hey," he asked, "did you lose a contact lens? I found one on the mountain." What was even more unbelievable was that the climber spotted the lens moving slowly across the face of a rock on the back of an ant.

Brenda's father, a cartoonist, drew a picture of an ant lugging a contact lens with the words, "Father, I don't know why You want me to carry this thing. I can't eat it, and it's heavy. But if You want me to carry it, I will."

Biggest Math Problem in the World

By faith they [Moses and the people] passed through the Red Sea as by dry land. Hebrews 11:29.

How did Moses feed 3 million people? It would take two freight trains a mile long carrying 1,500 tons of food every day. To cook the food would take two more trains carrying 4,000 tons of firewood each day and 11 million gallons of water transported by a freight train 1,800 miles long.

To cross the Red Sea in one night, the Israelites needed a space three miles wide so they could walk 5,000 abreast.

When they stopped each night to sleep, they would need a campground two thirds the size of the state of Rhode Island, or 750 square miles.

Do you think Moses sat down with a sheet of papyrus and a piece of charcoal to figure all of this out before he left Egypt? I don't think so. Moses believed that God would take care of all their needs.

However, the trip to the Promised Land should have taken 11 days. Instead it took 40 years. Moses trusted, but the people didn't. Yet even though the people didn't trust God, He made it so that their clothes and their shoes didn't wear out in all that time. Aren't you glad that God can be trusted even when we doubt Him?

Shipwrecked

I am the way. John 14:6.

The only survivor of a shipwreck washed up on a deserted island. At first he prayed for God to rescue him, but no one came. Feeling hungry, he explored the island for food. Then it began to rain. Shivering cold and miserable, he sulked under a broad-leafed bush. "You promised, Lord, to take care of me," he prayed.

When the rain stopped, he collected driftwood and palm fronds off the beach and built himself a hut to protect himself from the elements.

One day, after fixing a meager meal over a small campfire he maintained, the man went in search of food for the next day's meals. Seeing smoke curling up into the late afternoon sky, he returned to his camp to find his hut burned to the ground. Discouraged, the man crumpled onto the sand. "God, how could You do this to me?" he sobbed.

The next morning he awoke to the blast of a ship's horn and spotted a motorized raft approaching his island. They'd seen the smoke from the fire and had come to rescue him.

When things seem to be at their worst and I can't see the way I should go, God reminds me not only that He knows the way out of my troubles, but that He is the way.

Silly Tales and Serious Truth

I am the . . . truth. John 14:6.

Have you heard the one about the South American blush spider that hitched a ride to Blare Airport in Chicago on the underside of an airplane's toilet seat? It then attached itself to someone's trouser leg and traveled into the restroom of an airport restaurant, where it fatally bit five people. The same spider is currently flying back and forth across the United States on toilet seats, biting other unsuspecting victims.

Yeah, right. This story is an entertaining example of what is called an urban myth, a hoax. There were two giveaway clues: first, there is no such airport as Blare Airport in Chicago; second, a blush spider isn't a spider at all, but a kind of varicose vein.

Debunking hoaxes is David Emery's job. He receives 50 to 75 e-mail messages a day asking him about such stories. A little research on the Internet, and he can quickly identify the true stories from the urban myths or legends.

Satan, the father of lies, loves to spread urban myths about God and His Son, Jesus. Don't get taken, hook, line, and sinker. Jesus said, "I am the way, the truth, and the life" (John 14:6). A little research into God's Word and into who Jesus is will reveal God's truth and uncover the devil's lies.

27 March

Virtual Reality

I am the . . . life. John 14:6.

On a recent visit to Disney World I took a virtual reality trip. At one point a rattlesnake leaped right off the screen toward me. I screamed and ducked, even though I knew it wasn't real.

Rafting down the Colorado River by way of a video is nothing compared to actually rafting down the river. Even if video-makers could pipe in the spray of the water, the cries of the eagles, and the smells of the forest, it wouldn't be real unless you are there. Living someone else's adventure is never as good as experiencing it yourself. Some kids, and even adults, spend so much time playing virtual reality video games, they don't get to experience real life.

Watching the homeless scrounge food from garbage cans on TV isn't the same as being up close and personal, such as passing out sandwiches to the hungry at the local soup kitchen, weeding a housebound woman's flower garden, clearing garbage from a vacant lot in the neighborhood—that's what life is all about.

Jesus said, "I am the way, the truth, and the life" (John 14:6), God wants us to live life to the fullest, because He is life. Get involved with the reality of our world; don't settle for the make-believe reality viewed on a TV or computer screen.

A Thing of Beauty

The Lord looks not at the things man looks at. Man looks at the outward appearance, but the Lord looks at the heart. 1 Samuel 16:7, NIV.

The concert hall vibrated with anticipation as the lights dimmed and the curtains parted. Whispers of shock swept through the audience as an ugly little man walked across the stage to the piano and poised his hands over the keys. The muscles in his face swelled; the veins in his forehead stood out; his wide eyes rolled about wildly; his lips began to quiver.

"Look at his hairy little fingers. They can hardly stretch an octave," someone whispered. It was true, the backs of Beethoven's hands were densely covered with black hair. His fingers were so short, they could barely reach an octave. But when the music started, the audience forgot about the ugly-looking man and his stumplike fingers.

Critics described Ludwig van Beethoven's playing as "explosive," a titanic execution. He became a hit in the courts of Vienna and beyond—not because of his personal beauty but for the beauty he produced on the piano, the beautiful music that came from his heart.

God sees the beauty beneath the surface, in a person's heart. We, His children, are learning how to do the same.

29 March

Harnessing the Wind

Then He [Jesus] stood up and told the wind to be silent. . . . The sea became as smooth as glass. The men rubbed their eyes, astonished. "What's going on here? Wind and sea come to heel at his command!" Matthew 8:26, 27, Message.

Benjamin Franklin was a remarkable guy. Besides flying kites during storms to discover static electricity, the great American statesman was the first postmaster general, was an ambassador to France, and founded *The Saturday Evening Post.*

Big stuff, huh? But did you also know he was a first-class swimmer who invented the first wet suit and created webbed sandals—or flippers as they're called today? Sketches in his journal show a pair of water skis—barrel staves attached to his feet. And how would he propel himself across the water with gasoline engines almost a century away? A giant kite that he noted would "harness the wind."

Alas, poor Ben never tried out his invention, and he probably never imagined wind surfing, either. As far before his time as Ben might have been, Someone else had already "harnessed the wind" and the waves. But then, Benjamin Franklin was only an inventor, while Jesus Christ was and is the Creator.

God Majors in the Impossible

For with God nothing shall be impossible. Luke 1:37.

Be reasonable, Jackie. You can practice till the cows come home, but you will never make it to the big leagues."

The coach's words rang in his head as he returned to the dugout. The coach was right. He should resign himself to playing for the all-Black baseball league. No Negro ball player, no matter how well he played, would ever be allowed to play with the star White players.

In the early 1940s White Americans harbored dangerous hang-ups about people of different races. Jackie didn't know he would be one of God's chosen to begin changing people's notions. Through him, God would prove to be master of the impossible in the world of professional sports.

On July 5, 1947, Jackie Roosevelt Robinson found himself up to bat on an all-White, major league baseball team. And he struck out

However, Jackie proved his worth from then on. During his 10 years with the Brooklyn Dodgers, he maintained a .311 batting average, was chosen as Rookie of the Year in 1947 and Most Valuable Player in 1949, and in 1962 was the first Black player to be inducted into the Baseball Hall of Fame. Skill, not color or nationality, determines a player's worth today. Jackie Robinson did the impossible. Did he know that with God nothing is impossible? Do you?

31 March

Mule Day

Submit therefore to God. Resist the devil and he will flee from you. James 4:7, NASB.

Ever spend time thinking about the humble mule? And have you ever celebrated the day of the mule? Technically, March 31 is Mule Day in Columbia, Tennessee. That's the day farmers would bring their mules into town to swap or sell.

The mule has another celebration day set aside in its honor. On March 27, 1898, the town of Matanzas, Cuba, was bombarded by United States war ships during the Spanish-American War. After a day enduring heavy barrage, the citizens of Matanzas came out of hiding to discover that their casualties consisted of one mule. All that cannon fire and one mule dead.

Mules are known for their stubbornness. Did you ever hear anyone say, "He's stubborn as a mule"? Did you ever think that could be a compliment? It can.

A synonym for being stubborn could be resisting, the middle step in a great promise: First you submit to God; then you resist the devil; and after that, all the devil can do is flee from you. See? Stubbornness can be a good trait when it's first committed to God. Celebrate mule day by submitting to God, then resisting the devil with the stubbornness of a mule, and victory is ours! Yeah!

Atheists' Day

Fools say to themselves, "There is no God!" Proverbs 14:1, TEV.

Poor *Richard's Almanac* published the following verse in 1760: "The first of April some do say; is set apart for All Fools' Day. But why people call it so, neither I nor they themselves do know."

Whatever the reason, this day is called April Fools'. God's Word says that a fool is one who doesn't believe in God. These people call themselves atheists. Though the following is only a joke, I know you'll get the point.

An atheist is swimming in the ocean; suddenly a shark starts heading toward him. Swimming as fast as he can, the man cries, "Oh, God! Save me!"

Suddenly the man thinks he hears God saying, "You're an atheist. How can you ask for My help when you don't believe I exist?"

"It's true," the swimmer cries. "I don't believe in You, but how about the shark? Can You make him believe in You?"

God replies, "As you wish."

The atheist glances around in time to see the shark, who is ready to chomp down on the man's leg, pause, close his eyes, and say, "Thank You, Lord, for the food I am about to receive."

How many people wait until they're in trouble before believing in the God who can save them?

2 April

ATP Kids

Do for others what you want them to do for you. Matthew 7:12, TLB.

The first week of April is Golden Rule Week. Ten major religions of the world have the golden rule as part of their philosophy: "Do unto others as you would have them do unto you." No matter how you say it, the rule is quite simple: Treat others how you wish to be treated.

ATP kids are kids who live by the golden rule. They affirm the positive! The radio station KARM in Visalia, California, honors ATP kids by reading their names over the air during the Family Hour. I know because I host the program. I get to congratulate the ATP kids nominated.

Teachers in the area send me the names of kids who help others in and out of the classroom. Think about it: Schools honor kids who get good grades, who do well in sports and music. Why not kids who are kind, helpful, and have great attitudes?

You can start an ATP club at your school—make membership cards and posters; have a motto, a theme song, and a special meeting time. And it all starts with one person—you. If you ask God to help you find people to help, He will. And it can begin with one smile—yours!

Baby Vet

Let no man despise thy youth; but be thou an example of the believers. 1 Timothy 4:12.

No one suspected Calvin Graham was underage when he enlisted in the Navy during World War II and was assigned as a gunner on the U.S.S. *San Diego.* During the 1942 Battle of Guadalcanal, despite being struck by shrapnel, the boy dragged several of his fellow sailors to safety. His superior officers awarded Calvin several medals for bravery under fire and a purple heart for being wounded in action.

All was fine until they discovered Calvin's true age—12 years old. Immediately the Navy gave him a dishonorable discharge, revoked his military benefits, and stripped him of all his medals and honors. Baby Vet, as his buddies called him, returned home in shame.

It wasn't until 1988 that Congress voted to return Calvin's honors and benefits and to cleanse his record of the dishonorable discharge. Baby Vet died four years later.

Calvin's lie isn't what makes him a hero in America's record book. He's a hero because of his willingness to risk his life for his buddies, regardless of his age. To the men whose lives he saved, Baby Vet will always be a hero.

Let no one despise your youth. As with Calvin, your words and your actions will speak for you.

A Googol What?

*Your thoughts—how rare, how beautiful! God, I'll never compre-
hend them! I couldn't even begin to count them—any more than
I could count the sand of the sea. Psalm 139:17, 18, Message.*

The month of April is Mathematics Education Month. If a
Guide magazine is 8.25 inches long, how many *Guides,*
stretched end to end, would it take to reach the moon?
The moon is 238,857 miles from the earth. Answer:
1,834,421,760 *Guides* to reach the moon—almost 2 billion
magazines—a number truly out of this world!

God challenged Abraham to count the sand of the sea or
the stars in the sky. He couldn't do it.

Edward Kasner, a famous mathematician, wanted a name
for such a number—one that couldn't be counted. The number he chose was 1 followed by 100 zeroes. His 9-year-old
nephew named the number—googol.

Then the nephew came up with an even larger number—a 1
followed by as many zeroes you can write before you get tired.
He called it a googolplex. Webster's dictionary is more precise.
It defines googolplex as "1 followed by a googol of zeroes."

Let your imagination take you out of this world to God's
world. I wonder if the Creator of the universe counts stars in
googols and googolplexes too. Someday I'd like to ask Him.
And that's just one of the googolplex of questions I plan to
ask—someday. How about you?

Wacky Jell-O

May my spoken words and unspoken thoughts be pleasing even to you, O Lord my Rock and my Redeemer. Psalm 19:14, TLB.

Jell-O, I love Jell-O. I like the way it slides across my tongue, squishes through my teeth, and slithers down my throat. If it's black cherry Jell-O with minimarshmallows and fruit cocktail, it's all the yummier.

What I choose to put into my Jell-O is important. If I accidentally dropped nutshells into my Jell-O, I could strain them out before the gelatin hardened.

Your mind is a little like Jell-O. It's important to fill it with good things, such as today's text. God's Word memorized stays with you forever. But what about the bad stuff, the nut shells you might add, accidentally or on purpose? Once they're in, they're there for good. Only God can remove from our brains the bad stuff and make our minds clear and new again.

So think Jell-O when you choose a book to read, when you sit down to watch a TV program, or play a video game. Think Jell-O when you're tempted to hang out with kids who curse, swear, and have bad attitudes. Think Jell-O when you consider the "who" you want to be and the "who" you will one day become.

No Housework Day

Honor your father and mother, that you may have a long, good life in the land the Lord your God will give you. Exodus 20:12, TLB.

One afternoon Shelly and Jere came home to find total mayhem in the house. Their little brothers and sister were dressed in their pajamas, playing in the mud.

Inside was an even bigger mess. A lamp had been knocked over. There were toys scattered everywhere. Dirty dishes filled the kitchen sink; breakfast cereal spread across the counter; dog food spilled on the floor.

Worried that their mom might be sick or injured, the teens rushed up the stairs, stepping over toys and stacks of clothes. They found Mom curled up on the bed, reading a book. She glanced up from her book. "How was your day?" she asked.

"What happened here?" Shelly asked.

"You know how you come home from school and ask me what I did all day?" The mother smiled sweetly. "Well, today I didn't."

Sometimes members of the family forget that the dishwasher doesn't fill itself and the clothes don't wash themselves. Tomorrow is No Housework Day. I'm telling you one day early so you can give a big thank-you kiss to the person in your home who keeps things clean and running smoothly. Perhaps you can plan a special surprise, such as cleaning your room without being asked or emptying the dishwasher without complaining.

What Do You Say?

When God made a promise to Abraham, he backed it to the hilt, putting his own reputation on the line. He said, "I promise I'll bless you with everything I have—bless and bless and bless!" Hebrews 6:13, 14, Message.

You say, "It's impossible"
God says, "All things are possible" (Matthew 19:26).
You say, "Nobody loves me."
God says, "I love you" (John 13:34, TLB).
You say, "I can't do it."
God says, "You can do all things" (see Philippians 4:13).
You say, "I'm worried."
God says, "Cast your cares upon Me" (see 1 Peter 5:7).
You say, "I'm not smart enough."
God says, "I will give you wisdom" (see 1 Corinthians 1:30).
You say, "I'm afraid."
God says, "I have not given you the spirit of fear" (see 2 Timothy 1:7).
You say, "I don't have enough money."
God says, "I will supply all your needs" (see Philippians 4:19).
You say, "I feel all alone."
God says, "I will never leave thee, nor forsake thee" (Hebrews 13:5).

So tell me now, how do you feel? Rich? Blessed? Grateful? Remember, attitude is everything!

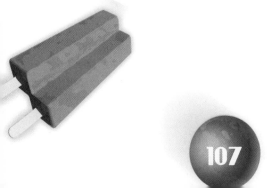

A Famous Man's Birthday

We are His. Christ died and rose again for this very purpose, so that he can be our Lord both while we live and when we die. Romans 14:9, TLB.

Today is Siddhartha Gautama's birthday. He was born in India on this day in 563 B.C. (before Christ) and died in 488 B.C. His name in Sanskrit means "the enlightened one." You know Siddhartha as Buddha, the founder of the Buddhist religion.

Abu al-Qasim Muhammad, prophet and founder of Islam or the Muslim religion, lived and died somewhere between A.D. 570 and A.D. 632. Confucius, or K'ung-tzu, as he was also called, lived in China from 551 to 479 B.C., and was a philosopher and founder of Confucianism.

Jesus Christ, prophet, healer, preacher, was born in Bethlehem of Judah sometime around 4 B.C. Theologians don't know the exact day, but they suspect it was sometime in the spring. They do know that Jesus, the founder of Christianity, was crucified on a Roman cross in A.D. 31.

Four religions; four individuals who, for a short time, lived outstanding lives, then died. But that's where the similarities end. In the first three men's graves, you would find human skeletons; in the fourth—nothing, because Jesus Christ is alive and well and living out of this world. We don't worship a dead prophet, but a living Savior. And that makes all the difference.

Troubled Runaways

In this world you will have trouble. But take heart! I have over-come the world. John 16:33, NIV.

Generals Lee and Grant met in William McLean's parlor in Appomatox Court House, Virginia, on this day to hammer out the details of the South's surrender to end America's Civil War. More than 500,000 Americans died in the bloody conflict.

That the surrender would occur in Mr. McLean's parlor is ironic since the first battle of the war, the First Battle of Bull Run, as well as the Second Battle of Bull Run, in 1862, took place on the McLean farm in northern Virginia. After a cannonball dropped down the farmhouse chimney into Mrs. McLean's pot of stew and exploded all over her kitchen, the terrified couple packed up and moved to southern Virginia, where they thought they'd get away from the war. Instead, the war followed them, right to their doorstep and into their parlor.

Are you turned off by civil wars going on in your home? in your school? in your church? in your heart? Have you considered running away to a better place? Running away isn't always the best answer. Just ask Farmer and Mrs. McLean—trouble is everywhere.

Jesus reminds us, "In this world you will have troubles, but I have overcome the world." He has the answer, no matter what your trouble may be.

10 April

Fly Like an Eagle

They that wait upon the Lord shall renew their strength; they shall mount up with wings as eagles; they shall run, and not be weary; they shall walk, and not faint. Isaiah 40:31.

When I was 5 years old, I wanted to fly more than anything in the world. Once I belly-flopped down our living room stairs, trying to fly. At 7, I tied the corners of a bedsheet to my wrists and ankles then jumped off the house roof. Ouch!

When my fifth-grade teacher took our class for a single-engine plane ride, I fell in love with flying. I still like it, seat belts, late flights, and all. I love looking down at the blanket of puffy clouds or seeing all the tiny lights below me in the night.

Someday I'll fly without the power of a Boeing 747. I don't know how God will attach my wings, but I want to soar with the eagles to the tops of snowy mountains and swoop down at breathtaking speeds into lush green valleys. I want to do spirals in the air that make me dizzy, along with back flips and somersaults that will be out of this world. But until Jesus comes, I'll wait on the Lord and dream of the day I'll fly with the eagles. How about you?

Creative Love Day

This is my command: Love one another the way I love you. This is the very best way to love. John 15:12, Message.

How do you say "I love you" the way Jesus does? There are a thousand different ways. Here are just a few: On Friday afternoons Tiffany and her friend Jackie wash and style hair at the nursing home near their home. Sela and Jeremy help make bologna sandwiches at the soup kitchen after school on Mondays and Wednesdays. Benji and Erin paint their faces, put on plaid, baggy pants, and "clown around" at the hospital ward for critically ill children. Kari, Michaila, and Darek conduct a once-a-week Bible puppet show for the younger kids of the inner city. Keith and Jacob baby-sit toddlers after school on Thursdays so two single moms can do their grocery shopping. Sean washes feet at the homeless shelter on Saturday nights while his dad, a physician, medicates their sores. What a bunch of creative kids!

National Youth Service Day, a two-day event, will be here soon. More than 3 million kids in 3,000 towns, cities, and suburbs across the country will be finding creative ways to serve others on those two days. I'm calling today Creative Ideas Day, the day you and your friends can plan how you be a part of the millions of kids who want to make their world a better place by demonstrating the love of Jesus.

12 April

Hiking on Thunder Mountain

Casting all your care upon him; for he careth for you. 1 Peter 5:7.

Malcolm and his friend Carl were roped together as they climbed the rocky face of Thunder Mountain. Malcolm watched helplessly as one of Carl's pinions slipped, sending him down the rocks' icy surfaces and hauling Malcolm behind him.

Their free fall stopped when Malcolm's leg got caught in a narrow crevasse, leaving Carl dangling several feet below. After much maneuvering, Carl managed to regain his footing, but had no way to reach Malcolm several hundred feet above him on the mountain. And Malcolm knew from the pain in his leg that he'd broken it in the fall. To compound their dilemma, the temperatures were dropping as the sun disappeared behind a cloud bank that shrouded the area where Malcolm found himself trapped.

Carl whipped out his cellular phone and called for help. Within minutes a helicopter arrived and airlifted Carl to safety. Rescuing Malcolm would be more difficult now that his position was obscured by heavy clouds. The national weather station predicted that the cloud cover would stay for seven to 10 days.

Carl did the only thing he could do: he prayed. "Dear God, please save my friend. He doesn't know You, but I do."

(to be continued)

Two Nights on the Mountain

He [God] ordered his angels to guard you wherever you go.
Psalm 91:11, Message.

Malcolm shivered from the cold as night fell. The temperatures dropped to –20° F. The climber burrowed into the snow as far as he could to avoid the winds that were stirring up the loose snow.

The next morning Malcolm heard the helicopters searching for him, then heard them leave. He doubted he could survive another night on the mountain. From somewhere in his memory his grandmother's voice came through: "He shall give his angels charge over thee," she said, "to keep thee in all thy ways. They shall bear thee up in their hands, lest thou dash thy foot against a stone" (Psalm 91:11, 12).

"God," the young man chuckled as he prayed, "I've definitely dashed my foot against a stone, and I think I've broken it. If You have a spare angel or two without much to do, I could use some of that help You promised."

Malcolm hoped he wasn't being sacrilegious talking to God like that. But he continued throughout the night. With the first light of morning Malcolm heard a helicopter. He looked up to see a small break in the clouds and a man being lowered on a rope to help him.

Malcolm survived with only a broken left leg and a sprained right ankle because of one tiny break in a 10-day storm on the mountain. Did this happened by chance? Out of this world!

Blooper of the Century

Pride goes before destruction and haughtiness before a fall.
Proverbs 16:18, TLB.

On April 15, 1912, the Baltimore *Evening Sun* published this headline: "All *Titanic* Passengers Safe; Transferred in Lifeboats at Sea." The *Sun's* famous mistake had many authors. They knew they were right, since everybody knew the mighty ship couldn't possibly sink.

The *Wall Street Journal* chided the New York *Times* for publishing the ridiculous story that the *Titanic* had sunk because everyone knew that the *Titanic's* bulkheads were watertight.

As you and I know, the famous "pride of the fleet" hit an iceberg. So certain that such a ship couldn't sink, the owners didn't stock enough lifeboats to hold the 2,224 passengers on board.

In July 1986 Jason Jr., a robot, searched the ship and discovered there was no gaping hole where the iceberg hit, but a series of little gashes that caused it to sink.

Nothing is invincible. The wisest man who ever lived wrote, "Pride goes before destruction." Fifteen hundred people drowned because someone forgot one simple proverb.

Miracle of My Sister

Declare his glory among the nations, his marvelous deeds among all the peoples. 1 Chronicles 16:24, NIV.

Let me tell you about my sister Connie. When she was born, she was 10 percent protein, 10 percent fat, 1 percent sugar, and 75 percent water. Connie dribbled 154 quarts of saliva before her first birthday. She crawled 93 miles before age 2. After age 2 she learned a new word every two hours for the next 10 years. By age 21 she had breathed over 3.5 million balloonfuls of air.

My sister's red hair, freckles, and blue eyes came from the 100,000 genes she inherited from her mother and father. Each of Connie's cells contains her full genetic code in her DNA. Her DNA is constantly replicating itself to make perfect copies of itself.

If the DNA in Connie's cells somehow get damaged, her cells will use the antioxidants vitamin C and vitamin E that Connie gets by eating her fruits and vegetables. Imagine, God knew what Connie's DNA cells would need long before she was born.

These facts apply to you and me as well—the drooling, the crawling, the DNA, all of it. God planned all of us even before He formed Adam's body out of Eden's mud. What's more marvelous is that He's still interested in every detail of our lives. Isn't God marvelous?

16 April

The Tournament

He doesn't treat us as our sins deserve. Psalm 103:10, Message.

In pro/am golf tournaments a professional golfer is teamed with an amateur. But the only score that matters is the professional's. As an amateur, you might not even know which end is up on a golf club. You may not know the difference between a wood or a putter or a five-iron. You may never break par. You may never hit the ball into even one of the 18 holes.

Yet, if your partner were Tiger Woods, you'd be on the winning team.

Imagine, along the way, having Mr. Woods show you how to hold your club correctly and which club to use for each situation. Imagine having him help you correct your slice. And when you made it to your first green, having him cheer for you.

That's how we play the game of life, too. Jesus is always by our side, helping, teaching, and cheering us on. But the best part is it's not how many holes in one we make or how many times we land in sand traps or in the "drink." Best yet, our score is erased. We win eternal life on His perfect score—His death on the cross. Incredible! The only way we can lose is by quitting the tournament and walking away from Him.

(Thanks to Max Lucado for the great illustration.)

Keep Your Focus

Let us fix our eyes on Jesus, the author and perfector of our faith.
Hebrews 12:2, NIV.

I love stories that come out of the Olympics, stories of victory and heart. One of my favorites is of the marathoner Frank Shorter.

Frank, far ahead of the pack, ran through the arch and into the arena. The cheers of the roaring crowd thundered against his eardrums with every exhausted step. Twenty-six miles, one run around the track, and he'd cross the finish line first.

As he headed down the track, the cheers from the grandstand suddenly turned to boos. What had he done wrong? He couldn't imagine. For an instant he stumbled, then considered stopping. But then his training cut in. Frank tuned out the censorious cries of the crowd and returned his focus to the prize—winning the race.

It wasn't until he burst across the finish line that Frank learned the boos hadn't been directed toward him, but toward some guy who had jumped from the stands and run onto the field. If Frank had let the booing crowd discourage him, he would have lost the race.

It's difficult to keep our eyes focused on Jesus when those around us boo or make fun of us, but as Frank learned, winning the race is worth it. Keep focused on Jesus.

Tug-of-war

The God of peace will soon crush Satan under your feet. The blessings from our Lord Jesus Christ be upon you. Romans 16:20, TLB.

Did you know that the game tug-of-war once was an Olympic sport just like running, swimming, and gymnastics? The contest called for one team to pull the other team six feet in five minutes.

In 1908 the British won because their team, eight police officers, wore heavy boots with steel plates in them that gripped the turf. The Americans accused them of cheating. At the next games in 1912, in Stockholm, the Swedish team defeated the Brits by holding the tug-of-war in sand instead of on a grassy field. The heavy boots couldn't grip the sand as they had the turf. Because of all the arguing and fighting, the Olympic officials voted to drop the tug-of-war competition from the games in 1920.

There's a bigger tug-of-war going on, not in the Olympics, but in people. God and Satan are battling for our hearts. Sometimes when we make bad choices and Satan gains ground, we end up with scrapes and bruises because Satan doesn't play fair. He cheats, lies, steals, bites, kicks, and gouges to get his way.

But I have good news for you. God's team already won by taking us all the way to the cross. Satan and his dastardly demons are crushed in the dirt under our feet.

A Timely Word

A man finds joy in giving an apt reply—and how good is a timely word! Proverbs 15:23, NIV.

Big words like "gigantic"; little words like "me"; long words like "supercalifragilisticexpialidocious"; short words like "hi." I like to play with words. I like the way they sound in my ears when they rhyme: "play, day, say, may, hay, ray, pay, Kay . . ." I like to pop them through my lips: "Peter Piper picked a peck of pickled peppers." I like to see them in my mind: . . . *the vast chasms of the universe . . .*

Did you know that the longest one-syllable word in English is "screeched?" And no words in the English language rhyme with "month," "orange," "silver," or "purple." Also, "dreamt" is the only word in English that ends with mt, and the only four words ending with dous are "tremendous," "horrendous," "stupendous," and "hazardous."

Word experts claim "cellar door" are the two most beautiful sounding words. I don't know about that. Personally, "I love you" and "I'm sorry" bring me more happiness. Add to that list of words that bring happiness, "You did a good job," "Thank you," and "Please," and you have quite a collection of words that will bring joy to others.

20 April

A Special Kind of Athlete

Make sure nobody pays back wrong for wrong, but always be kind to each other and to everyone else. 1 Thessalonians 5:15, NIV.

It was the final race. The crowd cheered as the runners took off like a shot, around the first bend and into the straight, around the second bend and the third and into the home stretch when suddenly one of the athletes tripped and fell. The audience gasped as the Olympian fell to the ground, his hopes for winning the heat gone.

If this had been your ordinary Olympic race for gold, the story would have been over. What happened next surprised everyone except the runners themselves. Instead of continuing to the finish line, every runner stopped to help their fallen competitor. After dusting off his knees and drying his tears, they linked arms and walked him across the finish line together.

Never happen in an Olympic race, you say? Well, it did. Not in the Olympic finals, but in the Special Olympics finals. The competitors in the Special Olympics were willing to sacrifice winning the gold medal to care for a friend in need. Sounds like those athletes had their priorities straight, huh? What about you?

The Red Baron

Put up thy sword into his place: for all they that take the sword shall perish with the sword. Matthew 26:52.

War is ugly. With all the violence on television, in the news, and in the movies, we sometimes forget that war is real. Real bullets kill real sons and daughters, fathers and brothers. And somewhere in the world right now, mothers, wives, sisters, and children cry real tears for those they lost because of war.

On this day in 1918 a famous pilot was shot down in the battle of Somme and died—Baron Manfred von Richthofen, the Red Baron.

Snoopy, the dog in the *Peanuts* comic strip, loved to climb atop his doghouse and pretend to shoot down enemy planes as the Red Baron did in World War I. And as humorous as that may have been in a cartoon strip, the real Red Baron was anything but funny.

Baron Manfred von Richthofen bragged of shooting down 80 planes in two years. Each of those planes carried a live, breathing pilot. The baron liked to boast, "My brother [in the German infantry] is a butcher. When I shoot down an Englishman, my hunting passion is satiated for at least 15 minutes."

The baron proved, once again, Jesus' words to Peter: "Those who live by the sword will die by the sword."

121

Justice for All

*Execute true judgment, and shew mercy and compassions. . . .
And oppress not the widow, nor the fatherless, the stranger, nor
the poor. Zechariah 7:9, 10.*

"But it's not fair," Esther wailed. "I was his wife! How can
the state take away my rightful inheritance?"

Her attorney shrugged. What could he do? New York
State's law discriminated against a woman inheriting her husband's business and wealth on his death.

In the 1850s a female couldn't vote, couldn't hold political
office, couldn't own property in her name, and couldn't represent herself in court. A woman even had to have a note from
her husband or her father giving her permission to ride a bicycle in town or to stay overnight in a hotel.

Frustrated with the laws, Esther Hobart Morris decided
the only way to change unfair laws was if women obtained the
right to vote. Moving to South Pass, Wyoming Territory,
Esther convinced William Bright, a member of the territorial
legislature, to introduce a women's suffrage bill. The legisla-
tors, as a joke, passed it two to one, and Governor John
Campbell signed it into law in 1869.

Wyoming wrote the first constitution in the world granting
equal voting rights for women. A year later Esther was appointed the first female justice of the peace in U.S. history.
While life isn't always fair, God's children can change things
for the better.

Not Even for Friends

Greater love has no one than this, that he lay down his life for his friends. John 15:13, NIV.

Nicolas Green and his parents were touring Italy in a rental car when suddenly they heard a shot, followed by the shattering of glass. They glanced in the back seat to see 9-year-old Nicolas slumped over, a bullet through his neck.

At the hospital Nicolas was declared DOA (dead on arrival). The police had no clues as to the source of the bullet. But the grieving parents weren't focusing on finding the guy who shot their son. Instead they did the unthinkable. They donated their son's organs to seven needy people.

Italians, famous for carrying out family vendettas (vows to "get even" for family slights), were stunned by the parents' generosity. The news spread through the country, then the world. International news reporters noted that over the years warriors had tried to conquer the country of Italy with elephants, cannons, and bombs; one little American had conquered it with the power of love.

Two thousand years ago a 33-year-old Man named Jesus willingly gave His life to conquer Nicolas Green's enemy— death—so that Nicholas, the people of Italy, and everyone in the entire world could one day live forever.

24 April

Scientific Goofs and Blunders

Since we've compiled this long and sorry record as sinners . . . and proved that we are utterly incapable of living the glorious lives God wills for us, God did it for us. Romans 3:21-24, Message.

One faulty and inexpensive O ring seal in a joint on the solid rocket booster caused the shuttle *Challenger* to explode 73 seconds into the flight, killing seven astronauts.

In 1999 a fossil smuggled out of China "proved" the missing link between birds and dinosaurs. The fossil "showed" a dinosaur with birdlike plumage. The whole thing turned out to be a hoax. A Chinese farmer had rigged together bird bits and a meat-eater's tail.

MTBE, methyl tertiary butyl ether, was sold as a gasoline additive in the early 1990s to help fuel in cars burn more efficiently and cut down on air pollution. In 1999 the government restricted the additive, for while it cut down on air pollution, scientists found they couldn't remove the dangerous chemical from drinking water.

Remember the Y2K scare? Because of the numbering systems of computers, we heard all kinds of doomsday disasters—planes falling from skies, no food, banks taking all your money. Thankfully it all got fixed . . . at a cost of $500 billion.

People goof, but God doesn't. And He has a great plan to save us from our own mistakes and sins.

Godfather of America

The eyes of the Lord are in every place, beholding the evil and the good. Proverbs 15:3.

You probably already know that America was named after Amerigo Vespucci, but did you know Mr. Vespucci wasn't the person who actually did the naming? That's right. The man who named America's two continents was Martin Waldseemüller, a European mapmaker. And in his "Cusmographiae Introductio," he chose to call the newly discovered land mass to the west of Europe Amerigo. But for one man's opinions, North and South Americans might have been called New Columbians after Christopher Columbus.

Mr. Waldseemüller affected future generations when he said, "Inasmuch as Europe and Asia received their names from women, I see no reason why anyone would object to calling the land of Amerigo after a man of great ability, Amerigo Vespucci."

Born in Florence, Italy, in March of 1454, Mr. Vespucci also wasn't the first to discover the continent, though he did sail from Europe to Brazil twice. His great contribution might have been his method of determining longitude for sailing ships. It was used for more than 300 years.

So whether you prefer being called an American or New Columbian, God's truth remains the same. God sees the good and the bad wherever you live on Planet Earth.

26 April

Devastation at Chernobyl

The tongue . . . is a fire. . . . It corrupts the whole person, sets the whole course of his life on fire. James 3:6, NIV.

April 26, 1986, is a day the world will never forget. At 1:23 a.m. one of Chernobyl, Ukraine's, four Soviet nuclear reactors exploded. A runaway chain reaction blew the steel and concrete lid off the reactor and created a fireball, releasing 100 times more radiation into the air than did the World War II Hiroshima and Nagasaki bombs combined.

While the Soviet government evacuated more than 100,000 people from the area, some 4,300 people eventually died as a result and more than 70,000 have been left permanently disabled. The inhabitants of the area had to leave so quickly that they couldn't pack anything to take with them. Everything—food, clothes, dishes, toys—is still in the empty houses and streets of the city. Seventeen years later the deadly poison still lingers over the city, in the drinking water, and in the soil.

While I've never been to Chernobyl, I've experienced the "fallout" of some mighty deadly poisons myself, in the form of words. That's right—words. Words have power to kill and destroy just as the radiation from an atomic bomb. A momentary explosion and *bam!* Poison is spewed in the air and in the minds and hearts of everyone. Only God can control the tongue, and only if we ask Him.

Things I Know

Who shall separate us from the love of Christ? Romans 8:35.

There are lots of things in the world I don't know. But I do know there are 293 ways to change a dollar bill and that rubber bands and batteries last longer when refrigerated. I know two thirds of the world's eggplants are grown in New Jersey and that peanuts are one of the ingredients in dynamite.

I know that the city of Los Angeles's full name is Nuestra Señora la Reina de los Ángeles de Porciúncula and that a cat has 32 muscles in each ear. I know it's the tiger's skin that is striped, not only the fur, and a goldfish has a memory of three seconds.

Some other truths I've learned along the way are: you can't sneeze with your eyes opened, and a giant squid has the biggest eyeball in the world. Also, there are 336 dimples on a regulation golf ball, and almonds are a member of the peach family. Imagine that!

Today's text asks, "Who can separate us from the love of Christ?" Do you know the answer? In Romans 8:38 and 39 you'll discover all the things that can't separate us from our precious Jesus. Death, life, angels, demons, height, depth, or any other creature. Have you guessed yet the only thing that can separate you from the love of Christ? (The answer is the eleventh word in the previous sentence.)

Can You Believe It?

Repent, then, and turn to God, so that your sins may be wiped out. Acts 3:19, NIV.

In Thailand people pierce their mouths with swords, umbrella sticks, cell phone antennae, anything to gain forgiveness of a year's worth of sinning. In Malaysia they put steel hooks in their backs and haul 50-pound shrines to honor their gods. Some people in India pierce their chests with knives or insert swords in one side of their bellies and out the other. Pakistani worshipers, even children, whip themselves with chains of knives.

People walk with bare feet on a bed of live coals or smear burning ashes on their bodies. In some parts of the Philippines men will allow themselves to be nailed to wooden crosses—all to prove they are sorry for their sins.

When I hear about people hurting themselves to earn forgiveness, I feel sad, because I know Jesus died for everybody's sins. We need only to ask.

He doesn't want us to scar, burn, or mutilate the beautiful bodies He's given us. On the contrary, He wants to restore us to the perfect forms He intended when He created us. That's His plan. We come to Jesus and repent—so simple, so beautiful, so like our loving God.

Wizards of Odd

Anyone who does not take his cross and follow me is not worthy of me. Matthew 10:38, NIV.

There are some pretty odd people in this world. Jack Mytton, a nineteenth-century English squire, owned 2,000 hound dogs. One day, seeking a cure for his hiccups, he set himself on fire. It worked, if you didn't mind the pain.

John Slater, from the Scottish Highlands, once walked the entire length of Britain barefoot, wearing red-and-green-striped pajamas. Four months, at 12 miles a day, he succeeded.

Jake Mangle-Wurzel built a waterfall of toilets. Seven toilets transfer rainwater from the roof of his cottage to a rain barrel. He has a motorcycle outfitted with a toilet seat and a kitchen sink. A lightning rod and a flagpole support a clothesline for his laundry.

Arthur Blessett's name is in the *Guinness 2000 Book of Records* for walking more than 33,000 miles carrying a cross. Since he started in 1969, he's walked across every country, past bamboo curtains, iron curtains, and Muslim curtains. He's walked with pop stars, presidents, preachers, and popes. Arthur's worn out three crosses and hundreds of pairs of shoes to draw attention to the story of Jesus Christ and His sacrifice for us. Odd, yes, but for a purpose greater than himself.

Person of Integrity

You belong to your father, the devil. . . . When he lies, he speaks his native language, for he is a liar and the father of lies. John 8:44, NIV.

What, a lie? A teensy, tiny white lie? Cheat on a quiz? Exaggerate about ourselves? Gossip about a friend? Weasel out of a responsibility? Whom does it hurt? Everyone does it, right?

Wrong! Today is National Honesty Day. Today the Honest Abe Award, or "Abies," will be given to last year's most honest individuals and companies in America. Dishonorable mention will be made for famous dishonest people. Oooh! Wouldn't it be awful to receive *that* prize?

Consider the importance of honesty the next time your dentist stands over you with a drill in one hand and a pick in the other. Would you have wanted him to cheat his way through dental school? And what about the pilot of your next commercial jet flight? Or the surgeon who is going to operate on your brain or your heart?

Also, I'd want an honest accountant handling my money, wouldn't you? And a pharmacist of integrity filling my prescriptions.

Albert Schweitzer, a famous missionary, wrote, "Truth has no special time of its own. Its hour is now—always."

May Day! May Day!

Be careful not to do your "acts of righteousness" before men, to be seen by them. Matthew 6:1, NIV.

Patti and Helen whispered to one another as they placed their scissors, construction paper, and glue bottles on the kitchen table. This was the day they made May baskets for friends and neighbors.

Their fingers moved quickly as they wove the brightly colored strips of paper into miniature baskets. While making the baskets and collecting the wildflowers from behind the Presbyterian church was fun, delivering them in secret was most fun.

The girls would ring their neighbors' doorbells and hide in the bushes to watch their happy faces when they discovered their baskets of flowers.

Over the years Patti and Helen's May basket list grew until they had to begin construction of the paper baskets two weeks before May 1, especially after a nursing home was built on the next block.

Patti and her sister developed a habit of giving with their May baskets. Today, Patti sets aside a portion of her paycheck to help someone else without their knowing who helped them. The fun is in keeping the secret. Try Patti's game for yourself. You'll like it.

Corporate Angels

God sent his angel to shut the mouths of the lions so they would not hurt me. Daniel 6:21, TEV.

Pilot Priscilla Blum had an idea after seeing company jets taking off and landing nearly empty. A few years earlier Priscilla had had breast cancer. She knew how expensive it was for the patients to travel to faraway places to get the treatment they needed. She thought, *Wouldn't it be great if we could fill those empty seats?*

After talking with her pilot friends, Priscilla started what is known today as Corporate Angel Network. Fifteen hundred jets and more than 500 companies carry patients to treatment centers whenever the jet's itinerary matches a patient's need.

Imagine if you were terribly sick and the only doctor who could help you lived on the other side of the country, or maybe even the world. Where would you get the money to make that trip? That's the kind of people the organization helps.

I'm proud of a pilot friend of mine who volunteers her time and her airplane to get sick boys and girls, men and women, to the right doctors who can help them get well. I think of Gwen as having angel wings. Aren't you glad God allows us, His kids, to become His angels—wings and all?

A New Name

I will . . . give him a white stone with a new name written on it.
Revelation 2:17, NIV.

William Brown was born the son of Elizabeth, a slave on a farm owned by Dr. John Young in Lexington, Kentucky. His overseer was a cruel man who enjoyed whipping Young's slaves. Because of his light skin, William found himself on the wrong end of the whip whenever a stranger mistook him for a member of the Young family. Worse yet, his fellow slaves shunned him for being "too white."

When finances grew tight for Dr. Young, he sold William for $500 to a St. Louis tailor, who later sold William to a New Orleans riverboat captain. When the boat docked in Cincinnati, Ohio, a free state, William escaped.

Nearly frozen and sick with fever, he wandered for six days, until he met Wells Brown. A Quaker, Brown gave the youth food and nursed him back to health. On learning that William had no family name, he offered his own, and the runaway slave became William Wells Brown.

William taught himself to read and write while helping more than 69 slaves escape to Canada in 1842 alone. He went on to become America's first Black novelist.

A new family, a new name—God has waiting for us. And as happened for William Wells Brown, along with the new name will come glorious new beginnings.

Psalm 118:8

It is better to take refuge in the Lord than to trust in man. Psalm 118:8, NIV.

For you math enthusiasts: It might be interesting to know how many dimples are in a regulation golf ball, but here's another piece of fascinating trivia I got from the Internet. I haven't tested it for accuracy. Maybe you would like to do the math for yourself. With a computer, it shouldn't take you very long. Here goes.

Psalm 118 is the middle chapter of the Bible. Just in passing, Psalm 117 is the shortest chapter and Psalm 119 is the longest chapter in the entire Bible. There are 594 chapters before and after Psalm 118. If you add up all the chapters of the Bible except for Psalm 118, you get a total of 1,188 (or Psalm 118:8).

Think about it. Is it pure chance or design that the middle verse of the entire Bible is verse number 1,188 or Psalm 118:8, which says, "It is better to take refuge in the Lord than to trust in man" (NIV)?

Chance or design, the advice given in the verse is the basic message of the entire Bible. The entire controversy on Planet Earth is God proving Himself to be trustworthy to the creatures made in His likeness. Over and over again, the Father demonstrates His faithfulness and love for us, His kids.

friend Indeed

A friend loves at all times, and a brother is born for adversity.
Proverbs 17:17, NIV.

Jeri's life collapsed when she learned that she had leukemia. She'd gotten top grades and had been star player on the girls' soccer team. But once she began her chemotherapy treatments she could barely make it to school, let alone study or play games with her friends.

To Jeri, the worst came when she lost her long golden curls. Looking at her bald head in a hand mirror, the young girl almost wished she could die. Ever since she was a toddler everyone had admired her sunshine yellow tresses.

"Mama, I don't want my friends to see me like this," Jeri wailed.

"We'll get a wig as soon as you're released from the hospital," her mother promised, tears glistening in her eyes as well.

At that moment the floor nurse stuck her head in the doorway. "You have some company, Jeri."

Jeri shook her head violently. "No! No!"

Ignoring the girl's protest, the nurse smiled and waved in her visitors. Jeri gasped as into the room walked her favorite uncle, her soccer coach, the entire soccer team, and her boyfriend, all with their heads shaved bald. The love of friends and family is sometimes expressed in unusual ways.

6 May

A Fairy Tale

*You are the light of the world. A city on a hill cannot be hidden.
. . . Let your light shine before men, that they may see your good
deeds and praise your Father in heaven. Matthew 5:14-16, NIV.*

O nce upon a time a king was looking for the right man to marry his beautiful daughter, Princess Sophia. Both he and his daughter wanted to be certain that the man she married was the smartest man in the kingdom.

They would hold contests to demonstrate the men's mental and physical strength. Hundreds of men tried, but alas, only three were left to participate in the final test, that of filling the king's largest horse barn. The one who filled it the fullest would win her hand.

The first man filled the barn to the second story with all the hay of the kingdom. The second man filled the barn to the rafters with corn. The third man emptied the barn, then removed several slats from the roof.

The next day the princess was stunned to see an empty barn until the creative young man pointed out that every nook and cranny of the building was filled with glorious sunlight.

Whether in a barn, a cottage, or a schoolroom, Christians fill their world with light. Jesus said it, and He can't lie.

Ode to Joy!

Make everyone rejoice who puts his trust in you. Keep them shouting for joy. Psalm 5:11, TLB.

On May 7, 1824, Austrian music lovers flocked to the concert hall in Vienna to hear the great Beethoven's latest composition, the ninth symphony. This is known as the "choral" symphony because of Beethoven's use of voices in symphonic harmony with the instruments. The maestro performed to a full hall.

At the end of Schiller's "Ode to Joy," which Beethoven included in his masterpiece, the soloist had to tug at his sleeve to get him to turn around and see the enthusiastic response. You see, Beethoven was deaf and couldn't hear the applause.

Imagine writing such a dynamic symphony and never being able to hear one note of it performed, especially the "Ode to Joy." Other than Handel's *Messiah,* I can't think of a piece of music that makes my spirit soar quite so high.

Imagine attending the out-of-this-world concert when Maestro Beethoven directs a heavenly choir composed of all the greatest earthly voices and a thousand or so of heaven's finest vocalists as they harmonize before the Creator singing, "Joyful, joyful, we adore Thee, God of glory, Lord of love."

8 May

No Socks Day

The time has come for . . . destroying those who destroy the earth. Revelation 11:18, NIV.

My friend John was shopping for a new pair of shoes when he tried on a pair of sandals, the most comfortable shoes he'd ever put on his feet. Turning to his wife, he asked, "What color socks should I wear with these?"

She eyed the brown leather-strapped shoes. "None. They're made to go with bare feet."

"Bare feet!" John exclaimed. "No way will I ever go without socks."

Lessons from childhood stick. John was born and raised in New York City where no mother would allow her children to wear shoes without socks, at least when John was a boy.

Today is No Socks Day—really! The idea is to give up wearing socks for one day to save on laundry, thereby contributing to a better environment. Kind of a stretch, huh? (No, you can't go sockless if your mom objects!)

This is only a humorous way to illustrate our responsibility to protect the world's environment. Animal and plant species are becoming extinct faster than scientists can catalog them. Can you imagine a world without lions, tigers, panda bears, and elephants? That's the kind of world your children will inhabit if my generation and yours don't do our part to protect God's beautiful planet.

Ouch! It Hurts!

Whoever sins is guilty of breaking God's law, because sin is a breaking of the law. 1 John 3:4, TEV.

Some people say God's laws aren't in effect today. I have news for you—they are! One day last March I decided to take a ride on my bike for exercise. I had no intention of proving any of God's laws, but that's exactly what I did when I attempted to skirt a speed bump.

These are the laws I proved that morning:

1. My front tire veered into the curb, causing a sudden stop—the law of friction.
2. I kept on going after the bike stopped—the law of momentum.
3. I fell to the ground—the law of gravity.
4. My left eyebrow and knee slammed against a concrete driveway (I wasn't wearing a helmet!)—the law of sudden deceleration.

I discovered that God's laws work, whether I believe in them or not.

The same is true with God's moral law, the Ten Commandments. It works whether or not I believe. My days will be longer on the earth if I honor my parents. I will be healthier if I rest on the Sabbath day.

God didn't zap me when I fell off my bike. Pain was just the natural result of my actions. Obeying God's laws saves us a whole lot of pain. If you don't believe, just ask me. Ouch!

10 May

The Iron Spike

All sins forgiven, the slate wiped clean, that old arrest warrant canceled and nailed to Christ's Cross. Colossians 2:13, 14, Message.

A deafening cheer arose from reporters, photographers, railroad workers, railway presidents, and government VIP's when Leland Stanford, president of the Central Pacific Railroad, swung the mallet and hammered the golden spike into the hole, officially linking the Atlantic Ocean with the Pacific. The place: Promontory, Utah. The time: May 10, 1869.

To be more accurate, the spike connecting the Union Pacific and the Central Pacific railroads completed a continuous track between Omaha, Nebraska, and Sacramento, California.

Almost before Mr. Stanford could turn around to accept congratulations, a railroad worker was digging the spike out of the ground and putting it in the hands of a security guard for safekeeping.

Another spike, at another place, 2,000 years ago made a much greater connection. The iron spikes hammered in Jesus' hands on the cross linked, not Nebraska and California, but earth with heaven, forever.

And remember God's laws and the natural result of breaking them that I talked about yesterday? Jesus took care of them that day. The scars in His hands are there to prove it for time and eternity.

Protective Force Field

Have you not put a hedge about him [Job] and his household and everything he has? Job 1:10, NIV.

I love the opening lines of the television series *Star Trek:* "To boldly go where no one has gone before . . ." Thinking about traveling in outer space has captivated people for generations. King David, as a boy watching his father's sheep in the fields at night, wondered about the majesty of the heavens. The nineteenth century author Jules Verne dreamed of space travel, as did the producers of *Star Wars* and the *Star Trek* series and its spin-offs.

I think space travel stirs my sense of freedom, living without boundaries. But all life has boundaries for our protection. In the *Star Trek* series the Starship *Enterprise* had a shield that protected the ship from alien attacks. All the lasers and explosions fired at it were repelled by this "force shield." Should the shield be lifted, the *Enterprise* would be vulnerable to sneak attacks from enemy forces.

The Ten Commandments act as a "shield" for the child of God. The devil described this protection as a hedge around God's children. One thing is certain, God's shield of protection is never a force shield. God never forces us to love Him or obey Him. But when that shield is removed, we are in mortal danger from Satan, our archenemy as well.

12 May

On Eagles' Wings

I carried you on eagles' wings and brought you to myself. Exodus 19:4, NIV.

High up in the Cascade mountain range a tiny eaglet pokes through his shell into a warm and downy world. He and his two sisters have nothing to do but grow and eat. Their parents keep the nest clean, protect them from predators, and keep their ever-hungry tummies full of juicy bugs and worms. What a life!

Then one day Mama nudges them from the only home they've ever known, onto a branch where Papa urges one of the little eaglets onto his back and takes off into the clouds.

Ooh! the baby eaglet thinks. *What fun!* Baby eaglet loves feeling the breeze rustle its tiny feathers until Papa drops out from under it and the little bird finds itself free-falling toward the ground! At the last second, when the precious baby will be dashed against the rocks, Papa eagle swoops beneath it and gently returns the terrified bird to its nest.

Day after day the babies suffer the trauma of near-death. And each time, Papa eagle is there just in time to save then. Then one day baby flaps its wings for dear life, catches an updraft off the mountain . . . and flies.

Father God is no less faithful in protecting His children while He teaches us to fly.

Picture Perfect

Let us come boldly to the very throne of God and stay there to receive his mercy and to find grace to help us in our times of need. Hebrews 4:16, TLB.

Three little boys were arguing as to whose dad was the best. The first boy said, "My father's a doctor. I can be sick for nothin'."

The second boy said, "My dad's a pilot. I can fly for nothin'."

Not to be outdone, the third boy said, "My dad's a preacher. I can be good for nothin'."

Good for nothin'? Good for everything. When Caroline Kennedy was a little girl, her father, John F. Kennedy, was president of the United States. The front of her father's desk in the Oval Office was an overhang. Caroline loved crawling into the little cubbyhole space and playing with her dolls.

Grown men wearing expensive silk suits, and Army generals with their chests covered with shiny medals would come into the office of the most powerful man in the world, their knees shaking and their palms sweaty. But not Caroline.

When her dad's office door was open, Caroline would boldly run into the office and leap into her father's lap.

The God of the universe holds all power in His giant hands, but His arms are always open to receive one of His kids.

The Jenkins Ear War

Don't be quick-tempered—that is being a fool. Ecclesiastes 7:9, TLB.

On April 9, 1731, near Havana, Cuba, a Spanish coast guard sloop called the *San Antonio* intercepted the British merchant brig, the *Rebecca,* on its way from Jamaica to London.

An argument broke out between Captain Robert Jenkins and the Spanish captain, Juan de Leon Fandino. Insulted by something Jenkins said, Fandino sliced off one of the English captain's ears with his sword.

Jenkins reported the incident and exhibited the severed ear to the British House of Commons. As a result, England declared war on Spain in October 1739.

Silly, huh? Getting angry enough to slice off someone's ear. Sounds a bit like the apostle Peter in the Bible. Of course, both events happened hundreds of years ago. Today we'd be smarter, don't you think?

Not so. The other day the evening news reported that a man was so angry at a customer for taking too many items through the supermarket express line that he accosted him in the parking lot and sliced off his nose. That's right! His nose.

Everyone gets angry sometimes. But losing control and lashing out, whether on the highway, in the grocery store, at home, or at school, leads to big trouble. It is a foolish thing to do.

Doomsday Clock!

Be still, and know that I am God. Psalm 46:10.

How will the world end? Here are 20 ways, in the order of potential, experts predict it will happen: asteroid impact, gamma-ray burst, collapse of our vacuum, rogue black holes, giant solar flares, reverse of earth's magnetic fields, volcanoes, global epidemics, global warming. (Need to catch your breath?) Failed ecosystem, biotechnical disaster, particle accelerator mishap, nanotechnology disaster, environmental toxins, global war, robot and computer takeover, mass insanity, alien invasion, divine intervention, someone wakes up and realizes life was all a bad dream.

What a list! Many of them I have no understanding of. I thought it humorous to get to "divine intervention." They're speaking here of wacko religious groups unleashing poison on society, not Jesus' coming to take us home with Him.

The last way is unusual, don't you think? A dream? The author quoted a philosopher who wondered if he's a man dreaming he's a butterfly or a butterfly dreaming he's a man.

Aren't you glad we don't need to be afraid of how the world will end? It's so simple. Jesus promised, "I will come again" (John 14:3). I can be still because I know God, and I know that He always keeps His promises.

More Wings of Mercy

One generation will commend your works to another; they will tell of your mighty acts. Psalm 145:4, NIV.

My 2-year-old grandson, Jarod, talks about flying airplanes to "faraway lands." He does this because his mother and father traveled around the world as missionaries before he was born. Jarod doesn't remember, but he celebrated his first birthday in Cuba. Jarod has a lot of growing to do before he will fly a real airplane to "faraway lands."

In the meantime, Jerry Witt risks his life every day flying his Cessna 182 into remote areas of the Mexican desert to reach people most of the world has forgotten. The high-risk conditions in the Mexican desert make landing and takeoff dangerous, but that doesn't keep Jerry from delivering much-needed medicines to the clinic doctors there. In the jungle, if he can't land, Jerry parachute-drops the supplies. The most unusual cargo he's flown in from the United States was bees. He's been robbed by bandits, ambushed by renegades, and shot at by drug runners.

With Jerry, mission flying is generational. His dad and grandfather before him were also bush pilots for the Lord. "We're nothing special," Jerry insists. "It's God who puts the desire in our hearts. Someday we'll be buried here in Mexico. . . . Somebody else will grab the torch and run with it."

Just My Kids

The only obligation you have is to love one another. Whoever does this has obeyed the Law. Romans 13:8, TEV.

A sociology class at Johns Hopkins University made a scientific study in one of the worst slums in Baltimore. Tabulations were made on cards, 200 of which were marked "headed for jail," along with the children's names, background, and prospects toward a life of crime.

Twenty-five years later another class found the cards and decided to check out the results. Only two persons on the cards marked "headed for jail" had gone to jail. How could the other class have been so wrong?

They discovered the question to ask wasn't How? but Who? The answer was Aunt Hannah, a schoolteacher.

Wherever the interviewers went, they found that something from the vigorous faith of this woman had rubbed off on her charges. Aunt Hannah's alumni include some of the most service-minded doctors, lawyers, preachers, and prominent businesspeople in the Baltimore area.

The college survey team visited Aunt Hannah in a local nursing home to report to her their findings. She had little to say, except, "I just loved them as if they were my own boys and girls."

Do you have an Aunt Hannah in your life? Someone who encourages you to do your best and do what's right? If not, God can help you see an Aunt Hannah in your neighborhood.

What Do You Need to Know?

I am the Good Shepherd. I know my own sheep and my own sheep know me. John 10:14, Message.

Twenty years ago the only mice people knew about ate cheese, bugs were something you killed with an aerosol poison, and viruses caused fevers. The computer changed things.

So what will you need to know 20 years from today? You might need to know how to talk to your house. As you step through the front door a laser beam will identify you, which in turn will trigger the lights to flicker on and the air-conditioner to kick in, and your dinner will heat in your state-of-the-art insta-cooker.

You'll drive a more animated and automated car. Like the toaster back home, the car's sensors will monitor the activity and destination you'll go.

When you awaken each morning, a computer will check your blood, saliva, and bodily waste. Should you be low in some vitamin or mineral, it will be inserted in your breakfast cereal.

When you fall in love, you can access your sweetheart's genetic map to see what diseases she or he is likely to contract before you decide to marry him or her.

These will be minor changes for those who allows themselves to be guided by the Good Shepherd and recognize His voice.

Darkness to Light

I delight to do thy will, O my God: yea, thy law is within my heart. Psalm 40:8.

On May 19, 1780, a strange darkness descended on New England in the middle of the day. Terrified that the world was coming to an end, people hid in their homes. Chickens went to roost for the night, and the cows came to the barn to be milked.

In New Haven, Connecticut, panic flooded the town council that was in session. One of the councilmembers made a motion to adjourn the meeting so they could rush home to their families.

Colonel Abraham Davenport opposed adjourning with this comment: "The way I see it, the day of judgment is either here or not. If it's not, then there is no cause to adjourn. If it is, then, personally, I would want the Lord to find me doing my duty when He arrives. I wish, therefore, that candles be lit."

And the council meeting continued regardless of the terror sweeping the northeastern United States. No scientific explanation, then or now, has ever been found for the strange phenomenon.

The world is filled with things that can cause us to be afraid. But if we are children of God who choose to live in God's will, we will never need to be afraid.

20 May

Making a Difference

Christ also was offered in sacrifice once to take away the sins of many. Hebrews 9:28, TEV.

While the minister preached, 7-year-old Trevor counted his birthday dollars. "One, two, three, four, five . . ." Just what he needed to buy a toy airplane he'd been eyeing at Wal-Mart.

Suddenly the pastor's story about a small boy in Ecuador who needed a wheelchair in order to attend school caught Trevor's attention. The pastor hoped to raise enough from the morning offering to meet the child's needs.

Trevor loved school. He couldn't imagine not being able to go to school. A frown deepened on the boy's forehead as he watched the deacons pass the offering plate. He shuffled the dollar bills between his fingers. They were so crisp and new.

When the offering plate was two rows away, the boy asked his father, "If I give a dollar, will it make a difference?"

Dad smiled and nodded. When the plate arrived, Trevor gave one of the dollars. Before the deacon moved to the next row, Trevor called to him and dropped the other four bills on the plate. "I want to be sure it's enough to make a difference," he said out loud.

Another boy gave his lunch to Jesus—all he had—and what a difference it made. God's Son gave His all on a rugged cross. And look at the difference His gift has made.

faith for Today

Become the kind of container God can use to present any and every kind of gift to his guests for their blessing. 2 Timothy 2:21, Message.

F
ifty-three years ago today a new program appeared on television. It was called *Faith for Today.* In 1950 preachers preached about the evils of television much as they do today. But one man, William Fagal, had a dream. He could see beyond the garbage that would be televised to the potential for sharing God's Word to millions of people all at one time.

Today his dream has been realized. Generations of people can trace their spiritual lineage back to this program. Hundreds of other religious programs have sprung up from this man's dream, or vision, as it is sometimes called. I wonder how many people will one day fall before the Lord in gratitude for this man's courage to dream bigger dreams.

Pastor Fagal had no idea that his dream would open the minds and hearts of people from every race, color, and continent to God's abundant love. Don't you just love the adventures God has for those are willing to "see" the possibilities through His eyes?

22 May

I Can Do That!

I can do all things through Christ which strengtheneth me. Philippians 4:13.

Have you ever had anyone say, "You can't do that! You're too big/too little/too weak/too whatever?" Today's text disagrees. "I can do all things . . ." with God!

Rick Hoyt has cerebral palsy. When he was a little boy the medical people told his father that Rick couldn't learn. The experts advised Rick's parents to put him into an institution and forget about him. The boy's family refused.

When Rick's brothers and sisters worked out a communication alphabet with him, the teachers said the kids were putting words into Rick's mouth. But his brothers and sisters persisted. They developed a computer voice for him so he could talk with the family. In time, Rick proved them wrong by graduating from college.

Rick loves sports. When he saw his first 10K run, he told his father that he wanted to enter. His father shook his head. But Rick persisted until his father began running and pushing Rick in his wheelchair.

A photo of Rick after their first race showed him wearing the biggest smile of his life. Today Rick and his dad have run marathons and triathlons together. The impossible? Hardly. So what's holding you back from working toward your dream? God and you can do anything!

Celebrating Little Things

Go to the ant . . . and be wise. Proverbs 6:6.

An ant is a little creature, hardly noticeable until one crawls onto your picnic plate of potato salad. When my daughter Kelli was a small girl, she decided ants would make great pets—red ants. After trapping several in a jar, she was ready to start her ant farm. Unfortunately, Kelli didn't tighten the lid, and you know what happened. They got out of the jar and into her bed during the night. Ouch! She learned more about ants than she intended, especially angry ones.

Another little thing is a paper clip—such a simple invention. It's been around a hundred years. Scientists predict that a hundred years from now, it will still be a useful tool to have.

Since the zipper was patented in the 1890s, nothing has come along to completely replace it, including Velcro. Some scientists tried using electromagnets, but that didn't work as well. The zipper idea came from studying nature in action in the form of the cocklebur, whose tiny "hooks" stick it to almost everything it touches.

God's natural world has many fascinating and useful lessons to teach us if we take the time to observe. A cause for celebration.

24 May

In 20 Years . . .

Heaven and earth will pass away, but my words will never pass away. Matthew 24:35, TEV.

Ever wonder what your future holds? Experts say that in 20 years we won't write our signatures on legal documents. Instead we will be known for our iris print, fingerprint, or voice pattern.

We won't visit video, record, or software stores. We'll order what we want through an earpiece and microphone inside our wrist watches.

Baldness will thin out, since doctors will know how to make scalp hair grow follicles. We won't go gray, either. Diabetics will say goodbye to insulin, as doctors will implant healthy islets of cells into the pancreas.

Plastic wrap will be replaced by a "bioplastic" made from cornstarch.

The same experts expect that the Super Bowl will still be around, as will the pencil, the earliest forms of which date back to the ancient Greeks. Books, money, passenger jets, and baseball are also expected to be a part of our lives. On the down side, traffic congestion, noise, poverty, and death will be here too. Another guarantee I can give you for the year 2023, if we're still on Planet Earth: God's Word will still be true.

The future can be scary with all the changes that will take place, but knowing God and His Word doesn't change. Makes me feel safer. How about you?

How About . . . ?

For behold, I create new heavens and a new earth; and the former things shall not be remembered or come to mind. Isaiah 65:17, NASB.

I like to think about the future. In 1957 author Robert Heinlein predicted that by 2000 we'd enjoy robot butlers, antigravity sleep, and cures for all diseases. Robot butlers? We need more exercise, not less. Antigravity sleep? Sorry, that's one of God's laws that won't change. And cures for all diseases? Satan, the father of lies, has a lot to say about that. It seems that the minute scientists find a cure for one disease, two more pop up from nowhere.

It's safe to say that in 20 years, Nintendo will go the way of the hula hoop and Pac-Man and will be remembered fondly by parents of a new generation of children.

The future I want to think about is the new heaven and new earth God promises. No matter how creative your brain may be, reality is going to be even more exciting.

I like to imagine what it will be like to deep-sea dive with dolphins and sharks without a heavy wet suit. What about soaring with eagles with my own wings? Or designing my robe of light into a rainbow paisley or wild plaid? Imagine perching yourself upon Jesus' lap while He shares with you the secrets of gravity, time, and Creation.

26 May

Love

If I speak with the speed of M.C. Hammer or sing like Britney Spears, but don't love, my words are like fingernails scratching over a chalkboard.

If I create a computer program that can break the codes at the CIA, the White House, and Wal-Mart; if I memorize the entire Bible in an hour or predict the winner of next year's Super Bowl, but don't love, I'm worth a ball of used dental floss.

If I give my new Nikes to my little brother and my new Skeeter to a poor kid at school, if I rescue a puppy from drowning or donate my kidneys to a stranger, but don't love, it's useless.

Love takes patience, even with a little brother's mess. Love takes kindness—no dissing a classmate, no jokes about the disabled. Love means no green-eyed jealousy when a friend becomes the captain of the softball team or gets the lead role in the Christmas play.

Love keeps my mouth shut when I get the top grades in math and English. Love never makes fun of the geek or the nerd. Love doesn't cheat on a math quiz. Love doesn't melt down over a bad call on the soccer field. Love trusts God to provide. Love hangs on to hope when mom and dad fight. Love is like the Energizer bunny—keeps going and going and going. . . . Only three things matter—faith, hope and love. And love is number one!

(1 Corinthians 13, Rizzo paraphrase. My apologies to the apostle Paul and to Pastor Karl Haffner.)

Claim to Fame

At the name of Jesus every knee should bow . . . and every tongue confess that Jesus Christ is Lord, to the glory of God the Father. Philippians 2:10, NIV.

Ever hear of Amelia Bloomer? Today is Mrs. Bloomer's birthday—May 27, 1818. If you've ever heard anyone refer to underwear as bloomers, then you've heard of Amelia Bloomer. Amelia's the woman who created a more sensible dress for women than the rib-crunching fashions of her day. While the costume was first worn in public by Elizabeth Smith Miller in 1849, the pants outfit became known as bloomers after its creator.

Another name you'll recognize is the Earl of Sandwich, all because during a card game (he was a despicable gambler) his valet brought him a slice of beef between bread.

Shakespeare for his writing, Mozart for his music, Da Vinci for his art, Johnny Appleseed for the apple trees he planted on his journey west. Today's famous, including former President Bill Clinton; Eminem, the rapper; Venus Williams, the tennis champ; Mark McGwire, the slugger; and many more—every human being, regardless of their fame, will one day bow at the name of Jesus. We have a head start, bowing at His feet and worshiping Him, not out of terror, but out of love. And aren't you glad the fame of the name doesn't matter when we worship God?

28 May

The Lowly Slug

Let the earth bring forth the living creature after his kind, cattle and creeping thing, and beast of the earth after his kind: and it was so. Genesis 1:24.

Years ago a musician wrote a romantic ballad about the swallows coming "back to Capistrano." As a result, tourists flock to the small town on the California coast to see the yearly arrival of the famous birds.

Unfortunately for the lowly slug, no one ever wrote a song about its arrival in Capistrano. Today is the day the slimy creatures come back to Capistrano—no fooling! If you plan to see for yourself, I recommend you wear shoes.

I have to admit, slugs are not one of my favorite creatures. In Oregon I hated the time of year when those chubby banana slugs would beach themselves on our sidewalks. It was almost impossible not to squish one under your feet, they were so plentiful. Yet even the lowly slug was created with intricate detail and with enough instinct to head south for the winter.

Scientists don't understand what makes birds or slugs migrate year after year to the same spots. I don't either; do you? But I know who does know. And someday I'm going to ask Him about migrating slugs, hibernating bears, and so much more.

Just Deserts

So they hanged Haman on the gallows that he had prepared for Mordecai. Esther 7:10.

Remember the story of Queen Esther? Somehow it seems only fair that when the king heard of Haman's dastardly deeds, Haman was hanged on the gallows he had built for his enemy Mordecai.

Scalpings were like that. The bloody practice didn't become widespread among early Native Americans until the British arrived with their steel knives and promised to pay the Indians so much for each scalp. Scalping spread quickly throughout the continent and was used against the very people who introduced the custom in the first place.

The great-great-grandmother of a friend of mine came across the United States in a covered wagon. She survived an Indian scalping—true story. The wound healed, but she always wore a cap to cover the scars on her hairless scalp. Granny was also one of the first Seventh-day Adventists to settle in northern California.

Did Granny wish bad on her attackers? No, she knew that vengeance was God's to deliver, not hers. Instead, she shared her love of Jesus with members of the local Indian tribe. She also knew that in the end the evil one will get his just deserts, just as the Bible promises.

30 May

Through Alaskan Wilderness

I will send my messenger, who will prepare the way before me.
Malachi 3:1, NIV.

In 1941, immediately after the Japanese attack on Pearl Harbor, Hawaii, President Franklin D. Roosevelt feared the Japanese would invade Alaska. More than a thousand miles of dense, tangled Canadian forest stood between the troops stationed in Washington State and Alaska. Ships would be vulnerable to attack, so the best route would be over land where no roads existed.

U.S. Army Corps of Engineers captain Alfred Eshbach and a team of men were assigned the task of surveying the best route for a road. Road builders would follow so closely that the surveyors could hear their heavy equipment plowing through the trees.

They plowed through hubcap-deep mud, shifty permafrost, and solid rock. At times the engineers climbed trees to find the best place to cut through the heavy briars and brambles of the forest. Eshbach's team and the road builders completed the task in record time, making it possible to secure Alaska for the United States.

Surveying and building the Alaska Highway was an incredible feat, but nowhere as marvelous as the way John the Baptist prepared for Jesus to come and win the war for the souls of you and me.

Drip. Drip. Drip

A false witness will not go unpunished, and he who pours out lies will not go free. Proverbs 19:5, NIV.

Drip, drip, drip—tiny droplets of water fell one at a time. No one noticed the tiny crack forming in the earthen dam. Heavy rains had been falling for days on the town of Johnstown, Pennsylvania. But the Conemaugh River Dam was strong, invincible—no one gave it a thought.

More and more water pressed against the walls of the dam. Drop after drop fell, pushing, melting, eroding the soil in the dam's unseen weak spot until—*swoosh!* The dam broke, sending tons of water crashing down the river into the town. Thousands of homes were washed away. Thousands of people were killed.

Lies are like the tiny droplets of water, at first hardly worth noticing—after all, everyone tells white lies, right? Then the lies are joined by other lies until there's no holding back the destruction.

You don't have to wait for a flood of your lies to destroy you. It's difficult to break the habit of lying, but with God it can be done.

Swords, Rockets, and House Cats

I find myself in a pride of lions who are wild for a taste of human flesh; their teeth are lances and arrows, their tongues are sharp daggers. Psalm 57:4, Message.

Ever since Cain killed Abel over a pile of fruit and David fought Goliath with a slingshot and stone, there have been wars. Bullets, bombs, AK-47s, stinger missiles, and germ warfare have long since replaced lances and arrows. But when was the last time you heard of a battle won by using cats?

King Cambyses II of Persia (Iran) holds the all-time record for ingenuity in devising weapons of attack. In the sixth century B.C. his troops found the walls of the city of Memphis, Egypt, too thick and too high to attack with their usual weapons.

Knowing Egyptians considered cats to be gods, the Persian king conducted a giant cat hunt, then hurled cats over the walls and onto the heads of the astonished Egyptians. Though the Egyptians were much stronger, they surrendered to the attacking Persians rather than see cats so mistreated.

Since I like cats, I think I would have sided with the Egyptians. In the book of Psalms David described his enemies not as housecats, but lions.

Temptations can be like cats. There are small ones, and there are lion-sized ones. And like King David, we find our only protection is in Christ Jesus.

Nobody Did It

Do not merely listen to the word, and so deceive yourselves. Do what it says. James 1:22, NIV.

Four Christians were named Everybody, Somebody, Anybody, and Nobody. At church Somebody asked for help at the local homeless shelter. Everybody knew that Somebody should do it. Anybody could help, but Nobody did.

Somebody got angry because it was Everybody's job. Everybody thought Anybody could help out, but Nobody realized that Everybody didn't. Everybody blamed Somebody when Nobody did what Anybody could have done.

Four Christians were named Everybody, Somebody, Anybody, and Nobody. One day Everybody noticed that Somebody was throwing gum wrappers on the school lawn. Everybody knew Somebody should pick up their litter.

A Christian named Everybody was picking on the new kid at school. Somebody knew he should stand up for him, and Anybody could have, but Nobody did.

Think about it. What do you see that Somebody should do and Anybody could do, but Nobody does? Change your world by refusing to become just another Everybody, Somebody, or Anybody. Turn love into a verb. Don't wait for Somebody else to do what you know you should do.

famous nobodies

Let another praise you, and not your own mouth; someone else, and not your own lips. Proverbs 27:2, NIV.

Dr. Samuel Prescott, William Dawes, Paul Revere—three men who warned the American colonists that the British were coming. So why do you recognize only one of the names?

Henry Wadsworth Longfellow chose to write his poem about Paul Revere because his name rhymed better. "Listen my children and you shall hear of the midnight ride of Dr. Samuel Prescott?" I don't think so.

None of the three men were alive by the time Longfellow wrote his epic poem. But if they were, it wouldn't feel too swift to sit back and let another become famous for what they did, would it?

History is full of nobodies who never received credit for making a difference in their world. Here are a few:

1. Philipp Melanchthon encouraged Martin Luther to translate the New Testament from Greek to German.

2. In a shoe store Edward Kimball asked the famous preacher Dwight L. Moody to give his life to Christ.

3. Onespihorus cared for Paul in the dungeon as he wrote his last letter to Timothy.

A bunch of nobodies who exalted Somebody—the Son of God. That Somebody knows their names and will reward their faithfulness. With God, there are no nobodies.

Outstretched Arms

You saw . . . the miraculous signs and wonders, the mighty hand and outstretched arm, with which the Lord your God brought you out. Deuteronomy 7:19, NIV.

Have you ever tried to picture what God's arm might look like? Is it big, hairy, and muscular, like your dad's? Can you picture Him grinning as you run like a little child into His arms, where He swings you off your feet and twirls you around in circles, laughing at your giggles?

Jarod, my grandson, squeals with delight whenever Mark, his father, "goes dizzy" with him (twirls him around in circles). Nothing makes the 2-year-old happier than to be in his father's arms.

My dad was a house painter. I don't remember seeing his strong muscular arms free of splotches no matter how hard he scrubbed them with turpentine to remove the paint. Paint-splotched or not, his arms were always outstretched toward me, ready to give me a big hug.

Today is National Hug for Health Day, and huggers of all ages are invited to make a difference in their world, one hug at a time, especially by hugging the elderly. It has been suggested that we should each get 11 hugs a day to stay healthy. So find your nearest grandma or grandpa and give them a hug, or adopt a grandparent to hug. Stretch out your arms today and let someone know you care.

Up. Up. and Away

Whoever wants to become great among you must be your servant. Matthew 20:26, NIV.

Do you know the names of the first people to fly? If you said Orville and Wilbur Wright, you'd be wrong.

Long before the Wright Brothers' famous flight, on June 5, 1783, coinventors Joseph and Jacques Montgolfier launched a 33-foot diameter *globe aerostatique,* or the first hot-air balloon, in France. The balloon reached 1,500 feet and traveled 7,500 feet for a 10-minute flight. This is the first recorded flight for such a sustained length of time. The Montgolfier brothers never imagined that one day, humans would send rocket ships to Mars and aqua robots to the bottom of the ocean.

Running the four-minute mile, swimming the English Channel, landing on the moon, and breaking Babe Ruth's hitting record were all pooh-poohed and laughed at, but that didn't stop people from doing it. The stories are exciting, but nowhere as exciting as those Bible heroes who were great in God's eyes.

Finding coins in fishes' mouths, surviving a fiery furnace, sleeping with lions, walking on water—there's no limit to the greatness you and I can achieve when God's in control.

Something Fishy

Take the first fish you catch; open its mouth and you will find a four-drachma coin. Take it and give it to them for my tax and yours. Matthew 17:27, NIV.

What kind of fish do you think it was that Jesus prepared for Peter?

Eviota zonura, or goby fish, live in the waters around the Marshall Islands. They seldom grow longer than a half inch, while the whale shark, measuring 45 feet from its snout to its tail, is more than 1,000 times longer. Then there's the toothed carp that feeds on mosquito larvae in the swamps of South Carolina and Florida; it's just three quarters of an inch long. What variety!

The goby from the Marshall Islands is so small that it takes 14,000 mature fish to weigh one ounce. This lightest of all vertebrates weighs only a 600 millionth as much as the whale shark, the biggest fish, and a 4 billionth as much as the biggest of all vertebrates, the blue whale. That's incredible.

When God prepared a fish for Peter, He had several from which to choose. However, the fish wasn't the point of the story, was it? Just what lesson did Jesus want Peter to learn from his fishing expedition?

7 June

Buzzing Bees

Let us continually offer to God a sacrifice of praise—the fruit of lips that confess his name. Hebrews 13:15, NIV.

Close observers of nature insist that honeybees talk to one another to indicate direction and distance of flowers from the hive. Most serious scientists declared this to be nonsense until Austrian zoologist Karl von Frisch proved that bees execute elaborate "dances" with other members of their hive. Each species has its own dance. For instance, the dwarf honeybee can't be understood by the Indian honeybee.

By an elaborate pattern of signals, the bee tells the others in the hive how far they must fly and in what direction. This is important, since studies indicate that it takes about 40,000 bee loads of flower nectar to produce 16 ounces of honey—or a total distance of two trips around the world for each pound of honey they manage to accumulate. So you can see why what the busy little bee "says" to the others is important. It's a matter of life and death for the hive.

Our words and actions—or "dance"—are a matter of life and death too. Our words and our "dance" should, dare I say, be as sweet as honey. Our sacrifice of praise will direct others to the Source of life-giving power.

Attack! Attack!

The thief comes only to steal and kill and destroy; I have come that they may have life, and have it to the full. John 10:10, NIV.

Today is the anniversary of two little-known events in America's history. In the spring of 1697, Indians attacked Haverhill, Massachusetts, capturing Hannah Duston, killing her baby, and killing and capturing 39 others as well. On April 29 Hannah killed 10 Indians with a tomahawk and returned to her people, bringing with her their bloody scalps. On June 8 she was awarded £25 of British money for her heroism, though it was given to her husband on her behalf, since women couldn't own anything back then.

The second occurred on June 8, 1874, when the fierce and courageous Apache chief Cochise died in his stronghold in southeastern Arizona. After his arrest in 1861 he escaped and launched the Apache Wars, which lasted for 25 years.

Stealing, killing, and destroying have gone on since the beginning of time. And while there are wars in such places as the Middle East, Ireland, and Africa, the evening news tells us about terrible events much closer to our homes.

But Jesus had a better idea. He came to give life. Not a ho-hum, breathe-in, breathe-out type of life, but exuberant life filled not with mayhem and murder, but joy, peace, and love.

Going Dizzy

He giveth power to the faint; and to them that have not might He increaseth strength. Isaiah 40:29.

Jarod never tires of "going dizzy." That's when his six-foot-five-inch dad takes his arms and whirls him in circles. I remember only once when Mark stopped spinning Jarod that the little boy staggered across our living room floor and complained of feeling a little sick. Otherwise "going dizzy"—whether with his dad or on a carnival ride—tops Jarod's preferred activities list.

Jarod's too young to know that he "goes dizzy" every moment of his life. Even when he's sleeping Jarod is whizzing around at 1,000 miles per hour because of the rotation of the earth on its axis. The earth circles the sun at the rate of 66,500 miles per hour. Are you dizzy yet?

Simultaneously, the solar system (sun, earth, planets, etc.) revolve around the hub of the galaxy (the Milky Way) at some 481,000 miles per hour. But that's not all. The Milky Way is believed to circle the core of a cluster of galaxies at 1.35 million miles per hour. Talk about going out for a spin!

That means Jarod, you, and I are traveling in five different directions at the same time! Mathematicians can't calculate the net speed achieved by combining all five movements. Despite all that power and action, God still takes the time to renew our strength every morning.

More Out-of-This-World Info

The valleys of the sea were exposed and the foundations of the earth laid bare at the rebuke of the Lord, at the blast of breath from His nostrils. 2 Samuel 22:16, NIV.

A blast of God's breath. What a powerful picture of Creation, going far beyond the simple words, "God spoke and it was done." However, it wasn't only done, but is maintained—year after year after year . . .

Take a deep breath. Inflate your lungs. Hold it for a few seconds, then exhale. Do this five or six times. With all the earth's whirling about its axis and speeding around the sun, how does its protective blanket of air keep from zinging off into outer space by the power of centrifugal force? You know, the force that controls your yo-yo when you use it as a lasso.

First, our blanket of air is a shield from the sun's radiation and sustains life. It weighs 4 billion tons! Second, the mysterious force of the earth's gravity and the weight of the earth hold the air to us. Without both, our atmosphere would fling into outer space.

Imagine God thinking about all these things while He was designing our planet: the ideal weight of the planet, the gravitational pull, the perfect temperatures for sustaining human life. Why not celebrate God's life-sustaining "breath" by singing "What a Mighty God We Serve."

What Flood?

The waters flooded the earth for a hundred and fifty days. Genesis 7:24, NIV.

On September 12, 2000, Robert Ballard announced that his team of scientific explorers had found evidence that humans once lived in an area covered by the Black Sea—perhaps inundated by the biblical Flood. They found ancient hand-carved wooden beams, a stone chisel, and two other stone tools at a depth of 300 feet.

A surprise? To a Christian, no. To the rest of the world, absolutely! This represents the first concrete evidence (other than God's Word) that the bottom of the Black Sea had once been inhabited. Scientists exploring the area using remote-controlled underwater cameras and vessels believe this find will rewrite history.

It may rewrite some people's history books, but mine? Hardly. God's Word, the Bible, is right on target. There's no mystery in those pages. It's all very clear. God told Noah to build a big boat. He gave Noah and his sons precise measurements for this boat, as well as specifying the wood to use. Gopher wood is not the easiest wood to saw. Did Ham or Shem ever ask their dad to use maple or pine instead? I don't know. But I do know Father Noah followed God's command. As a result, he and his family survived. Is it any wonder? Following God's commands brings life, and believing God's Word is wise.

Amazing Facts

When he cries out to me, I will hear, for I am compassionate.
Exodus 22:27, NIV.

Hi, I'm Geri. I'd like to tell you what I learned from my 5-year-old brother, Greg. He's a real pain sometimes. At least that's what I thought until the day I was baby-sitting while Mom ran to the store. I was reading a great storybook, and he wanted help building a snowman. Exasperated, I distracted him with a bagful of trail mix and his favorite Veggie Tales video. That lasted for 20 minutes. Soon I found him standing beside me.

"Geri, whatcha doin'?"

I gritted my teeth. "I'm studying."

"I want to study too," he replied, running to his room and returning with an armload of storybooks. "Will you read me a story?"

"Greg, I'm busy right now. You read to yourself, OK?"

He didn't object, and plopped himself beside me on the sofa and began "reading" his books out loud—and I do mean loud. The exasperated little boy was trying to get his big sister's attention.

Suddenly I thought, *Does God get frustrated sometimes trying to get my attention?* Then to my brother I said, "Hey, kiddo, ya still wanna build a snowman?"

A Good Kid

"Why do you call me good?" Jesus answered. "No one is good—except God alone." Mark 10:18, NIV.

Janey considered herself a good girl. Everyone said so. Janey always obeyed her teachers and her parents. She attended church each week and hung out with other good kids at school. When there was work to do or a good deed to perform, Janey was the first to volunteer. Sometimes she resented the way people expected so much of her, but she loved the attention she received once the job was done. Yes, Janey was a good girl. Everyone said so.

When the pastor came to her school for a Week of Prayer and asked who would like to give their hearts to Jesus, Janey followed the example of her classmates, even though she didn't need forgiveness like the other kids did. She just knew the other kids would be right back to their naughty ways by next week.

When the pastor organized a baptismal class, she, of course, joined, because it was the "good" thing to do. She studied the lessons faithfully. As she neared her baptism date, Janey became sullen and depressed. At school she stopped volunteering to help the teacher. At home she hung out alone in her room. Her family and friends couldn't figure out what was wrong with her.

(to be continued)

No Way

"Who has any chance at all?" they [the disciples] asked. Jesus was blunt: "No chance at all if you think you can pull it off by yourself. Every chance in the world if you let God do it." Mark 10:26, 27, Message.

Thursday night before Janey's scheduled baptism, the girl announced that she had decided not to be baptized with her friends.

"Honey," her mother asked, "what is it? What's wrong?"

Janey's lips tightened.

"Please tell me what's wrong," Mom insisted.

A tear slid down Janey's face as she explained to her mother, "Mom, all the other kids need to be baptized. I don't. I'm a good kid; everyone says so. I've never done anything bad; not really. So how can I be baptized? Wouldn't I be lying if I did?"

Mother smiled and said, "No one can enter heaven without Jesus. Remember the story about the rich young man who came to Jesus?" She continued, "Everyone sins, including you. You pride yourself in being good. Pride is one of the most difficult sins to overcome."

The Holy Spirit tugged at the girl's heart. "Maybe I'm not as good as I thought. . . . You're right. I need to give my heart to Jesus. And I need to be baptized just as much as my friends."

Tears sprang into her mother's eyes. "Janey, you've just made the most important decision of your life."

Winging It

Show the wonder of your great love. . . . Hide me in the shadow of your wings. Psalm 17:7, 8 NIV.

If you're afraid of being surprised by a burglar, you might install a fancy alarm system with bells and whistles and flashing lights. But if you lived 1,000 years ago, you might choose birds as your alarm system.

That's what William the Conqueror of Rochester, England, did. He built his famous White Tower in 1078. Whether or not he planned it as such, ravens found the tower to be a perfect nesting place between flights into the surrounding woods for garbage.

Six hundred years later, when the enemies of Charles II tried to capture the tower at night, they startled the ravens awake. The birds croaked so loudly that the tower guards awoke and fought off the assault. Grateful, the Merry Monarch (that was Charles's nickname) ordered that the birds be protected and fed.

In 1967, with the price of horse meat (the ravens' food) rising, the chancellor of the exchequer approved an increase of 42 cents a week in the household budget for the Tower of London.

Bible writers use the symbol of a bird's wings to illustrate how God hides and protects us from our enemies. I like to imagine snuggling close to God as He wards off my enemies, don't you?

Committed Chameleons

Make it as clear as you can to all you meet that you're on their side, working with them and not against them. Philippians 4:5, Message.

When I was in college a visiting minister preached about being a chameleon. He explained that these tree-dwelling reptiles rapidly change colors to match their surroundings. These creatures have a layer of outer skin that is almost transparent. This allows the pigment cells to imitate what's on the outside. Light and temperature also affect this "miraculous" change.

However, scientists tell us that the most powerful element that causes the change is the reptile's emotions. That's right, emotions—the same way my emotions affect how I respond to other people, whether I try to get along or to resist.

The preacher's words bothered me at first. I remembered the early Christian martyrs, beginning with Stephen. They didn't bend to other's opinions. Aren't we supposed to stand for the right though the heavens fall?

By the end of his sermon I understood the meaning of his illustration. The minister wasn't advising us to go against our consciences. He was saying, "Wherever possible, get along with people. Be kind, agreeable, loving. Be committed to Jesus and His commands, but don't be stubborn about having your own way." That's God's way.

17 June

Perky Paula

How beautiful on the mountains are the feet of those who bring good news, . . . who bring good tidings. Isaiah 52:7, NIV.

Good morning, Sandi; welcome to church," Paula said, her eyes scanning Sandi's hairstyle and passion-pink suit with matching sandals. Drawing closer to the newest arrival, Paula added, "Honey, your skirt looks a little tight this morning. Putting on a little weight?"

Sandi gave the church greeter a pale smile and walked into the sanctuary. When Tiffany arrived, Paula confidently suggested she try Clearasil on her latest outbreak of acne. Then Paula pointed out a tiny run developing in Brook's pantyhose.

Every week it was the same, being greeted by perky Paula and her mentioning something wrong or out of place in each of her friends' appearances. The girl had a knack. Worse yet, she did so with the sweetest smile on her face. This made her friends wonder if they'd misinterpreted her remarks. But every week?

No one discussed the problem among themselves or with Paula. They merely steered clear of the girl. And Paula wondered why she didn't have any close friends at church or at school.

What do you think? Truth and kindness—where do you draw the line between being helpful and being hurtful? Could you be Paula's friend? What advice would you give to Paula? to the other girls?

(to be continued)

Paula's Problem

Why, then, do you look at the speck in your brother's eye and pay no attention to the log in your own eye? Matthew 7:3, TEV.

When Paula greeted Dina with "Honey, your new haircut is too severe. You need a softer look," the spitfire brunet sputtered to herself throughout song service. To make matters worse, Paula had special music. And she had a great voice!

Someone needs to do something about that snake, Dina seethed. The angry girl didn't have long to wait.

As Paula walked toward the podium, Dina noticed that the hem of Paula's peasant skirt was tucked into the back waistband of her pantyhose. Should she stop her and warn her?

Before Dina could decide, the girl was on stage. The audience gasped, as with Paula's every step an unplanned bustle of skirt bounced, revealing a four-inch-wide snag in her pantyhose that ran from her heel to the bustle.

Did Dina do wrong not telling Paula? She could have stopped her from being embarrassed. How would you have handled the situation? Would you have told her before or after the solo? Considering honesty, compassion, and the golden rule, what should both Paula and Dina learn from this embarrassing experience?

19 June

Moonstruck

You . . . must be ready, because the Son of Man will come at an hour when you do not expect him. Luke 12:40, NIV.

As a little girl riding in the back seat of my dad's car at night, I couldn't understand how the moon stayed with us no matter how many miles we traveled. The mountain range, trees, and houses—we left those behind, but not the moon.

As I grew older, I learned that the phenomenon happened because my eyes were playing tricks on me. The moon, being 2,160 miles in diameter and an average of 240,000 miles away, doesn't change sizes like a mountain range, which is so much smaller and closer. The moon's size gives the illusion of being close to us.

The opposite can be true too. If you close one eye and hold a quarter in front of your open eye, you can completely block out the moon. For that matter, hold the coin close enough and you can block out the faces of your parents, your siblings, everyone and everything around you.

Both examples are optical illusions, tricks the eyes play on us. Many people who focus their attention on money are believing a dangerous illusion, that money is more important than helping others. However, it's no illusion to view heaven as being as close and real as the moon on a clear night.

Troubles

I've told you all this so that trusting me, you will be unshakable and assured. . . . Take heart! I've conquered the world. John 16:33, Message.

Achoo! Another cold! I hate colds. Sneezing, coughing, stuffed nose, headache! Yech! Did Jesus ever had a cold when He lived here on earth? Did His eyes water and His head ache from pesky cold germs? I don't know, but I do know He experienced troubles just as I do.

Long before He lived on Planet Earth, Jesus our Creator planned for the possibility of infections by being redundant—two lungs, two eyes, two ears, etc. How about your two nostrils that bring oxygen to your lungs, heart, and blood? That's right, two nostrils that give you stereo smell when you don't have an infection, and stereo stuffiness when you do.

Each of your lungs is controlled by one of your two "Schnozzles." Without a flow of oxygen for a prolonged period, the corresponding lung would be threatened.

God planned for this, too. When you sleep, the stuffiness in your two nostrils shifts from side to side, freeing one nostril to do the breathing for you. One nostril stuffed is better than two. Yeah, Jesus conquered the world and its cold germs, too.

21 June

Practice Pays

My people come to you, as they usually do, and sit before you to listen to your words, but they do not put them into practice. Ezekiel 33:31, NIV.

You throw like a girl! Ever hear that, or maybe say that? There used to be a theory that females had one extra bone that prevented them from throwing like a boy. Not so.

Psychologists have discovered that up until ages 10 or 12, boys and girls have similar scores in athletic ability. Then, with the onset of puberty, the males who were tested outthrew girls two to one.

Before you guys cheer too loudly, that was a test of throwing with the dominant arm. When the boys threw softballs with the opposite arm, they "threw like girls."

The difference is in the practice. The study concluded that upon reaching puberty, boys were encouraged to continuing practicing their throw while girls were not. The scientists also observed that right-handed girls threw with their right foot forward. Simply shifting their left foot forward increased their throwing distance and improved their throwing form.

Male or female, if you don't want to "throw like a girl," practice is the key. Any skill requires practice. Playing the piano, drawing, learning a second language, throwing softballs, or obeying the Word of God—practice pays.

My Mystery List

Do not let your hearts be troubled. Trust in God; trust also in me. . . . I will come back and take you to be with me. John 14:1-3, NIV.

Achoo! Not again! Didn't we talk about colds a couple days ago? Today's topic isn't about colds, but sneezing—well, not about sneezing, but about things that trouble me, such as Why do we close our eyes when we sneeze?

Some people believe closing our eyes when we sneeze keeps our eyeballs from popping out. Troubled with that answer, I read books and logged on to the Internet. While I found no better answer, I don't plan to test the theory next time I'm about to sneeze. I guess I'll have to wait and ask Jesus when I get to heaven.

Other mysteries that trouble me are: What makes gravity work? Is there a back side to a black hole? Was there ever an "abominable snowman" or a "Loch Ness monster"? Did people before the Flood build and fly airplanes? What colors do angels see that I can't? Do fish sleep? Why is yawning contagious?

My more troubling mysteries are about death: my dad's death, about the day Lucifer become Satan, and the day Jesus said goodbye to His Dad in heaven. Most important, I will ask why He loved me enough to die so I could live forever.

23 June

Chris's Dad

What we have seen and heard we announce to you . . . so that you will join with us in the fellowship that we have with the Father and with his Son Jesus Christ. 1 John 1:3, TEV.

Chris wrinkled his face and shook his head violently. "Hang out with the Father?" he snarled. "I hate the word 'father'!"

When Chris was 5 years old his father punished him for spilling milk on the floor by hog-tying his hands and feet, gagging him with a dirty rag, and locking him in a coat closet, where the child stayed all night. Another time Chris's dad punished the boy for playing with matches by burning the child's fingertips.

During a snowstorm Chris's father came home drunk. Terrified, the boy ran outside with his younger brother, Jed. Barefoot and wearing cotton PJs, the two boys hid behind a lilac bush all night. Chris never understood why his mother didn't help them. Finally the boys were taken from their parents and moved to a loving foster home.

Nightmares plagued Chris throughout his childhood and teen years. When he learned of Jesus Christ, he wanted to give his heart to Him. He accepted Jesus as his Savior and the Holy Spirit as his Guide, but the Father? How could he be expected to fellowship with any Being called Father? "I can't," he said. "Don't ask me to, Lord."

(to be continued)

Honor Your Father

Honor your father and mother, that you may have a long, good life in the land the Lord your God will give you. Exodus 20:12, TLB.

Chris struggled with his concept of Father God until he married Ali and she became pregnant. One night, alone in the darkened parlor, Chris fell on his knees. "Dear F-f-f . . ." He could barely make himself say the word. "Help me, Lord," he prayed aloud, starting again. "Dear Father . . ." There! The word was out. Chris asked the Father to forgive his stubborn heart, to accept him as His son, and to help him to forgive his biological father, wherever the man might be.

One afternoon Chris learned that his dad was in the state prison dying of cancer and that he wanted to see him. Could Chris "honor" his father's wish? He wasn't sure.

Reluctantly he walked into the prison hospital room and saw the man he'd known as a boy. "Dad?" he whispered.

The man opened his eyes. "Chris? I was afraid you wouldn't come, but I had to see you before I died." The man wheezed. "God has changed me. I'm not the same person you remember. Can you forgive me for how I treated you?"

Chris's eyes filled with tears. "I already have, Dad. God changed my heart too." Joy filled Chris's heart when his father helped him locate Jed, his long-lost brother.

Arms in Prayer

Be merciful to me and hear my prayer. Psalm 4:1, NIV.

M-m-m-m! Hot freshly made pretzels. Who can pass a pretzel stand and resist the temptation? Ever wonder who the genius was who invented pretzels?

No one knows the name of the first pretzel person, though researchers have traced the doughy snack to Italy in A.D. 610. Many believe it was invented by a monk as a reward for students who could recite their catechism properly. Not an accident, the shape was meant to resemble the arms of a child praying.

The Italian word for pretzel, *bracciatelli,* means "small arms." In medieval times people prayed by putting their arms across their chest, their hands on opposite shoulders in the shape of a cross. Pictures of pretzels can be found as page borders in early Bibles. Since that time some Europeans have worn the pretzel on a ribbon around their necks as a good luck charm.

While the unknown monk had good intentions, no pretzel or good luck charm is needed to remind God's children to communicate with Daddy God. And nothing we do can make God any more willing to answer our prayers. He is a generous God who loves to give us the desires of our hearts.

Believe It or Not

I will put my laws in their hearts, and I will write them on their minds. Hebrews 10:16, NIV.

When two trains meet, each shall come to a full stop and neither shall proceed until the other has gone." Huh? Believe it or not, that is a law in the state of Texas. It seems a state senator didn't want a certain bill to be voted into law, so he attached the above "train law" to keep it from passing. Unfortunately, the other senators didn't notice the attached "train law" and passed both.

If you think that law is crazy, did you know that it is against the law to fish from horseback in Utah?

In Memphis, Tennessee, it is illegal for a woman to drive a car unless a man either walks or runs ahead of it waving a red flag to warn approaching motorists and pedestrians.

In Devon, Connecticut, you can't walk backwards after sundown. Don't try to catch fish with your bare hands in Kansas. And Pennsylvania prohibits singing in the bathtub.

In Baldwin Park, California, you can't ride a bicycle in a swimming pool. And you can't carry an ice-cream cone in your pocket in Lexington, Kentucky.

These are genuine laws—no kidding. Aren't you glad God's laws make sense and were given because He loves us and wants to protect us?

A Knock at the Door

Listen! I stand at the door and knock; if any hear my voice and open the door, I will come into their house. Revelation 3:20, TEV.

Before she would listen to a child's heartbeat, the pediatrician would first plug the instrument into the patient's ears and let them listen. She loved watching their eyes light up with awe at the sound. When 4-year-old David came for his checkup, she tucked the stethoscope in his ears and placed the disk over his heart. "Listen," she said. "What do you suppose that is?"

Puzzled for a moment, the boy drew his eyebrows together and listened to the tap-tapping inside his chest. Suddenly his face broke into a wondrous grin. "It's Jesus knocking, isn't it?"

On David's bedroom wall was a painting of Jesus knocking on a door. At bedtime David and his mother would talk about the painting. "Jesus stands knocking at the door of your heart, David. See? There's no doorknob. You can open it only from the inside."

The same is true for you and me. Jesus will never force His way into our hearts or lives. We must open the door. Have you invited Him into your heart? It's the most important decision you will ever make.

Heaven's Grocery Store

All things, whatsoever ye shall ask in prayer, believing, ye shall receive. Matthew 21:22.

The following is an adaptation of an e-mail message I received from a friend. While it originated in the Netherlands, God's children everywhere can appreciate the message.

If I did my shopping in God's grocery store, angels would welcome me, hand me a cart and say, "Shop with care. Everything you need is here for you."

They would direct me to a row with shelves of patience on one side and tons of love on the other. In the next aisle I'd toss a box or two of wisdom into my cart, along with giant-sized bunches of strength and courage. And of course I would need a generous amount of grace and faith. As I filled my basket I would be sure to include peace and joy, along with several songs of praise. I'd also help myself to a day's supply of prayer, hope, and salvation.

When I reached the checkout line, I'd ask the Checker behind the counter, "How much do I owe You?"

The Savior would smile and say, "I paid your bill in full a long, long time ago. Remember?"

To which I would reply, "Thank You, thank You, thank You, dear Jesus. How could I forget?"

How Wise Are You?

I am sending you out like sheep among wolves. Therefore be as shrewd as snakes and as innocent as doves. Matthew 10:16, NIV.

Ready for a quiz? Try these questions on for size.

1. Do they have a fourth of July in England? Yes or no.
2. How many birthdays does the average man have?
3. Some months have 31 days; how many have 28?
4. Is it legal in California for a man to marry his widow's sister?
5. If there are three apples and you take away two, how many do you have?
6. How many animals did Moses take into the ark?
7. If a butcher is 5'10" tall, what does he weigh?
8. A plane crashes on the Canadian-U.S. border. In which country do you bury the survivors?

Answers: 1. Yes; it comes after July 3. 2. Everyone has only one birthday. 3. 12—every month has 28 days. 4. No—because he's dead. 5. 2—You took them, remember? 6. None—it was Noah, not Moses. 7. A butcher weighs meat. 8. Neither. You don't bury survivors!

While our word tricks were done in fun, Jesus said there would be people who would try to trick and deceive His disciples. We can be as shrewd as snakes and as innocent as doves by studying His Word and asking for His wisdom.

Keeping Your Cool

A gentle answer turns away wrath, but a harsh word stirs up anger. Proverbs 15:1, NIV.

You know how water fights start: first with a flick of wet fingers, then a handful, followed by a cup, until everyone is racing for a bucket.

King Solomon gave some pretty sage advice that the seven men between the ages of 18 and 29 who received three- to four-year jail sentences in Kingston-on-Thames, England, in 1979 should have listened to. The brawl started when one of the men threw a french fry at another while waiting for the train. One thing led to another . . .

With the violence on the street, on the roads, and in the schools, kids and adults should heed Solomon's advice as well. Television shows would have you think that quarreling and "duking it out" with fists, knives, or worse is the way to settle your differences. Not so. That's the fool's way of dealing with conflict. Any jerk can mouth off when offended, but the toughest person is the one who has the guts to walk away. So if you want to be a he-man or a Wonder Woman, buff up your self-control muscles. The time to stop trouble is before it starts. Staying cool is a wise choice that could save your life.

Sage Advice

A cheerful heart is good medicine. Proverbs 17:22, NIV.

Feel grumpy this morning? Ready for a few chuckles? Read the following advice given by some of your peers:

Never give up, because life gets harder as you get older. After preschool the road of life keeps getting bumpier and bumpier. Angela, age 11.

Never blow in a cat's ear. If you do, after three or four times he'll bite your lips. And he won't let go for at least a minute. Lisa, age 9.

A realist is more correct about things in life than an optimist. But the optimist has more friends and more fun. Megan, age 14.

When people run around in circles, we say they're crazy. When planets do it, we say they're orbiting. Kurt, age 10.

Most books say our sun is a star, but it still knows how to change back into the sun in the daytime. Shelly, age 9.

Many dead animals in the past changed to fossils while others preferred to be oil. Joe, age 12.

A vibration is a motion that can't make up its mind which way to go. Amy, age 13.

Doctors agree with King Solomon: "A cheerful heart is good medicine." Remember that the next time you wake up with sniffles.

192

Scared Silly

Flee the evil desires of youth, and pursue righteousness, faith, love and peace. 2 Timothy 2:22, NIV.

Driving home late at night over a country road in Pennsylvania, I slammed on my brakes when my headlights reflected off the terrified form of a giant buck standing in the middle of the road. I laid on my car horn and swerved to miss hitting the majestic creature, only to find a doe in my path a few feet further.

With a prayer on my lips, I swerved to the opposite side of the road, barely missing her as well. Shaken, I pulled to a stop to collect my wits. Why in the world would these two swift-moving animals freeze instead of run at the sight of my headlights? Did they have a death wish?

No. All animals have a survival instinct, including deer. It is believed that the animal is temporarily blinded by the lights and hears the rumble of the approaching auto, so its fear hormones take over. As prey instead of predators, deer react by freezing or hiding to avoid detection.

Ever been blinded by a terrifying temptation? Do you momentarily freeze, rather than run from it? Unlike the deer, God's kids don't have to become the devil's roadkill. Through the power of Jesus Christ you and I can not only run from evil, but defeat it.

It's Over!

"It's done . . . complete." Bowing his head, he offered up his spirit. John 19:30, Message.

Aroomful of tourists sat on the bleachers at the Gettysburg Battlefield Memorial, watching an electronic reenactment of the July 3, 1863, Battle of Gettysburg. Susie, her parents, and her older brother, Ronnie, listened intently as the narrator told how the battle had raged for more than an hour, the heaviest cannonade of the war.

"At 3:00 p.m. Confederate General Pickett and 15,000 men charged across a mile wide field, hoping to take a hill known as Cemetery Ridge from the Union Army." The uniformed guide continued, "In less than an hour 7,000 Confederate men had been killed or wounded in the battle that determined the outcome of the entire war."

During the morning ride to the memorial Ronnie had baited his sister by defending the South's position in the war. Confused, 6-year-old Susie whispered to her dad, "Who won?"

"The North," her father answered.

With a gloating smile the little girl poked her brother. "Ha-ha, my side won," as if the 138-year-old victory had just occurred.

Two thousand years ago God's Son, Jesus, won the war between God and Satan. It's all over! Finished! We won!

Declaration of Independence

If you hold to my teaching, you are really my disciples. Then you will know the truth, and the truth will set you free. John 8:31, 32, NIV.

We hold these truths to be self-evident, that all men are created equal." On July 4, 1776, the members of the Second Continental Congress officially signed the Declaration of Independence. When they did, they put their lives on the line. The outcome of the war was in the hands of a bunch of ragtag farmers and adventurers.

As John Hancock scratched his sprawling signature on the parchment, he knew he was signing his death warrant.

Not every American greeted the news with dancing and re-joicing. Loyalists sat in silence behind closed doors and barri-caded windows; some fled to Canada in fear. A third group received the news with indifference. They didn't care one way or the other.

Fifty years later to the day, two of the daring signers of that historic parchment died. John Adams and Thomas Jefferson died free men in a country they helped build on the principles of freedom.

Jesus' government is built on freedom too, the freedom to make your own choices, the freedom to live forever. But some people reject or fear that government because of Satan's dis-torted facts. If you check it out, you will know: God's truth will set you free.

Accidents Happen

All the ends of the earth will remember and turn to the Lord, . . .
for the dominion belongs to the Lord. Psalm 22:27, 28, NIV.

While motorcycling through Hungary, Cristo Faletti came to a railway line as the crossing gates came down. He was joined by a farmer with a goat. For some reason the farmer tethered the goat to the crossing gate. A few moments later, a horse and cart drew up behind Faletti, followed by a man in a sports car.

When the train roared through the crossing, the horse startled and bit Faletti's arm. Furious, Faletti punched the horse in the head. Indignant, the horse's owner jumped down from his cart and began scuffling with the motorcyclist.

Frightened, the horse backed away, smashing the cart into the sports car, causing the sports car driver to leap out of his car and join the fray. When the farmer came forward to pacify the three men, the crossing gate rose and strangled his goat. The insurance companies are still sorting the claims.

The poor goat didn't do anything wrong, yet he suffered the most. Accidents happen. In this world people do stupid things and the innocent suffer. Knowing God is ultimately in control puts life into proper perspective.

Suicidal Moths

Watch out that you are not deceived. For many will come in my name. . . . Do not follow them. Luke 21:8, NIV.

A commercial on television has a young actor telling the audience how great a new computer is, while an older man looks on. In his spiel the younger man says, "It's bad, really bad!"

Horrified, the older man shakes his head. "You can't say that. Our computer isn't bad. It's very, very good."

Of course, you know in today's lingo "bad" means exactly the opposite. It means great, right?

In a world of constant change, keeping things straight can be difficult. Take, for instance, the humble moth and your porch light. The moth isn't mesmerized by the light; it's confused.

Moths sleep during the day. At night they'd much rather be searching for food or for a mate than circling a lightbulb. Since the beginning of time the moth used light from stars as a reference point. This worked well until Thomas Edison invented the lightbulb.

The moth makes smaller and smaller circles, trying to keep a constant angle on the light, until it becomes so confused and disorientated, it can't escape.

Knowing God's Word and keeping in touch with Jesus will keep us from confusing Satan's artificial light with God's genuine Light.

7 July

Mrs. Tibbits' Stress Relaxers

Peace I leave with you; my peace I give you. . . . Do not let your hearts be troubled and do not be afraid. John 14:27, NIV.

Jenny clutched her head with her hands. "I can't take any more," she wailed. "I can't."

Mrs. Tibbits, the school's guidance counselor, saw the stress in Jenny's distorted face.

"If things don't let up, I swear I'll pop a blood vessel!"

During the past few months Jenny's grandmother had died of cancer, her older brother had crashed his motorcycle and died, and her mother and father had filed for divorce. And now her favorite teacher had sent Jenny to the guidance counselor after the girl burst into uncontrollable tears following a bad grade on a math quiz.

"Jenny, you couldn't prevent your grandmother's or your brother's death, nor your parents' decision to divorce. But I have a few suggestions for relieving your stress and improving your math grade."

"First, stop! Spend 10 minutes every morning with God. Claim the peace He promises is yours. Second, look for blessings every day and write them down. Third, listen to the world around you—birds, laughter of little kids, sounds of living. Give God praise. And fourth, run! When you feel you can't take another minute, exercise."

Mrs. Tibbits' advice for finding peace worked for Jenny. And it can work for you.

Attitude of Gratitude

The prayer of a person living right with God is something powerful to be reckoned with. James 5:16, Message.

Two-year-old Jarod was fussy and irritable in the back seat of the family Honda. The car's air-conditioner had stopped, and they were at a standstill, trapped in a traffic jam 50 miles from home.

Tears of frustration welled up in Jarod's exhausted mother's eyes. All she wanted was to be home and soaking in a hot tub. With the boy wailing in the back seat, Kelli began whining aloud to God about her situation.

Suddenly Jarod stopped crying. "What was that?" he asked.

Kelli sniffled and replied, "Mommy was just praying to Jesus, that's all."

Jarod's response stopped Kelli's tears. He prayed, "Oh, OK. Dear Jesus, thank You for Mommy and Daddy and Kiki and jet planes and trees . . ."

The traffic jam remained the same, the air-conditioner stayed broken, but Kelli's attitude changed, as did her prayer—to one of thankfulness and praise.

It's easy to imagine your parent's prayers changing you, but what about your prayers affecting your folks? Try it and see what a difference your prayers can make.

9 July

Children's Letters to God

O Lord, our Lord, your greatness is seen in all the world! Your praise reaches up to the heavens; it is sung by children and babies. Psalm 8:1, 2, TEV.

Dear God, in school they told us what You do. Who does it when You're on vacation?"—Jane.

"Dear God, I didn't think orange went with purple until I saw the sunset You made last night."—Larry.

"Dear God, did You mean for the giraffe to look like that, or was it an accident?"—Annie.

"Dear God, instead of letting people die and having to make new ones, why don't You just keep the ones You have now?"—Jane.

"Dear God, the bad people laughed at Noah, but he stuck by You. That's what I would do."—Neil.

"Dear God, thank You for my baby brother, but what I prayed for was a puppy."—Mikey.

"Dear God, I read Thomas Edison invented light. In the Bible it says You did. I bet he stole the idea from you."—Kurt.

"Dear God, I think about You sometimes, even when I'm not praying."—Ali.

God loves the prayers of His children. No prayer we pray is too trivial, no thought too unimportant. He always loves to hear from us.

God's Gardening Tip

Be not deceived; God is not mocked: for whatsoever a man soweth, that shall he also reap. Galatians 6:7.

When I was a preschooler, I helped my mother plant vegetables in our plot of the community garden. It was my job to open the seed packets of beans, peas, and carrots and hand the seeds to her one by one. Then I helped by covering them and patting down the soil on top of them.

On my own I'd carefully collected some seeds of my own from our backyard. I thought I was being helpful when, during a break, I planted a handful of seeds in the middle of the garden. Weeks later my mother discovered a short but orderly row of weeds growing in our pumpkin patch.

I learned a valuable lesson that summer. You reap what you sow.

It makes sense, this reaping what you sow. When you are in need, give something *good* to others, and you'll get back 10 times as much. The poor widow wasn't foolish to give her last mite. She believed in the miracle of this simple tip straight from the Master Gardener. Do you?

11 July

Name That Fruit

But the fruit of the [Holy] Spirit [the work which His presence within accomplishes] is love. Galatians 5:22, Amplified.

A preacher was about to fly between Atlanta and New York when a couple with four children boarded the plane he was on. Because the flight was full, the parents had separate seats close to the minister. As they chatted back and forth about how excited they were about visiting New York for the first time, the pastor thought, *I wish they'd shut up so I can sleep!*

After a few moments, the Holy Spirit spoke to the minister. "Why don't you give them your seat so they can sit together?"

"Oh, please," he silently groaned. "This is my assigned seat. I'm sleepy, and I'm not moving!"

As the pastor tells the story, he says, "Immediately I heard the voice of the Lord audibly scream at me. 'Name that fruit!' It startled me so badly, I jumped up and offered to trade seats with the wife."

The pastor knew that love, joy, peace, long-suffering, gentleness, goodness, faith, meekness, and temperance are the fruit (or evidence) that the Spirit of God lives within a person. Name the fruit of your actions. If you don't find it in God's list, it isn't one grown by God.

Gun-slinging Granny

Professing themselves to be wise, they became fools. Romans 1:22.

The story is told about a grandmother living in a rough neighborhood of Houston, Texas. Her three sons, having moved to the suburbs, urged her to move out of the dangerous area of the city.

Failing to convince her to move, they bought her a pistol and convinced her to take firing lessons. Reluctantly she did so, to please her boys.

Two weeks later Granny came out of the mall and discovered three teenage guys sitting in the front seat of her car. Removing the gun in her purse, she waltzed up to the car, where she aimed her pistol at the boys and ordered, "Get your hands up and get out of that car now!"

The boys started to protest. "Don't give me any lip," she snarled. "Just do as I say. I know how to use this thing!"

Frightened, the boys fled into the mall. Granny congratulated herself on her fast thinking as she tried to start the car, but the key wouldn't fit into the ignition. Suddenly Granny realized it wasn't her car. She hopped out and spied her car three rows away.

Later in the paper she read about a police report of a gun-toting granny who'd tried to hijack a teenager's car in the mall parking lot. Sometimes our leap-to-conclusions wisdom leaves us feeling mighty foolish.

13 July

A Chip off the Old Spud

But when he, the Spirit of truth, comes, he will guide you into all truth. John 16:13, NIV.

Earl Wise had a problem. His supplier had delivered too many potatoes to his restaurant. They'd spoil before he could use them all.

While contemplating his problem, Earl began peeling a potato, then another and another out of the first gunny sack. Exposed to the air, the peeled potatoes began turning brown. Rather than waste them, he dumped the thinly sliced potatoes into a pot of hot grease bubbling on the stove. Voila! A new snack! Eat any Wise potato chips lately?

Penicillin was discovered by a similar accident, as was safety glass and silly putty. The term for such accidents is serendipity. That's the process of discovering one thing while looking for something completely different.

A friend of mine discovered the truth of the Sabbath while trying to prove Sunday was the biblical day of worship. Another friend studied the Bible to prove that Jesus wasn't God, only to come to love Him. Of course, these last two examples aren't really serendipity since the Holy Spirit made the difference. The Holy Spirit working on your heart or mine is never an accident. He's just doing His job.

In Times of Trouble

The Lord is good, a refuge in times of trouble. Nahum 1:7, NIV.

An early spring storm in Alabama switched to a tornado with 300-mile-per-hour winds while the Baptist church choir was rehearsing for the upcoming Sunday services. Children's Bible classes were meeting in other rooms when the church custodian announced, "A tornado is coming! Take cover."

He directed everyone to an enclosed hallway where there were no windows. The teachers had already herded the children to the protected area. Parents, teachers, and children huddled and waited.

Children screamed as the deafening sound of a rushing freight train filled the air, followed by the sound of the roof being ripped from above their heads and debris whirling by in the night sky. The twister destroyed the town and the church, but the 69 people were safe.

The National Weather Bureau reports hundreds tornadoes each year. And I have no idea how many hurricanes, earthquakes, and other disasters occur.

I live in California where the earth sometimes shakes. My sister Connie lives in tornado alley. My daughter Rhonda lives in the shadow of volcanoes. And my sister-in-law, Fran, lives in the land of hurricanes. I would worry and fret for our safety if I didn't know that the only safe place for God's children to live on this earth is under the protection of God's love.

A-Mazing Thrills

Beware that you don't look down upon a single one of these little children. . . . I, the Messiah, came to save the lost. Matthew 18:10, 11, TLB.

Maze lovers say the thrill of running mazes are the dead ends and the wrong turns. When I visited England, I toured a maze. A maze is a giant puzzle, like the Pac-Man board, where you become the player. For one who is claustrophobic (hates small spaces), I confess I got panicky even though I knew that, sooner or later, I would safely escape.

The latest maze craze is found at the 24 cornfield mazes in Europe, America, Australia, and Canada. Fifty thousand visitors will pay as much as $8 each to get lost in these amazing and carefully planned labyrinths this year.

Becoming addicted to tobacco, alcohol, or drugs is similar to running a maze. Those who don't know better might, at first, think they're having fun. But sooner or later, after hitting too many dead ends, terror sets in, as it did for me in the English maze. There's no way out!

Experimenting with smoking, alcohol, or drugs is stupid, and we who don't experiment might say, "Don't they know any better?"

It's true. Mistreating one's body is not smart. But let's not "put down" those lost in Satan's mazes but lift them up. For Jesus is their Savior too.

God's OK: I'm OK

Don't fret or worry. Instead of worrying, pray. . . . Before you know it, a sense of God's wholeness, everything coming together for good, will come and settle you down. Philippians 4:6, 7, Message.

Sandi worries about her dad, a policeofficer. Eric frets over where to go to college. Larry is anxious about passing his math test. What are you worried about? And why? God knows everything, right?

When He says, "Don't worry," what does He mean? He means don't worry. When He says, "Don't be anxious." What does He mean? Don't be anxious! When He says, "Don't fret," He means don't fret. Duh! It's so simple, it's hard—if you don't know God.

Imagine winning a prize—10 minutes with God. When you get there, you ask Him, "Do You know everything?"

He answers, "Yes."

"About me?"

"Yes . . ."

"How do you keep from getting it all mixed up in Your head?"

"I'm not you."

"Do You watch over me all the time?"

"Yes. Don't worry; everything you need for the rest of your life, I've already provided. On your best days I fill you with joy. And on your worst days I get you through."

When your 10 minutes are up, you return to earth forever changed. No more doubts, because you've seen Him; you know Him. Ten minutes with God is no fantasy prize. It can be yours every day through prayer and His Word.

17 July

Toast, Popsicles, and Black Holes

By faith we understand that the universe was formed at God's command." Hebrews 11:3, NIV.

If you could heat the head of a straight pin to the temperature of the core of the sun, it would kill every man, woman, and child on the planet.

The sun is like a 4 trillion ton atomic bomb exploding continuously. Yet only one 2-billionth of that energy reaches the earth. If more reached us, we'd be toast. Any less, we'd be Popsicles. God's precision reveals His love to us.

A black hole is a collapsed star with gravitational pull that reduces objects to zero volume. It would crush our sun to two miles in diameter and the earth to a half inch in diameter.

Every galaxy has black holes. Scientists tell us that there is a point called "event horizon," the last step before an object is absorbed by a black hole. Beyond that means total annihilation. Do you think God can go beyond the "event horizon" and win against a black hole's power? Absolutely. God wins. He controls the universe, including black holes and the sun's atomic blasts. The more scientists learn about the universe, the more they have to admit: God is real. He created and controls a powerhouse beyond our wildest imaginations.

A Little Misunderstanding

Come, and let us go up to the mountain of the Lord, . . . and he will teach us of his ways. Micah 4:2.

The National Education Association of Sciences recently shared the answers some students gave on science tests.

1. "The body consists of three parts. The branium contains the brain; the borax, the heart and lungs; and the abdominal cavity contains the bowels, of which there are five—a, e, i, o, and u."
2. "H_2O is hot water, and CO_2 is cold water."
3. "When you smell an odorless gas, it is probably carbon monoxide."
4. "Blood flows down one leg and up the other."
5. "The moon is a planet just like the earth, only it is even deader."
6. "The tides are a fight between the earth and the moon. All water tends toward the moon because there is no water on the moon, and nature abhors a vacuum. I forget where the sun comes in."
7. "The pistol of a flower is its only protection against insects."

For centuries adults believed that the earth was flat—that the night sky was a giant upside-down cup. Stars were holes in the cup that let through light. We will never, on this earth, have answers to every question, but God promises to teach us everything we need to know to live with Him forever.

19 July

Liar! Liar!

Would you like to enjoy life? Do you want long life and happiness? Then keep from speaking evil and from telling lies. Psalm 34:12, 13, TEV.

In Salem Village, Massachusetts Bay Colony, Sarah Goode, Sarah Osborne, and Tituba, an Indian slave from Barbados, were charged with practicing witchcraft. The date: March 1, 1692. Under coercion, the terrified slave confessed to the crime. Hysteria swept through the town, until more than 150 men and women from the area were accused of witchcraft.

One way the authorities determined if an accused was guilty was by the "dunking stool." If a person tied to a stool was guilty, then lowered into the water she would float and would be executed. If the accused drowned, she was innocent. Either way she was dead. The accusations have since been proved to be lies.

But that was long ago. Such a thing couldn't happen today, could it?

A softball glove is missing from the classroom. Joey has a new mitt; therefore, Joey must have stolen it even though he claims it's a birthday gift. The new girl at school transferred because she _____ . You fill in the blank. Or better yet, don't. And refuse to listen when someone else does.

Brain Power

And you must love him [God] with all your heart and soul and mind and strength. Mark 12:30, TLB.

The dizzying scent of Trish's perfume filled Kurt's nostrils as she leaned close to him and flipped her long golden hair carelessly over her shoulder. "What is it, Kurt?" she asked, batting her baby blues. "Don't you like me?"

Kurt had dropped by Trish's house to return the history book she'd accidentally left in his car. Before he learned they were alone in the house, Kurt found himself on the den sofa and the girl pressed close to him.

"I gotta get out of here." He pushed her away. "My dad wants me to mow the backyard lawn this afternoon."

"Stay a while," she cooed, unbuttoning the top button on his sport shirt. "I'll help you do the yard later." He had the worst desire to kiss the girl's pouting lips.

Television and movie script writers would have you believe Kurt was hopelessly trapped by his emotions. But Kurt knew a higher Power. He knew he was a son of God, not of an ape. With God controlling his mind, Kurt controlled his emotions and senses, and fled the temptation.

21 July

Feeling Brainy?

I will put my law in their minds and write it on their hearts. I will be their God, and they will be my people. Jeremiah 31:33, NIV.

The human brain is a relatively small part of the body. It isn't the size and the weight of the brain that determines intelligence. How smart you are is determined by the number of ridges and grooves on the brain's surface and the interconnections between nerve cells. Each fact you learn adds a new wrinkle.

The brain is divided into the cerebrum and the cerebellum. The cerebellum keeps you breathing and walking. The cerebrum distinguishes you from your goldfish or from your cat.

What blouse will I wear tomorrow? Should I cut my hair? Should I become a doctor or a teacher when I grow up? Do I want a chocolate or butter pecan ice-cream cone? This is where you make choices—good and bad.

Remember Kurt? It wasn't an accident that he resisted Trish's advances. Long before the temptation to "mess around" with Trish came, Kurt made a choice to put God's law in his mind and heart, and therefore wasn't blindsided by what could have been an overwhelming situation.

Make a list of the decisions you want to make today to keep you from "messing up" your life with bad choices.

Two Times Foolish

Do not be wise in your own eyes; fear the Lord and shun evil.
Proverbs 3:7, NIV.

Have you ever done something to make you feel foolish? I have. There was the time I realized in the middle of a presentation before 300 people that I'd accidentally wore shoes from two different pair—a black one and a brown one. Then there was the time I made a stop at the bank on my way to the grocery store and left my shoes in the bank parking lot. (The heels were too high to drive in safely, so I slipped them off when I climbed back into the car.) Nothing too serious, except to my ego.

The same can't be true of Anna Taylor, who on October 24, 1901, climbed into a specially designed barrel and rode it over Niagara Falls. Fifteen minutes later Anna climbed out of the barrel at the bottom of the falls and waved to the cheering crowd. Bruised and battered, the schoolteacher advised reporters, "Don't ever try it. It was a very foolish thing I did."

Both Anna and I were wise in our own eyes. Both of us were wrong. And both of us vowed to be more careful in the future. To make a mistake once is human, but not to learn from one's mistake is truly foolish.

Belief or Doubt

Believe on the Lord Jesus and you will be saved, and your entire household. Acts 16:31, TLB.

Is there really a hole in the earth's ozone layer? Does secondhand smoke kill? Is marijuana dangerous to your health? Did humans really land on the moon?

Believe it or not, I heard a public figure declare that the hole in the ozone layer is a myth promoted by environmentalists to get the government to support their agenda. A friend of mine is certain that secondhand smoke never hurt anyone, that the story is told to harass smokers. And many people truly think that marijuana is safe to use.

As to the question about humans landing on the moon, up until the moment my mother died, she honestly believed that God would never allow humans to touch the moon's surface. To her, the moon landing would always be nothing more than a cleverly filmed movie made in Hollywood; the astronauts were actors playing their parts.

I don't tell you these things to poke fun at anyone. Yet, the answer is yes to each of the questions, regardless of what anyone, including my mother, might believe. However, the most important truth to know is that by believing in Jesus, you will be saved.

Speak No Evil

Whoso keepeth his mouth and his tongue keepeth his soul from troubles. Proverbs 21:23.

Hear no evil; see no evil; speak no evil"—wise counsel to one who wishes to stay out of trouble. Today's mother may say, "Mind your own business." Again, that's good advice. My mother used to say much the same thing when she advised, "Mind your own p's and q's."

(Speaking of p's and q's, did you ever count the number of p's and q's in a can of Campbell's alphabet soup? And are there equal numbers of each letter? The Campbell Soup Company actually hires a vice president of letter distribution. He assures me that all letters are equally represented. However, the company won't guarantee that while letters and soup are being inserted into a can, things won't get messed up.)

Actually, the saying "Mind your own p's and q's" originated sometime around 1780. Schoolboys, confused by the lowercase letters p and q on their chalkboard, would check their answers against their neighbors. Hence, the teacher would say "Mind your own p's and q's."

When I was a kid, I took on everybody's cause, fighting every Goliath I saw. My mouth got me into heaps of trouble, most of which wasn't mine in the first place. Often I learned the hard way when to speak and when to "mind my own p's and q's."

Down to Your Toenails

Never fear, you are far more valuable to him than a whole flock of sparrows. Luke 12:7, TLB.

Did you ever wonder why birds perching on a tree limb can sleep without tipping over? The Creator came up with a built-in security system that controls their toes. They have special tendons in front of their knee joint and behind their ankle joint that lock around the perch. Other tendons located under their toe bones keep them from losing their balance.

What about you? Look in the mirror. What do you see? Freckles? An oval-shaped face? An upturned nose? Or a schnozzle just like dad's or Grandpa Joe's? No matter how similar you may look to another, you are uniquely you, right down to your toenails. Even if you're one of identical twins, you are still one of a kind.

Look at your hands. Your fingerprints are you. Take a peek at your eyes. The pattern in the irises of your eyes spells you. Stick out your tongue and see your very own tongue map. That's right—tongue map.

You do have something important in common with birds—not special tendons for perching on limbs, but the fact that God loves and cares for you.

Dead Men Hearing

The time is coming . . . when the dead shall hear my voice—the voice of the Son of God—and those who listen shall live. John 5:25, TLB.

Here's an experiment you might want to try. Roll a sheet of poster board (18" x 24") into a cone shape, leaving a hole (half inch to an inch across) at the pointed end. Tape the edge into position. Go outside and put the small end of the cone to your ear. What tiny sounds can you hear that you missed hearing without the cone?

Your poster board cone works like a satellite dish that detects signals from satellites in space. Wouldn't it be neat if you heard God's voice with your cone or with your dad's satellite dish? What would He have to say?

The Bible is God's Word. I "hear" God speaking to me through its pages. So I understand how the living can hear, but the dead?

Here's the key: "The time is coming" when Jesus will return to take us home with Him. On that day the living and the dead will hear His voice. The dead will pop out of their graves. Abraham Lincoln, Grandma Jones, Uncle Peter, baby sister. Won't that be something?

By listening to His voice today, I'll hear His call and be ready to go home with Him on that incredible day. How about you?

That's Quite a Yarn

As high as the sky is above the earth, so great is his love for those who honor him. Psalm 103:11, TEV.

Today I want to take you (your mind, anyway) out of this world. On July 29, 1999, *Deep Space I* flew past the asteroid Braille, which is roughly 117 million miles (190 million kilometers) from Earth.

Do you know how far that is? If you had a piece of yarn that long, it would weigh 88,000 tons. That's enough yarn to make sweaters for every person in the United states. If you made a ball of that yarn, it would be 330 feet high—as tall as a 32-story building or two times as tall as the Statue of Liberty. And that's not very far from earth at all compared to the other places astronomers can see through a telescope.

Yet no matter how far a spaceship can travel or an astronomer can see through their telescope, God's love for you and for me is even greater. Actually, it's infinite; it has no end or limit. (Log on to the Education Planet home page [www.educationplanet.com] and discover even more fantastic facts about how big and wide and deep and tall God's universe really is. It will make you love Him all the more.)

A Secret Code

The knowledge of the secrets of the kingdom of God has been given to you, but to others I speak in parables. Luke 8:10, NIV.

Did you ever invent a code so that you and your friend could write notes, but no one else could understand them? Here's a simple code you can use: Think of the alphabet as a circle. For every letter in a word, count forward five letters. The word code would look like this: htij. Simple to those who know, but gibberish to those who don't.

Victory over Japan during World War II was due to a secret code. During the darkest months of war in the Pacific, the government couldn't stop the information leaks to the enemy. Code after code was devised and broken. All attempts to invent an unbreakable code failed.

Then communications experts remembered that Navajo is one of the most complicated and least-known languages in the world. The plan worked. Four hundred twenty Navajos became the radio "talkers," ending the loss of secrets to the opposing forces.

Jesus spoke in code, or parables, to keep the lessons of the kingdom from being understood by His enemies too. To teach the important lessons about the kingdom of God without the wrong people understanding, Jesus told stories or parables. God's code still works today through the power of the Holy Spirit.

29 July

The Chosen Ones

You are the ones chosen by God, . . . chosen to be . . . God's instruments to do his work and to speak out for him. 1 Peter 2:9, Message.

To be chosen of God—isn't it neat to be "special"? Feels good, huh? I doubt the 290,000 Japanese *hibakusha* feel special. These are the "living ones" or the "survivors" of the atomic bombs dropped on Hiroshima and Nagasaki, ending World War II.

Before the bombs fell, Hiroshima's population was more than 300,000 and Nagasaki's about the same. More than 120,000 citizens died instantly. Many others lived a few days, then died.

Today 60 percent of the *hibakusha* are still alive. These people have formed a separate culture of their own in Japan. Instead of being grateful for being alive, many *hibakusha* feel guilty for surviving when their friends and loved ones perished in the blast.

At the end of time there will be a group of *hibakusha*—living ones—who will survive the final destruction of Planet Earth. These chosen ones will have shared the good news of God's love with their family and friends. They won't share a sense of guilt for surviving, but joy for what God has given them—eternity.

The Playful One

Even a child is known by his actions, by whether is conduct is pure and right. Proverbs 20:11, NIV.

When I was a child, I had a nickname—haywire. I wasn't very proud of it. Wire wrapped around a bale of hay can suddenly, without warning, snap and fly about dangerously. (I had an unpredictable temper, you see.)

I'd like to tell you about another girl's nickname, Matoaka's. Matoaka's father was an Indian chief, which made the girl a princess—a playful princess, so history tells us. She was known by everyone in her tribe as "the playful one."

When she was 11, Matoaka saved the life of a 27-year-old Englishman by throwing herself upon him and claiming him for her own. Her father granted his beautiful daughter's wish.

Seven years later, having been taken prisoner by the English, the young girl captured the heart of John Rolfe, married him, and changed her name to Rebecca. Rebecca Rolfe went down in history, not as Rebecca or as Matoaka, but as Pocahontas, "the playful one."

What are you known for today? Temper? Kindness? Giggles? Being honest? Happy? Grouchy? Snoopy? Sympathetic? Helpful? What nickname has your attitude earned for you? If it's not so nice, how can you change it?

Space Talk

They know nothing, they understand nothing; their eyes are plastered over so they cannot see, and their minds closed so they cannot understand. Isaiah 44:18, NIV.

A few days ago we talked about secret code. Today's code isn't secret. It's used in almost every home in the United States. The spacecraft *Voyager*² uses the code to communicate with NASA scientists. Using only ones and zeros, the signals *Voyager*² sent to earth show us pictures of Jupiter, the fifth planet from the sun; Saturn, the sixth from the sun; as well as Neptune and Uranus.

This special language looks like this: 1101 0010 1001 0101 0000 1011. It's like speaking with your kitchen light switch—on and off. Spacecraft engineers and computer scientists solve humongous problems with this language. Seems like the machines are very smart, huh?

Actually, none of these machines are smart enough to speak English or Spanish or German or any other human language. It takes a human to invent the language, understand the messages, and program the computers in the first place.

People with eyes and minds closed are kind of like the machines that, at first, seem so smart. They spout all kinds of nonsense. The real "brainy ones" are God's kids who listen and obey His Word.

A Healing Jesus

People brought anybody with an ailment, whether mental, emotional or physical. Jesus healed them, one and all. Matthew 4:24, Message.

My grandfather was an herbal doctor in a remote area of western Pennsylvania where medical doctors were rare. Grandpa had an elixir, tea, or salve guaranteed to cure "whatever ails ya." However, his strongest medicine he gave to every patient he saw—prayer.

Science has come a long way since Grandpa Ball knelt beside the beds of his patients to pray for them. The following remedies recommended by aspiring physicians ages 8 to 10 will probably not be included in the medical books of the new millennium.

1. Before giving a blood transfusion, find out if the blood is affirmative or negative.
2. To remove dust from the eye, pull the eye down over the nose.
3. For a dog bite, put the dog away for several days. If it has not recovered in several days, kill it.
4. For a head cold, use the agonizer to spray nose until it drops in your throat.
5. To keep milk from turning sour, keep it in the cow.

The best medical advice in the world hasn't changed since Grandpa's day, because Jesus hasn't changed. He's still the one who wants to heal the diseases of our minds, our bodies, and our hearts.

A Blade of Grass

My presence shall go with thee, and I will give thee rest. Exodus 33:14.

During World War II the Nazi regime of Germany imprisoned and executed millions of Jewish people and their sympathizers. Dutch citizens Corrie ten Boom and her sister were cast into a prison camp for helping Jews escape to freedom.

With maggot-infested cornmeal to eat and cold, filthy, crowded barracks to live in, Corrie became depressed. One night as she listened to the other prisoners snoring, weeping, and coughing in their sleep, she cried out to God.

"Where are You, God? You said You'd always be with me, but I can't see You in this terrible place."

Somehow she fell asleep with that question on her mind. Corrie awoke in the morning to a shaft of sunlight illuminating a single blade of green grass beyond the walls of her prison. She smiled and thanked God for reminding her that God could make new life grow even behind prison walls and that He would never leave nor forsake her.

A single blade of grass. You might not be in a concentration camp where the world is gray and bleak, but right now, where you sit, God is reminding you that He loves you and will never desert you.

Hitting It out of This World

This resurrection life you received from God is not a timid, grave-like life. It's adventurously expectant, greeting God with a child-like "What's next, Papa?" Romans 8:15, Message.

Baseball coach Tommy Lasorda led the United States Olympic team to victory in the 2000 Summer Olympics. While firing up the athletes before the games he gave this illustration. "It's the bottom of the ninth with one out in the World Series. The other team's strongest home run hitter is at the plate. What are you praying?"

An athlete in the back of the locker room answered, "Please don't let him hit the ball to me." Everyone laughed—after all, who wants to be the one to fumble the ball and lose the game as well as the series?

Mr. Lasorda shook his head. "Wrong! If you want to be a winner, you are praying, 'Please, Lord, let him hit it to me!' Winners think positively!"

The Olympics coach wasn't talking to an audience of believing Christians. For us, being positive should be as natural as breathing. We know the end of the story. We're on the winning team! Not for what we do, but for what Jesus did. Each morning we can confidently ask God, "What's next, Papa?" And each night we can praise Him for the day's adventure.

4 August

A Gentle Push

They returned to Lystra . . . encouraging them to remain true to the faith. Acts 14:2, 22, NIV.

What does it take to push NASA's *Deep Space 1* spacecraft through space? The weight of a single piece of notebook paper resting in your hand. Using an ion propulsion system, the spacecraft accelerates from zero to 60 miles per hour in two and a half days.

Yet four days after it's launched, *Deep Space 1* will be about 600,000 miles from Earth. That's more than twice as far as the moon.

Walking that far would take you eight hours every day for your whole life. To drive it at 60 miles per hour, you would have to drive 24 hours a day—without stopping for gas, to eat, to use the bathroom, or to stretch your legs—every day for a year plus one and a half more months! It would take a jet six weeks without stopping. All because of a gentle nudge.

The ion propulsion system on *Deep Space 1* is nothing compared to the gentle nudge of an encouraging word. "You look extra nice today." "Great job on your science project." "You're a very kind person." Encouraging words, a gentle push in the right direction, can help move God's kids from here to God's eternity.

Gift of Dyslexia

Be not be overcome of evil, but overcome evil with good.
Romans 12:21.

When Don Winkler sang in church as a child, he would belt out the songs, sometimes using the wrong words. Instead of "Praise God," he might sing "Praise dog." The other kids would giggle, thinking he was cutting up.

He wasn't, nor was he slow or lazy. Don Winkler, CEO of Ford Motor Credit Company, had—and still has—a learning disability called dyslexia, a condition in which the brain sees the words backwards or upside down. Sometimes the letters dance on the page.

Broker Charles Schwab, television writer Stephen Cannell, politician Troy Brown, and presidential honor guardsman Terry Johnson have turned the disability of dyslexia into a blessing.

Author Fannie Flagg grew up feeling stupid. "I'd compensate by acting silly. I don't know if [dyslexia] is a gift, but it is a character builder."

Dyslexic polar explorer Ann Bancroft says, "The disability has . . . forged my iron will and given me strength." The first woman to cross the ice of both the North and the South Pole, Ann jokes, "I get to talk about being crummy at math and still get to navigate."

Rhodes scholar and weight lifter Tom Gray, once considered the class clown because of his learning disabilities, says, "The hardest experiences I've faced have given me my greatest strength."

6 August

Twinkle. Twinkle

What supports its [Earth's] foundations, and who laid its corner-stone, as the morning stars sang together and all the angels shouted for joy? Job 38:6,7, TLB.

Use your imagination: God the Father, God the Son, and God the Holy Sprit are about to create the world. Breaking the silence of space, the Creator's booming voice commands a mass of nothing to become Planet Earth. Then as an Olympic shot-putter, He hurls the globe into the sky, causing it to begin spinning on its axis at just the right speed to support the life He is about to create.

A loud cheer goes up from the angels. "Hooray! Jesus is king!" What song do you think the stars might have sung?

When I see them twinkle, I like to imagine they are still singing that song to their Creator. Of course, science might better describe the twinkle of a star as light passing through 300 miles of Earth's atmosphere, during which the light-bending properties of the different layers of light cause the light to bend and jiggle, thus causing it to twinkle. Make sense?

Yeah, but I like my version better. I wonder if some day, when God takes us out of this world, beyond the far reaches of space . . . I wonder if we will get to hear the stars sing? H'mmm; I wonder.

How Did They Do It?

You claim to know nothing about him, but the fact is, he opened my eyes! . . . If this man didn't come from God, he wouldn't be able to do anything. John 9:30, Message.

The Great Pyramid of Giza built during the reign of Khufu (2575-2465 B.C.) rises 481 feet, covers 13 acres, and weighs almost 6 million tons. The 2.3 million blocks would build a wall around France 10 feet high and one foot wide. The pyramid's stones are cut so accurately that you can't fit a sheet of paper between them. How did they do that?

The rocks were hewn at quarries 600 miles away, then floated down the Nile on rafts in flood season. A massive stone causeway was built on the banks of the Nile where the stones were dragged on wooden sledges resting on rollers to the building site. Here the stones were smoothed.

Some scholars suggest that the stones were moved into position on enormous ramps. A stone would be pushed to the tip of the ramp, then placed on a bed of liquid mortar (or mud) and left to set.

When Jesus placed mud and saliva on the blind man's eyes and the man could see, people asked, "How did He do that?" Building a massive pyramid was a marvelous undertaking. But restoring the eyes of a man who'd been born blind took a miracle act of creation.

8 August

Awesome God

O Lord . . . you are a great and awesome God; you always fulfill your promises of mercy to those who love you and who keep your laws. Daniel 9:4, TLB.

Before you begin today's reading, it will help you to know that 6 taken to the power of 10 is 6 multiplied by 6 10 times. The problem would look like this:

6 x 6 x 6 x 6 x 6 x 6 x 6 x 6 x 6 x 6 = ?

Got that figured out?

Try thinking about these numbers:

1. The number of electrons (10 to the eightieth power) that pass through the filament of a lightbulb is equal to the number of droplets of water that flow over Niagara Falls in a century.

2. The "Coney Island number" (10 to the twentieth power) is the number of grains of sand on the beach at Coney Island.

3. The number of atoms you breathe in one breath is 10 to the twenty-first power.

4. The number of oxygen atoms in a thimble is 10 to the twenty-seventh power.

5. It took 10 to the thirtieth power of snowflakes to form the ice age.

What a math whiz God is! His precision in His created order is 10 to the tenth to the 127th power. When He says, "Don't worry about anything," what do you think He means?

A Little About You

Go to God. . . . For he does wonderful miracles, marvels without number. Job 5:8, 9, TLB.

Look in the mirror. What do you see? Do you see the 10,000 trillion trillion atoms—more than the stars in the universe—that make up your body? Did you know that your body replaces 1 trillion atoms every 1 millionth of a second?

Our bodies leak atoms through sneezes, common breathing, going to the bathroom, flowing rivers, and the jet stream, just to name a few ways. The released atoms move on to others. Red, Yellow, Black, White—we all share the same atoms. Some of the carbon atoms that resided in you when you were a baby are now at work in the body of a child in Afghanistan. And some of his father's carbon atoms are probably residing in your teacher, or your grandmother, or even you.

Every cell of your body has 1 trillion atoms; your entire body has 10 to the 100 trillion! The body makes more than 2 billion new cells every day. You sluff off 40 pounds of skin in a lifetime!

Take a deep breath. You just inhaled 150 millioon air molecules, some of which Jesus breathed when He was on this earth. Imagine Jesus doing mouth-to-mouth resuscitation on you all the time! Go ahead—shout, dance, and sing praises to our incredibly awesome God!

See How They Run

He makes my feet like the feet of a deer; he enables me to stand on the heights. 2 Samuel 22:34, NIV.

Sixty-two-year-old Patty Rossback wins races with her nerves of steel and with legs made of carbon fiber and titanium. Patty lost her legs in a childhood accident. Today she runs races and marathons. Recently she completed the New York Marathon in four hours and 15 minutes—faster than many runners with two natural legs.

Chris Waddell has won nine medals for the USA Alpine Ski Team at the Sydney Paralympics. (The Paralympics is competition for the physically challenged, while the Special Olympics is for the mentally challenged.) Chris, both legs amputated as a child, was clocked at 65 miles per hour on his mono-ski.

Janey Goldman lost her legs from frostbite after being stranded for days in a snow storm at age 19. Ten years later she calls herself the "Bionic Woman." Her new legs allow her to be a full-time track and field athlete.

Leg amputee Todd Huston broke the able-bodied man's record by 64 days for climbing the highest peak in every state, including the treacherous Mount McKinley in Alaska. His dream is to conquer Everest!

So what's your excuse? Got any mountains to climb? Any races to run? God and a little science can change your "I can't" to "Yes, I can!"

Medals and Prizes

Everyone who competes in the games goes into strict training. They do it to get a crown that will not last; but we do it to get a crown that will last forever. 1 Corinthians 9:25, NIV.

As we watch the Olympics, it's easy to forget that every person running, swimming, jumping, skiing, wrestling— whatever their sport—is already a winner. They've "bested" the best of hundreds of others to make it on the Olympic team. Yet many don't feel like a winner unless they "medal" with gold, silver, or bronze.

Studies have shown that those who win the gold medal aren't always happy. They're afraid they can never do it again. The silver medalists feel as if they're second best. Of the three, those who earned bronze are often just grateful to have made it into the medals. They're the happiest group of Olympians.

The same is not true of the athletes in the Special Olympics. Remember the runner who stumbled and fell. Instead of rushing on to the finish line, the other competitors stopped to help the fallen athlete to his feet, then walked beside him across the finish line. These athletes understood God's Olympics. God doesn't help those who help themselves. He helps those who help others.

12 August

Happy Mother's Day

I'm thanking you, God, from a full heart, I'm writing the book on your wonders. I'm whistling, laughing, and jumping for joy; I'm singing your song, High God. Psalm 9:1, 2, Message.

That's me—laughing, jumping, and singing God's song. Today is my day. "Happy Birthday to me . . ." Sure, I share it with every other person born on this day. But I don't mind, because no matter how many babies have been born on my day, I am still special to my heavenly Father.

It doesn't matter that I don't look like a Barbie doll or that my hair is brown and straight and that freckles dance across my nose and my knees. It doesn't matter that I can't whistle— not a note. I like being special to my heavenly Daddy.

But today isn't only my day. It belongs to my mother. She did all the work. I didn't have anything to do with being born; I just was. Instead of wishing myself a happy birthday, I want to wish my mother a Happy Mother's Day.

How about it, kids? On your next birthday, whether it's today or eight months from now, write a little note thanking Mom for being your mother. She had a choice, and her choice was you. More important, you are God's choice. That's reason enough to sing, to dance, to whistle today.

God's Hand on Ben's Shoulder

Listen to your father and mother. What you learn from them will stand you in good stead; it will gain you many honors. Proverbs 1:8, 9, TLB .

In fifth grade Benji's classmates called him dummy. Raised in extreme poverty by a single mother of two, Benji had no hope of ever making anything of himself. But God had his hand on Benji's shoulder in the form of his praying mother. Benji's mother couldn't read, but she was determined that her sons would.

When it became evident that the street gangs were winning with her boys, this mother took the situation in her own hands, beginning with reading. She insisted that her sons read two books a week. Within 18 months Benji loved reading so much that he rose from the bottom to the top of his class. Through reading he could go anywhere and be anything he wanted to be.

Today Ben Carson is a neurosurgeon at Johns Hopkins University Hospital. He is known around the world for his surgical skills and for his faith in God.

As for Ben's mother? She learned to read, returned to school, and today is the second Dr. Carson in the family. God uses praying mothers to keep His hand on the shoulders of His precious sons and daughters.

Sing. Birdie. Sing!

He put a new song in my mouth, a hymn of praise to our God.
Psalm 40:3, NIV.

How can the study of little tweetie birds teach us any-thing? University of Chicago researchers have discov-ered that when zebra finches sleep, they dream of singing new and intricate song patterns.

Singing is serious business to birds. The neuron patterns in the bird brains make the same activity pattern when they're singing as when they are dreaming. The researchers hope to unhook the system so they can monitor the singing of a dreaming bird. The beautiful songs of birds could teach us about how we learn and how we dream.

How's your dreaming? Do you lie awake unable to sleep? Maybe you need a fresh supply of new songs. If your heart is filled with troubles all day and your face looks like a Kansas tornado, when you sleep your dreams will be frightening too, and God's song won't be able to break through your fears.

What new song is God trying to teach you today? (Or should I say, tonight?) Is He teaching you to praise Him through your troubles? Is He teaching you to praise away your fears? If you sing praises in the daytime, He will put a new song in your dreams (and mouth) at night.

Brothers and Sisters

If you are offering your gift at the altar and there remember that your brother has something against you, leave your gift there in front of the altar. First go and be reconciled to your brother; then come and offer your gift. Matthew 5:23, 24, NIV.

A Sabbath school teacher was discussing the Ten Commandments with her 5- and 6-year-olds. After explaining the commandment to "honor thy father and thy mother," she asked, "Is there a commandment that teaches us how to treat our brothers and sisters?"

Without pause, one little boy answered, "Thou shalt not kill." While God probably chuckled at the child's answer, the first murder was committed when one brother killed the other—Cain and Abel.

When I was a child, my sister and I fought like the proverbial cats and dogs. Connie was my bossy older sister, and I was her bratty kid sister.

Today we are best of friends. Other friends have come and gone since I did somersaults on the front lawn and she played with baby dolls. She's my link to my past, and I'm hers. We understand one another like no one else can, not our husbands, not our children—no one.

If you're blessed with a brother or a sister—or 10 of them—heal the grudges and hurts you share. Become friends—best friends—for life.

16 August

The Big Inning Team

Bless those who persecute you; bless and do not curse. Romans 12:14, NIV.

Communist leader Fidel Castro has restricted Christianity in his Caribbean island country of Cuba. This makes it difficult for most Christians to visit Cuba. But not for the Hampton Christian Warriors. Their passion is baseball. Mr. Castro loves baseball too.

Hampton Christian High School in Hampton, Virginia, recently formed a league—with high schools in Cuba. They call themselves the Big Inning Team. They travel to Cuba to play the baseball teams of 14 rural schools, one team in each of Cuba's 14 provinces.

While touring these small towns, they visit churches, share their love for Jesus with young people like themselves, and worship with fellow believers.

These teens and their coaches have found a creative way to bless and help strengthen the spiritual convictions of Cuban young people—through baseball.

For 40 years Cuban Christians have been persecuted, imprisoned, killed, and tortured. Those outside prison walls have found ways to worship God and to maintain their faith in secret. But this secret life can be lonely.

Those imprisoned by government, ideology, health problems, and adverse circumstances need our prayers to remain strong in the face of adversity.

Three Prayers

For the Lord is watching His children, listening to their prayers.
1 Peter 3:12, TLB.

Fifteen-year-old Peter knelt to pray. "Dear heavenly Father, bless my family . . ." Outside his bedroom window police sirens filled the less than silent night. He could hear the shouts of neighbors, the wail of Mrs. Burns's colicky infant in the apartment above his. And always he heard the relentless beat of heavy metal through the walls of his next door neighbor's apartment in ghetto U.S.A.

Eleven-year-old Pierre knelt to pray. "Dear heavenly Father," he whispered in French, his father's native tongue. "Please watch over my family through the night . . ."

The walls shook as government forces bombarded the rebel stronghold. Pierre prayed for his father, hiding in the hills behind the small Central African village.

Thirteen-year-old Pedro's stomach growled as he knelt to pray within the adobe walls of his parents' home in northern Mexico. "Dear heavenly Father, please be with my family tonight." The few spoonfuls of rice and beans he'd eaten that day couldn't stop his hunger pangs. His heart ached for his 5-year-old sister whimpering on the mat on the other side of the room.

Three Peters; three prayers; three different parts of the world. No wall, no enemy, no situation, can stop them from reaching God.

18 August

Macho Man

"Not by might nor by power, but by my Spirit," says the Lord. Zechariah 4:6, NIV.

George Washington—the father of our country. I imagine him to be a real macho man. You know the vigorous and hearty type, slogging through dense forests and swamps, leading his men to victory in two wars, one against the French and the other for America's independence.

In truth, physicians have combed the Revolutionary records for first-hand data on the father of our country. His diaries and letters reveal that my hero was afflicted with a host of diseases.

As a boy, he nearly died of diphtheria. As a public surveyor in southern Virginia, he contracted malaria and suffered with it, off and on, for the rest of his life. Add to the mix smallpox, typhoid fever, pleurisy and wooden false teeth! Poor George would have run for a third term as president except for persistent respiratory infections.

Doing remarkable things when you feel healthy and strong is noteworthy, but accomplishing great tasks when you feel lousy takes a truly great man or woman.

George Washington led the infant country, not by his might nor by his power, but by God's Spirit. All old George needed to be was willing.

Wise Guys

It is the Lord who gives wisdom; from Him come knowledge and understanding. Proverbs 2:6, TEV.

$E = mc^2$ is the mathematical formula for Einstein's theory of relativity, which made it possible for humans to land on the moon. Long before Einstein shared his mathematical theory with the world, another mathematician demonstrated it in a children's book, *Alice's Adventures in Wonderland.*

In 1862 Charles Lutwidge Dodgson, a philosopher of mathematics, loved to entertain children with magical stories. One day he took three sisters rowing on the Thames River in England. After the outing one of the girls, Alice Liddel, begged him to tell the girls a story with "lots of fun in it."

Using his knowledge of higher mathematics as a basis for the story in which all kinds of strange but mathematically logical things happened, Dodgson told the famous tale. Family members were impressed with the fanciful story and encouraged him to publish it.

Afraid that his reputation as a serious scientist would be damaged by such "nonsense writings," he chose to publish the tale under the name of Lewis Carroll. Dodgson lived to see the children's story go around the world.

Two mathematicians, living in two different areas of the world, and in two different centuries—it makes sense since God is the source of all wisdom, all knowledge, and all understanding.

20 August

Mary's Little Lamb

O Lord, I know that the way of man is not in himself: it is not in man that walketh to direct his steps. Jeremiah 10:23.

Sarah Josepha Buell Hale (1788-1879) edited the first national women's magazine for women, *Godey's Lady's Book.* Copies of this magazine rolled west in covered wagons, sailed on ships across oceans, and were hoarded by missionary wives and high society matrons alike.

In addition to her thousands-plus articles, critics applauded her 1853 book on women's suffrage called *Woman's Record: Or, Sketches of All Distinguished Women From the "The Beginning" Till 1850.* Her novel *Northwood* was billed as the most exciting of 1827. Yet we remember her for an 1830 poem she wrote about a true event that happened in Massachusetts. Mary's school is still standing.

> Mary had a little lamb,
> Its fleece was white as snow,
> And everywhere that Mary went
> The lamb was sure to go;
> He followed her to school one day,
> That was against the rule;
> It made the children laugh and play
> To see a lamb at school.

As Sarah, we can't know our futures. Whether God uses us in some great and mighty way, or through the lines of a children's poem doesn't matter. What matters is that we're willing to let Him direct our paths no matter where they lead.

Out of Your Mind

Set your minds on things above, not earthly things. Colossians 3:2, NIV.

Are you left-handed? right-handed? Are you color-blind? Do you have chromesthesia? Whichever you are, you probably got it from your folks, who got it from their folks, who got it from their folks, and so on.

So what is chromesthesia? Chromesthesia has to do with hearing, "colored hearing." To a person endowed with chromesthesia, the act of listening to music produces a brilliant display of colors in their minds.

Many of the great composers had "colored hearing." Rimsky-Korsakov described D major as a "golden key." He pictured the sound of F sharp major as parrot green. Beethoven spoke of B minor as the "black key." Conductor Franz Liszt would demand of his musicians "more black," "less pink," etc.

Even more unusual, these people would, on a single note, "see" the colors differently. Alexander Scriabin saw violet on the same tone that Serge Koussevitzky pictured strawberry red. The combination of these "color tones" would produce completely different music from one composer to the next.

Take the theory of chromesthesia "out of this world." Imagine the colors we'll "see" in heaven when the angel choirs break into song, praising God our Father. Don't you just love it?

Walking With Heroes

Point me down your highway, God; direct me along a well-lighted street; show my enemies whose side you're on. Psalm 27:11, Message.

Did you ever wonder how all our roads came into being? Some routes, such as the Alaska Highway, were laid out by civil engineers. Most country roads began as a dirt footpath cutting through heavy grasslands, tangled thickets, and lush forests.

Running alongside the Erie Canal, U.S. Route 20 is one of those roads: the best way to go from Massachusetts to New York's Finger Lakes and Niagara Falls, across the Mid-western plains and the Rocky Mountains to the Pacific Ocean—3,365 miles through 12 states and four time zones—the nation's longest continuous highway.

To walk or ride along this highway is to walk or ride with genuine heroes of years gone by. Iroquois warriors, French Jesuits, and fur traders used this route before America was a nation. Revolutionary troops marched over it. Pioneer wagons rolled over it.

When you let God direct you on the right pathway, you walk on God's highway with such heroes as Abraham, Esther, Moses, David, Peter, Dorcas, Martin Luther, David Livingston, Ellen White, and Mother Teresa.

Be Kind to Humankind

So overflowing is his kindness towards us that he took away all our sins through the blood of his Son, by whom we are saved. Ephesians 1:7, TLB.

This is Be Kind to Humankind Week.

Sacrifice Our Wants for Others' Needs Sunday is a day to give up something for someone else. It's easy to share a cookie when you have two, but much harder when you have only one.

Motorist Consideration Monday. Even if you don't drive a car, there is traffic in the halls of your school and traffic outside the bathroom as you get dressed in the morning. Be considerate to them.

Touch-a-Heart-Tuesday is the day to say "I love you" to Mom or write a love note to your grandparents or to your pastor at church.

Willing to Lend a Hand Wednesday. Mom's folding the laundry? Help her. Little brother or sister can't find a favorite toy? Stop what you're doing to help them.

Thoughtful Thursday. Ask God to open your eyes so you can see the possibilities for thoughtfulness around you.

Forgive Your Foe Friday. Forgive by the teaspoonful, you'll receive a teaspoon of forgiveness. Forgive by the bushel—you do the math.

Speak Kind Words Saturday. Kindness builds up; mean words tear down. Wow! Is it going to be a great week or what?

The Redcoats Are Coming!

The name of the Lord is a strong tower; the righteous run to it and are safe. Proverbs 18:10, NIV.

On this day in 1814 British troops surrounded Washington, D.C., for an invasion. President James Madison's aides tried to hurry Dolley, his wife, to safety. "Begging your pardon, ma'am, we have to leave now, before the Redcoats block our only escape from the city."

The first lady shook her head and stomped her foot. "I'm not leaving without President Washington's portrait!"

"Take the painting!" the officer in charge demanded of his men as he escorted Mrs. Madison from the president's house. President and Mrs. Madison, along with the other government officials, fled the city just ahead of the British, who proceeded to burn the Capitol, the president's house, and most of the other government buildings.

The American Army retook the city from the British two days later. (The painting Mrs. Madison saved is now on the dollar bill.)

When Satan, our enemy, attacks, we can always run to Jesus. God and His mighty army of angels can and will keep us safe.

Little-known facts About Our Leaders

Know the Lord: for all shall know me, from the least to the greatest. Hebrews 8:11.

Here are some facts you might not have known about our former leaders: George Washington turned down the opportunity to be crowned king of the United States. Andrew Jackson, the seventh president, killed a man while defending his wife's honor in a duel. James Buchanan, the fifteenth president, was proud of his tiny feet. Abraham Lincoln stored letters, bills, and notes inside his stovepipe hat. Ulysses S. Grant, our eighteenth president, had his name changed from Hiram Ulysses Grant because he didn't like his monogram, HUG.

Our twentieth president, James Garfield, liked to show off by writing Greek with one hand and Latin with the other—at the same time. William Taft weighed more than 300 pounds and had an oversized bathtub installed in the White House. Twenty-eighth president Woodrow Wilson grazed sheep on the White House lawn.

Gerald Ford turned down offers to play professional football with both the Green Bay Packers and the Detroit Lions. And Ronald Reagan, fortieth president, rescued 77 people from drowning as a young lifeguard in Illinois.

Interesting, but not important to know. However, as citizens of God's country, no fact is too small to discover about our heavenly Leader, Jesus Christ.

I'm Having a Wife?

Instruct the wise man and he will be wiser still; teach a righteous man and he will add to his learning. Proverbs 9:9, NIV.

At Sabbath school 5-year-old Johnny listened intently as the teacher told about the Creation week. "God made man in His image. And God removed one of Adam's ribs to make his wife, Eve," the teacher instructed.

On Monday Johnny developed a pain in his right side. When he told his mother, she rushed him to the doctor. The boy cried when the doctor poked the little boy's side.

"H'mmm," the doctor said. "Looks like appendicitis."

Through his tears Johnny shook his head. "No, it's not my appendicitis, doctor," he lisped. "I think I'm going to have a wife."

After the surgery Johnny's mother explained Eve and Adam's unusual circumstances. "When it's time for you to have a wife, God won't take a rib from your side."

Johnny rubbed the tender spot on his side where he'd had his appendix removed. "I'm glad, because this smarts too much."

The teacher was right, but Johnny misunderstood the facts. You and I are a lot like Johnny. We learn the truth a little at a time. The more we learn, the better we can understand God's plan for us.

Getting Your Facts Straight

So don't criticize each other any more. Romans 14:13, TLB.

A middle-aged man pulled into a mall parking lot just as a young guy parked his pickup truck in a handicapped space. Upset because the younger man would use a space meant for an individual with a disability, he jumped out of his car and ran to the younger guy as he was getting out of his truck. "Hey, who do you think you are parking in a handicapped space? Move that truck, or I'll report you to the authorities!"

The younger guy, wearing shorts and a T-shirt, looked stunned by the man's anger. "Sir, I have a disability. I have a fake leg."

The older man glanced down at the guy's leg. His leg looked fine, except for the Ace bandage wrapped around one knee. "How dare you claim such a thing!" the man shouted for all to hear. "You should be ashamed of yourself."

"But sir, I . . ."

Furious at the younger man's repeated claim, the middle-aged man grabbed the younger guy's leg and gasped when the leg came off in his hands. The younger man had lost his leg in an accident some years before. The joints were invisible under the stretch bands.

The astonished man threw a $20 bill at him and ran into the mall. Criticizing others is not the way God would have us treat one another—besides, we may be wrong!

28 August

A Choice Yarn

There are seven things that the Lord hates . . . a proud look, a lying tongue, hands that kill innocent people, a mind that thinks up wicked plans, feet that hurry off to do evil, a witness who tells one lie after another, and someone who stirs up trouble among friends. Proverbs 6:16-19, TEV.

Telling lies isn't so bad, is it? Here's one that came out of the Civil War:

The Battle of Gettysburg, in which 7,000 men were killed along with thousands of horses, mules, and other livestock, attracted hordes of scavenging vultures who return every winter to the battlefield, waiting around for another banquet. Yeah, right!

Vultures do live a long time by bird standards—30 years, but not 140. And the big birds do congregate at Gettysburg, Pennsylvania, every year, not because they remember the great feast, but because it is a peaceful area with plenty of roosting sites and food.

What's wrong with a little lie? The story doesn't hurt anyone, right? When King Solomon listed the seven things God hates, and two of them had to do with lies, he didn't say God hates lies only when they hurt someone. Think about it. The Bible text simply says that God hates "a lying tongue," and "a witness who tells one lie after another."

Set Free!

He [the Lord] has sent me . . . to proclaim freedom for the captives and release from darkness the prisoners. Isaiah 61:1, NIV.

On this day in 1839, 53 Africans who'd been kidnapped from their home in Sierra Leone and sold in Cuba as slaves revolted while being taken to another part of the island on the ship *Amistad*. They seized control of the ship and demanded that the crew return them to their home.

The crew secretly changed course in the night and landed at Long Island, New York, where the ship's cargo was seized as salvage. The *Amistad* was towed to New Haven, Connecticut, where the Africans were thrown into prison. Future president John Quincy Adams believed the Africans were being treated unfairly and took their case all the way to the Supreme Court. And on March 9, 1841, the men were set free and allowed to return to their families in Africa.

Great story with a happy ending. Today's text is an even better story. You and I were slaves, kidnapped by the evil one and thrown into prison. Jesus took our case and fought for us all the way to the cross, where He died so that all those who want to accept Him as their lawyer and Savior are forever free and will go, not to Sierra Leone, but to a much better home in His incredible kingdom.

Apples, Oranges, and Space

The eyes of the Lord are in every place, beholding the evil and the good. Proverbs 15:3.

If you could fly, how would your world look if the trees were different colors instead of a blur of greens? While you're zooming high in the sky, you spot your favorite apple trees. You swoop down and pick your fill.

There are people at NASA space center working on just such a project. Not so astronauts can more easily identify their favorite gala apple, but to find ways to solve earth-bound problems.

From Landsat satellites scientists can see the entire earth surface. To make these images from space better, they built a special spacecraft, Earth Observing-1 (EO-1), that tests an instrument called Hyperion, which is so sensitive it can see clearly the difference between one tree and another from outer space.

Besides sorting out trees, it can report land changing, farmland and rain forests shrinking, rivers flooding, wildfires burning, volcanoes erupting. All of this from outer space. Our technological eyes help us understand and take better care of our planet.

Remarkable until you recall what God sees from His outer space vantage point. He sees you and me, right down to our growing fingernails—and He loves us still.

Versions of the Bible

Thy word have I hid in my heart, that I might not sin against Thee. Psalm 119:11.

Printers of the Bible are very careful to get every word right. Yet in the earlier editions, such as the Vinegar Bible, there were several mistakes. The printer titled Luke 20 as the "parable of the vinegar" instead of the "parable of the vineyard."

The Camel Bible was published in 1823 with a typographical error: "Rebecca arose, and her camels . . ." (instead of "damsels" [Genesis 24:61]).

In a Bible printed in 1702, instead of "princes," David complained, "The printers have persecuted me without a cause" (Psalm 119:161). Another edition said, "Blessed are the pacemakers" (Matthew 5:9).

The Wife Hater Bible said in Revelation 12:11 that the overcomers "loved not their wives [instead of "lives"] unto death." The Wicked Bible was named because the printer accidentally omitted the word "not" from the commandment "Thou shalt not commit adultery" (Exodus 20:14).

You can be sure that today's versions of the Bible have been checked and rechecked by religious scholars. In addition, if we get confused, the Holy Spirit promises to lead us into all truth. All we have to do is put scriptures to memory, and He'll make sure we get the message straight and, in His time, understand what God would have us do.

Throwing Your Heart

Be careful how you think; your life is shaped by your thoughts.
Proverbs 4:23, TEV.

Keith loved the circus. He dreamed of becoming a flying trapeze artist. The problem was, he would panic whenever it came time to fly from one swinging bar to the other. Again and again he missed his cue or crashed to the net below. Finally a veteran trapeze artist gave him the secret to succeeding: "Throw your heart over the bar and your body will follow."

Businesspeople and rocket scientists have discovered this advice works for them, too. By falling in love with (or throwing your heart over) their job, they've found success.

The botanist Luther Burbank fell in love with plants. Thomas Edison fell in love with inventing. Henry Ford fell in love with automobiles. The Wright brothers fell in love with airplanes. Einstein fell in love with math. Mother Teresa fell in love with the dying. Work isn't boring when you love what you're doing.

Do you have a dream? Is it worthy of your heart? your time? your energy? Is it God's plan for your life? Ask Him, and He will direct you to do that which you are best suited to do. But even then, when you know God is leading you, you must "throw your heart over" the bar to make it happen.

Crazy Races

The sun lives in the heavens where God placed it and moves out across the skies . . . as joyous as an athlete looking forward to a race! Psalm 19:4, 5, TLB.

A race you won't see in next year's Olympics is the Klondike Outhouse Race. Crazy outhouses of all kinds on wheels race the 1.5-mile course through Dawson, Yukon Territory. The winners will be announced at "Diamond Tooth Gertie's Gambling Hall."

Not to be outdone, Nome, Alaska, conducts the Great Bathtub Race every Labor Day. Five-member teams race tubs, mounted on wheels, down Front Street. One of the team rides in a tub of water (with bubbles). The other four must wear large-brimmed hats and pants with suspenders, and carry a bar of soap, washcloth, towel, or bath mat for the entire race. The winning trophy is a statue of Miss Piggy and Kermit taking a bath.

These athletes anticipate their big contests with excitement. But their joy is nowhere near what true Olympians feel as they race for a gold medal. All the preparation, work, and struggle to reach the moment they represent their country before the entire world is suddenly worth it. Ah, what a moment!

A poetic verse, isn't it? Describing the sun as a joyous athlete before a race? Scripture says all creation praises the Creator. Are you praising your Creator as you begin your race today?

3 September

Too Little Too Late

Who will rise up for me against the evildoers? or who will stand up for me against the workers of iniquity? Psalm 94:16.

It isn't fair!" Silas struggled with feelings of shame and humiliation. "That isn't what happened. How can I prove he is lying?"

In the early days of the Civil War, Brigadier General Silas Casey discovered that lies become fact to many people. To cover his own bad judgment, Casey's commander, General George B. McClellan, reported that Silas and his men "ran from the field of battle at the Battle of Seven Pines."

Worse yet, McClellan hadn't even been there to see what had happened. He took the word of another and spread the slanderous gossip that ruined a man's reputation and life. By pointing at Casey and his men, McClellan avoided criticism and disgrace for his own bad judgment on May 31, 1862. Years later General McClellan said he regretted the faulty report he'd made.

But the damage was done. In libraries across America there are regimental histories that still perpetuate the story of Brigadier General Silas Casey's cowardice. During his life no one stood up for Silas Casey. But one day both generals will stand before a God who makes all wrongs right. The entire universe will know the truth.

Stinky Feet

Now that I . . . have washed your feet, you also should wash one another's feet. John 13:14, NIV.

Rhonda loved to tease her younger sister by touching her with her toes. Kelli would scream, "Mama, Rhonda's putting her stinky feet on me!" To this day, as a mother of two children, Kelli still hates to touch someone else's bare foot. She makes an exception when she takes Communion.

A doctor friend of mine had the same problem. In her first year of medical school, Donna was sent to the local shelter for the homeless, where she was expected to wash and treat people's sore feet. Unable to sleep, she turned on the light and gazed at the painting of Jesus' face at the foot of her bed. "Dear God, help me do my job tomorrow."

The first person who needed her help was an old man named Jake. Jake had long matted hair, missing teeth, and a grizzled beard. He had body odor.

Setting the basin of water on the floor beside him, Donna knelt down and removed his shoes and dirt-encrusted socks. She gasped when she saw his feet, covered with festering sores and caked-on dirt. Gulping, she glanced up at him and forced a smile. Instead of seeing the stranger's pockmarked, unwashed face, she saw the smiling face of Jesus. Her task was no longer difficult or distasteful to perform.

Scaredy-cat

You do not realize now what I am doing, but later you will understand. John 13:7, NIV.

I hate needles!" Kay sniffed. "I'd rather get polio than get a shot." Of course, Kay didn't know much about the dreaded disease called polio, or she never would have said such a thing.

A clinic in town had offered free vaccinations for all children on the fifth of September. And Mother was determined that Kay would be protected. At breakfast she told Kay, "I'm taking you to the clinic for your shot at 11:00, so don't leave the backyard."

All morning Kay watched the hands of the clock turn closer and closer to 11:00. At 10:30 Kay bolted from the backyard and ran into a field of tall grass behind her house. From her hiding place Kay could hear her mother calling, "Kay. Kay! Where are you?"

Mama must hate me to want me to get hurt by the needle, Kay reasoned. Although she knew she'd be punished for not coming when called, the 6-year-old stayed out of sight. Soon Mother stopped calling. Kay smiled to herself.

Her scheme didn't work, though. For when she went home, Kay not only got the vaccination but punishment too.

"I want to protect you, not to hurt you. Someday you'll understand," Mama said. And you know what? Mama was right. Today I do understand.

Two Worry-free Days

Do not fret—it leads only to evil. Psalm 37:8, NIV.

Are you a worrywart? Do you worry, like Chicken Little in the children's story, that the sky will fall? If you are, I have good news for you. You have two days each week when you don't need to worry.

The first is yesterday. Yesterday is gone. You can't undo it. You can't bring it back. You can't erase one single word from it. All you can do is learn from it.

The other day you needn't worry about is tomorrow. Tomorrow is unborn. It is beyond your control. The sun will rise, maybe behind clouds, but it will rise. Any problems that might come tomorrow, you can't do anything about today.

Today is the only day you have, and only one minute at a time, at that. If you have a math test you're worrying about, study. A piano recital? Practice. This is the day to put into practice the lessons you learned yesterday.

The tennis-playing sisters Venus and Serena Williams became champions not by fretting over a poor swing but by hitting a tennis ball over the net, one ball at a time. Olympic figure skater Tara Lipinsky learned to do a triple salchow one thrust of her skate at a time. Even the brainy Albert Einstein had to learn to add and subtract before he could solve the complicated equations of the universe.

7 September

The Ripple Effect

An anxious heart weighs a man down, but a kind word cheers him up. Proverbs 12:25, NIV.

Jason sat on the sofa, his head buried in his hands. He hadn't done anything, regardless of what Mrs. Gold might say. Attitude! Humph!

His dad hung up the phone. "Come on, Jason; let's take a walk."

"A walk?"

"Yeah, I think you and I need some fresh air."

Without a word they strode to the park and to the footbridge, where Dad tossed a nickel into the quiet pond.

Ever-widening ripples flowed out from the point where the coin disappeared beneath the water's surface. Dad leaned on his elbows. "Look at that. The nickel disappeared, but the ripples from it spread all the way to that bird's nest by the shore." He tossed a quarter and watched as the ripples spread in every direction. "You're a leader, Jason. Whether you like it or not, your attitude influences your entire classroom, just as the coins affect the pond."

"Dad, I don't have a choice. Mrs. Gold is . . ."

"No, you always have a choice, regardless of your situation," Dad said. "And you are responsible for the influence of your negative choices on others, just as the coin affected the ripples in the pond."

A Day to Rejoice!

This is the day which the Lord hath made; we will rejoice and be glad in it. Psalm 118:24.

What an incredible, absolutely fabulous day! In 1921 Margaret Gorman believed it to be terrific when she won the first Miss America title, in Atlantic City, New Jersey; as did Mark McGwire in 1998 when he broke Roger Maris's 1961 record for the most home runs in one season of baseball, at Busch Stadium in St. Louis.

Dr. Don did too. At least those are the words he sang when he leaped into the Bering Sea, seconds before his plane crashed. He continued singing those words past the 13-minute grace period a human has before freezing to death in frigid water. He sang those words throughout the entire 45 minutes before he was rescued by the Coast Guard. Was it a fabulous day for him and his six companions?

It surely was. When God made September 8, He knew Dr. Don's plane would crash. He knew that Mark would hit home run number 62 and that Margaret would win the Miss America title. He knows everything that will happen to you today, too, the good and the bad. You can celebrate, because this day is completely in God's care and keeping, and so are we.

A Study in Uniqueness

Know this: God is God. . . . He made us; we didn't make him. We're his people. Psalm 100:3, Message.

Use your magnifying glass to examine the flower I am giving you, then write down your observations." Miss Larson made her way down one aisle and up the next, placing a different kind of flower on each desk. A rose, a peony, a hollyhock, a pansy—no two blossoms were alike.

"Study the shade of the leaves, the symmetry of the flower petals, the shades of color, size, texture. Then record every detail about your plant."

After each student turned in a page of observations, the teacher sent them back to their desks to discover 10 more things that they'd missed about their flower. Fifteen minutes later she asked the class to enumerate the ways the blossoms were similar, then different.

"What was special about your blossom?" the teacher asked?

The seventh graders were eager to answer. "People are like flowers," Miss Larson added. "Each one is different, carefully crafted by the Creator, beautiful in his or her own way. Just as He did with people, God endowed each flower with traits and talents you would never have known if you hadn't taken the time to admire their uniqueness."

Honey. Ugh!

If you find honey, eat just enough—too much of it, and you will vomit. Proverbs 25:16, NIV.

Long before wars were fought with Agent Orange, a poisonous chemical used during the Vietnam War, peasants in rural Spain were using chemical warfare to defeat their enemies. They knew that bees who eat nectar from a common form of azalea produce a special kind of honey that contains impurities dangerous for humans to eat.

The people of the ancient world never tasted Twinkies or Little Debbies. They'd never eaten hot fudge sundaes or caramel apples. The only form of sweet known to them was honey.

When Pompey the Great marched against his foes in the mountains of Spain, his men were delighted to find great pots of honey left behind by the villagers. The Roman soldiers wolfed down the azalea-produced honey until the pots were empty. As a result, Pompey's 1,000 men were so sick they couldn't fight. When the soldiers felt the sickest, the villagers attacked and defeated the nauseated soldiers.

Fortunately for the villagers, the Romans hadn't read their Bibles and the words written by the wisest man who ever lived. If they had, the Roman army would have been much wiser.

Raining Cats and Dogs

He causes his sun to rise on the evil and the good, and sends rain on the righteous and the unrighteous. Matthew 5:45, NIV.

How many times have you prayed for it to be sunny on your school picnic day and to snow during Christmas vacation? I have many times. Living in California's Central Valley, I'm learning to make my prayers a little less selfish. For on the days I may want sunshine, the fruit growers may be praying for rain. And on the days I wish it would rain, the raisin growers are needing to dry their raisins in the hot California sunshine.

While I've heard people say that it's "raining cats and dogs," I've never heard that it's "raining fish, frogs, and eels." But that *has* happened in England. Storms can whip up small tornadoes that have hovered over a pond long enough to suck the water and the living creatures up into the funnel and drop them a few miles away. Tornadoes have lifted fish high enough into the clouds to freeze them, then drop them to earth as frozen fish.

I am glad that my God shows His love for the good people and the evil by showering them equally with rain and sunshine. (I'm not so sure about the fish, though.)

Ice Hotel

I will lie down and sleep in peace, for you alone, O Lord, make me dwell in safety. Psalm 4:8, NIV.

In January 2002 North America had its first "ice hotel." The people of Quebec built a 10,760-square-foot hotel out of 4,750 tons of snow and ice. Along with the ice-bed suites, there was a bar, movie theater, and art gallery. The complex was open only for three months before it melted away in the spring. The idea came from Sweden.

The cost was $100 a night. As of July 2000 more than 1,000 hearty people had placed their reservations for this chilly vacation. I imagine that no one asked if the rooms were air-conditioned! The idea of sleeping on ice doesn't sound too appealing to me. To each his own, I guess. Talk about slipping into bed . . .

If you want a night's sleep that is truly out of this world, try out the sleeping quarters near the Orinoco River on the moon. Such a resort is in the planning stages of a Texas-based company, Lone Star Space Access.

I like knowing that wherever I lay down my head at night, I can be at peace. For God is with me.

A Not-So-Silent Night

Those who sow in tears will reap with songs of joy. Psalm 126:5, NIV.

On the night of September 13, 1814, the sky over Fort Henry was ablaze with cannon fire. A battle raged between British and American troops. Aboard a ship that was delayed in the Baltimore harbor because of the battle, passenger Francis Scott Key could only stand and watch the British attack. Amid the smoke, fire, and booming cannons, he had no idea which side was winning. At dawn he anxiously searched the horizon to determine if his side had prevailed. There above the fort waved a limp and battle-weary American flag.

So thrilled by the sight, Mr. Key penned verses to the tune of a popular bar song: "O say! can you see, by the dawn's early light . . ." Poor Mr. Key had no idea the song would one day be his country's national anthem. That wouldn't happen for 117 more years.

I wonder how many tears Mr. Key shed during the night—how many times it had seemed the British would squash the fledgling American Army. Sometimes when things are going badly for me I sow real tears too. But I remember the promise from my heavenly Dad assuring me that when morning comes I'll sing a song of joy, and I am happy once more.

Chicken Hearts

Let's send out spies to discover the best route of entry, and to decide which cities we should capture first. Deuteronomy 1:22, TLB.

Recently Canada enlisted a troop of 600 to infiltrate the general population. They weren't given weapons or uniforms or any special training. The secret flock of *chickens* strutted along the Canadian-U.S. border to detect the presence of West Nile virus in Canada.

In 1999 the virus, which is believed to be spread by mosquitoes that have eaten the blood of infected birds, had been found in the northeastern United States.

You'll be relieved to know that none of the domesticated fowl tested positive for the disease. And only one human Canadian contracted the West Nile virus during that time. Since then the secret protectors have been discharged from their military duties, as the virus is no longer a threat.

A general in another army many years earlier dispatched 12 spies on a fact-finding mission. When they returned, only two, Caleb and Joshua, trusted the Lord to win the battle for them. The people listened to the 10 chicken hearts and never entered the Promised Land.

15 September

Snakes Alive

I am afraid that your minds will be corrupted . . . in the same way that Eve was deceived by the snake's clever lies. 2 Corinthians 11:3, TEV.

Snakes! Yikes! At the very mention of snakes, my sister Connie screams and runs for cover. Service representatives had temporarily removed our window air-conditioner to work on it. Leave it to Connie to come upon a small green lizard that had crawled inside to get out of the hot July sun.

A friend of mine was camping in the New Mexican desert one night when he discovered he wasn't alone in his sleeping bag. A rattler had found the down-filled bag warm and cozy against the desert's chilly night. Slowly, carefully, my friend exited the bag without getting bitten. He slept in his SUV the rest of the night.

More than 1 million people receive snakebites each year, and 30,000 to 40,000 of them die. Tied for having the most potent bites are the Australian inland tiapan and the Australian brown snake. One snake has enough venom to kill 100 people.

Since Eve's encounter, people have been fearful of snakes. Most snakes don't deserve the bad rap they've received. Yet as deadly as many of our snakes might be, Eve's serpent, the devil, is a thousand times more deadly, for he can kill not only your body but your soul.

Power of Words

Pleasant words are a honeycomb, sweet to the soul and healing to the bones. Proverbs 16:24, NIV.

What was the first poem you learned? "Jesus loves me! This I know"? Or "Now I lay me down to sleep"? Writing poetry can be difficult for some and easy for others. Yet we've all been poets if we've finished the rhyme "Roses are red, violets are blue . . ."

While you may have heard of America's earliest male poets, you might not know the name of our first female poet. Anne Bradstreet's book of poems, *The Tenth Muse,* was published in England on this day in 1650.

At 18 Anne came to America in 1630 along with her husband, Simon; her father, Thomas Dudley; and John Winthrop, the Commonwealth of Massachusetts' first governor.

Along with the daily chores of running a pioneer household (i.e., making candles, spinning yarn, weaving cloth, baking bread, washing clothes by hand), Anne wrote poetry. Without her knowledge, her brother-in-law published the poems. Many people were blessed by her words.

You might not be a poet like Anne Bradstreet, but your words at home and at school can heal or injure those around you.

Turn the Lightning On

For as lightning that comes from the east is visible even in the west, so will be the coming of the Son of Man. Matthew 24:27, NIV.

You may have heard someone say, "Lightning never strikes the same place twice." While that might be true, it does strike the same person more than once. According to the *Guinness Book of World Records,* park ranger Roy Sullivan was struck by lightning seven times between 1942 and 1977. The chances of that happening are one in 2.8 million.

In the United States about 100 people are killed each year by lightning. Seventy percent of all injuries and fatalities occur in the afternoon. U.S. waterways, such as the Mississippi, Ohio, and Hudson rivers, increase the risk, as do the Rocky Mountains. But the highest number of injuries and fatalities from lightning strikes is along the Gulf Coast.

Other places of danger include the Empire State Building in New York City, tall trees, and golf courses (where a golf club acts as a lightning rod). And then there's always standing under a tree in a thunderstorm or flying a kite.

While I don't plan to go out of my way to be struck by everyday lightning, I can hardly wait to see the lightning that will accompany Jesus' return. That's one light show I don't want to miss. How about you?

The Watcher

She watches over the affairs of her household. . . . Give her the reward she has earned, and let her works bring her praise at the city gate. Proverbs 31:27-31, NIV.

At a time when the word on the streets of America was "The only good Indian is a dead Indian," Harriet Maxwell Converse chose to see Native Americans as her brothers and sisters and to help fight for them in the U.S. courts. Harriet learned to care for the tribal people from her parents. Throughout her life she fought for those who couldn't fight the prejudices against them because of their birth.

On this day in 1891 the Six Nations Tribe at the Tonawanda Reservation, New York, made her a chief. They gave her the Seneca name Ga-is-wa-noh, meaning "The Watcher," because she watched out for their people. Harriet extended the borders of her household and watched over those who couldn't do it for themselves, and she was rewarded for her compassion and bravery.

It's easy to speak up for someone being picked on when the crowd is on your side, but to challenge unfairness when everyone else is wimping out isn't so easy. Harriet "Ga-is-wa-noh" Converse didn't do it to become a tribal chief. She did it because she cared about others.

19 September

Second Fiddle

This is the Great Reversal: many of the first ending up last, and the last first. Matthew 19:30, Message.

A music lover asked a famous conductor of a world-renowned orchestra which instrument he considered the most difficult to play. The conductor thought for a moment, then answered, "Second fiddle. I can get plenty of first violinists, but to find one who can play second fiddle with enthusiasm—that's difficult. And if an orchestra has no second fiddle, we have no harmony."

The conductor is right. Think about it—music created by a one-note orchestra. What makes the music so rich and alive are the integrated tones blending to produce beautiful harmonies. That can happen only when one instrument takes the lead and another follows that lead.

"Me first! Me first!" Whether playing baseball, being in the school band, or acting in a school play, everyone wants to be the star. No one likes to play "second fiddle" to someone else's brilliance—for harmony or otherwise. Some of the fiercest battles between Christians are over who's going to be "head elder" or who'll get the solo line in the church choir.

Jesus said, "The last shall be first, and the first last." Perhaps He was talking about more than fiddlers and orchestras. What do you think?

Working Together

All things work together for good to them that love God, to them
who are the called according to his purpose. Romans 8:28.

When I was a little girl my dad would take my mother, my sister, and me for a Sunday evening drive for ice cream cones. Anderson's Dairy Store on Route 40 made the best ice cream around. And now, many years and many ice cream cones later, Anderson's ice-cream cones are still number one—to me.

It was at the St. Louis World's Fair in 1904 that the first ice-cream cone was sold. A man from Syria named Hamwi had come from Damascus to sell *zalabia,* a Syrian-type waffle, at the fair. Next to Hamwi's concession booth was an ice-cream booth.

One day, when the operator of the ice-cream booth ran out of clean dishes in which to serve the ice cream, Hamwi rolled up one of his still-soft *zalabia* into a cornucopia and handed it to the ice-cream vendor, who filled it with ice cream. Voilà! The first ice-cream cone. A new treat was born.

A tragedy for the ice-cream vendor turned out to be a blessing. I don't know if Hanwi or the ice-cream vendor loved God, but in the case of ice-cream cones, I'm glad that all things did work out for good. Yum! Very good!

21 September

No More Forever

The Lord's servant must not quarrel; instead, he must be kind to everyone, . . . not resentful. 2 Timothy 2:24, NIV.

One of my heroes is Mut-Too-Yah-Lat-Lat, or Nez Percé chief Joseph. His famous words "I will fight no more forever" came after shepherding his weak and tired tribe to within 40 miles of the Canadian border, where they hoped to escape to freedom.

When the chief had to choose between leading his people into a war with the United States Army in which hundreds would die, or being resettled on a reservation where his people would lose their identity as Nez Percé, he chose to try to escape to Canada. Many died.

After three months and more than 1,000 miles of being hounded by the U.S. Army, Chief Joseph surrendered. The few survivors of the long trek were relocated to a reservation in Washington, while the chief was moved to an Oklahoman reservation. He kept his promise even when others tried to convince him to lead a revolt. Chief Joseph died on September 21, 1904, never again seeing his beloved ancestral land.

Chief Joseph's heart was too big to allow any more of his people to suffer and die. While his enemies managed to capture his body, they never succeeded in breaking his honor. Sometimes the kindest act means to surrender one's pride for the good of others.

A Wise Guy

The Lord protects the simple and the childlike; I was facing death and . . . He saved me. Psalm 116:6, TLB.

S o you're the boy who wants to join the Mafia." The 90-year-old nursing home resident's hand shook as he greeted Andy. "Your teacher's been telling me about you. I used to be a wise guy for Al Capone."

Andy's eyebrows shot up into his hairline. "Al Capone?"

"Yes, sir."

Andy knew about—and admired—the cruel and vicious outlaw of the 1920s. He told everybody that he wanted to be a Mafia wise guy someday.

The old man nodded. "I'm the only wise guy from his gang who is alive to tell about it."

"Wow! That's cool. He's my hero!" Andy scooted a folding chair next to Mr. Moreno's wheelchair and sat down. To think he hadn't wanted to visit the nursing home with his fifth-grade class!

"Pretty lousy hero!" Pain entered the old man's eyes. "I was five minutes late for Chicago's St. Valentine's Day massacre. I could have died in the shooting, but I didn't because I couldn't find a place to park near the warehouse."

"Really?" The boy had heard the story about the massacre at the old Chicago warehouse.

The man shook his head sadly. "I made many bad choices as a lad. Fortunately, God had better plans for my life."

(to be continued)

A Wiser Guy

Is not wisdom found among the aged? Does not long life bring understanding? Job 12:12, NIV.

How did you meet Capone?" Andy asked.

"My brother introduced me." Mr. Moreno pursed his lips. "During the 1920s it was against the law to sell liquor. I ran bootleg whisky from Kentucky to Chicago for Capone, then I met my future wife."

"Eww, a love story . . ." Andy groaned.

"Not quite. My wife was raised a Christian but rebelled and ran away to the city. That's where I met her. We were living what I thought was 'the good life,' until the massacre."

Andy's eyes glistened with excitement. "Go on . . ."

"On the morning of the massacre, I had to park a block away. As I climbed out of Capone's car specially designed to carry whiskey, I heard the machine guns and knew what was happening. So I left the car parked beside the street and hurried home to my wife. We packed a few things and hopped a train for Oregon."

"Why?"

"I knew that if I stayed with Capone, I'd probably be killed sooner or later."

"Wow!"

"In Oregon I got smart. I joined up with a different Boss, not a crime lord who stole from, killed, or maimed people, but One who died so I could live. Al Capone would never have given his life for me." The man nodded. "I've been a 'wise guy' for Christ ever since. And I've never been sorry!"

Breaking Records

What is man, that you think of him; mere man, that you care for him? Psalm 8:4, TEV.

So you think Olympic gold medal athletes are the best in the world at their sport? Think again. In 1963 Robert Hays set the record for the 100-yard sprint at 27 miles per hour. Big deal. A cheetah can sprint at more than 60 miles per hour. Even greyhounds and red foxes sprint at more than 40 miles per hour.

Zhu Jianhua of China high-jumped 7 feet 10 inches. An Australian red kangaroo jumped a 10-foot-high stack of lumber in 1965.

Russia's Alexander Gunyashev lifted 1,025 pounds in 1984; gorillas have been known to lift as much as 1,800 pounds. Humans can barely swim more than five miles per hour; sailfish average 68 miles per hour on a bad day. Even a waddling penguin moves through water at more than 10 miles per hour. Kind of puts human athletes in their places, huh?

So why is God mindful of humans if His other creatures can outrun, outlift, outjump, outswim the fittest of us? Because of our special gift—we are made in the likeness of our Creator. Monkeys look like monkeys; giraffes, giraffes; and zebras, zebras. But people were made in the image of God, our Creator.

25 September

Standing By

Everyone who exalts himself will be humbled, and he who humbles himself will be exalted. Luke 14:11, NIV.

A traffic accident on a busy corner immediately drew a crowd. When it was obvious that one of the drivers needed medical attention, a woman rushed out of the crowd and tried to help him, only to be pushed aside by a man who announced, "Step back, please. I know first aid."

The woman did as ordered, but stayed by to watch the man administer aid to the victim. After a few minutes she tapped the man on the shoulder. "Sir, when you get to the part where you tell someone to call a doctor," she said, "I'm already here."

Embarrassment! Jesus gave good advice to His disciples when He told them not to push ahead of others for a better seat at the banquet table. He said that it would be better to sit in a less important spot and be asked to move up than to sit in a prime seat and be asked to move to a less important position.

Thinking yourself more important can cause you much embarrassment. Television ads selling everything from cars to clothes to weekend vacations push the idea that "I deserve it!" Jesus said it won't be the proud and pushy who inherit the new earth, but the meek and the humble.

Apple Man

Keep me as the apple of your eye; hide me in the shadow of your wings. Psalm 17:8, NIV.

"An apple a day keeps the doctor away." I love apples, apples of every kind—McIntosh when reading on a cold, wintry night; Fujis for chomping on anytime; Granny Smiths for apple pie; crabapples in jelly . . .

John Chapman, also known as Johnny Appleseed, was born in Leominster, Massachusetts, on September 26, 1774—two years before Americans declared themselves to be independent of English rule. He became famous, but not for his ability to fight or make money or write books. At a time when men were rough and tough, carrying guns and knives, John was a kind and gentle man. History calls him "a friend to man and to animals." To the American Indians, he was a medicine man.

Johnny carried a bag of apple seeds wherever he went. He became famous for planting apple orchards across the continent, hence his name. There wasn't an apple John didn't like. Apples were his thing. You could say apples were the "apple of Johnny's eye."

With God, you and I are the "apples of His eye." Like Johnny and his apple seeds, God plants us where we will grow best. Unlike Johnny Appleseed, God doesn't plant us, then abandon us. He stays with us, watching over us and protecting us as we grow.

27 September

Change of Orders

Don't harm my chosen people . . . touch them not. 1 Chronicles 16:22, TLB.

Ask anyone. Everyone knew Juan was a troublemaker. It was no surprise when he dropped out of school and joined a street gang. School friends expected to hear he'd either been killed or arrested.

When a preacher, a former boxer, came to the "hood" to hold meetings, one of the gang's main lieutenants became a Christian. Worse yet, the guy was going to become a preacher himself!

"Kill him!" the gang leader snarled at Juan, his steely gaze adding the "or else" to his order.

I can do that, Juan thought, pride tweaking the corners of his mouth. He'd already knifed two members of warring gangs.

Slipping into the back row of the meeting hall, Juan sought to be inconspicuous. After everyone exited the building, he would stab the preacher and leave without anyone being the wiser.

Juan counted dots on the ceiling tiles to escape words such as *love, forgiveness,* and *grace.* Finally the last prayer was prayed. As he eased his knife from his pocket, the words of today's text rang out, loud enough for everyone to hear, or so Juan thought.

(to be continued)

A New Voice

Speak, Lord, your servant is listening. 1 Samuel 3:9, TEV.

Huh? What?" Juan whipped around to discover who had spoken to him. He glared at the wizened old church deacon standing by the back wall. The old man looked surprised, but returned a smile.

As the people streamed past his row to shake hands with the young preacher and to exit the building, Juan heard the order again, this time from a woman. But when he looked, no woman was near enough to have spoken.

The boy's hand shook. What was going on? Who was messing with his mind? Steeling his nerve, Juan stepped into the aisle behind the last worshiper only to hear the preacher's voice boom over the public address system, "Do not harm My chosen people!"

The rattled assassin snapped his head around toward the microphone on the podium. No one was there; not a soul!

"Is something wrong?" A hand reached out and touched Juan's shoulder. The boy leaped away. The knife slipped from his grasp and clattered onto the tiled floor.

The boxer-preacher bent down and picked up the knife. "Is this yours?"

Juan's eyes bugged from their sockets as he stared at the glinting knife in the man's hands. *He's going to kill me,* Juan thought, *with my own knife!*

(to be continued)

29 September

A New Direction

See if there be any wicked way in me, and lead me in the way everlasting. Psalm 139:24.

Wake up! Wake up!"

Juan opened his eyes to find himself no longer in the church auditorium, but on a sofa in a small cluttered office. He'd passed out from fear.

A halo of light from a desk lamp supplied the only light in the room. The boxer sat beside him holding a glass of water in his hand. "You must be thirsty, son. Here, drink this."

Juan eyed the preacher skeptically, remembering the voice. "How'd you do it? How did you throw your voice?"

"Throw my voice?" The boxer looked questioningly at him.

"In the church," Juan explained. "You knew I was going to kill you!"

"I didn't, but my Boss did."

"Your boss?"

"Yes, let me tell you about Him. He's one tough Dude."

Juan listened throughout the night to tales about the prophet Samuel, the prophet Balaam, and the apostle Paul. "God wanted to get your attention, Juan. He has a job for you. Think you're tough enough to do it?"

Jesus became Juan's new "Boss" that night. He become a preacher, along with three of his gang's five remaining lieutenants. The gang leader who ordered the "hit" died before he could carry out his threat to kill God's newest servants.

Behave!

I will behave myself wisely in a perfect way. Psalm 101:2.

There are two kinds of rules: (1) God's rules—not lying, not taking God's name in vain, honoring my parents; and (2) human rules—not speeding on the highway, not leaving my dirty socks in the middle of the floor, not yelling in the car, not talking with my mouth full of food.

Here's a 130-year-old list of rules that Wells Fargo enforced on stagecoach passengers. "Forgo smoking, as smoking and odor are repugnant, especially to the ladies. Gentlemen must refrain from using strong language. Don't snore loudly, or friction with fellow passengers may result. Firearms may be kept, but don't fire them for pleasure—the sound frightens the horses. Gents guilty of unchivalrous behavior toward lady passengers will be put off the stage. It's a long walk back."

It's fun to see how rules change over time and new rules come into being, such as how close to stand behind a person at the ATM machine and the "no tolerance" policy at schools. The wise child of God obeys both kinds. While traffic laws may change, God's laws remain the same because He is always the same—yesterday, today, and forever.

1 October

The Real Thing

It is the one who sins who will die. Ezekiel 18:20, TEV.

rmy paratroopers were aloft for their very first jump. One after another, the men leaped from the plane shouting "Geronimo!" and sailing into thin air until the last man prepared to make his jump.

"Hey, wait a minute!" his commanding officer shouted above the roar of the plane engine and the wind outside the open hatch. "You're not wearing a parachute!"

"Oh, that's OK. I don't need one." The soldier laughed. "We're just practicing, aren't we?"

Practicing or not, that young recruit would have had a hard landing had he jumped. I've heard kids say, "You can't get pregnant the first time you have sex," or "None of my friends would be infected with AIDS." I've heard kids tell their friends, "The drug ecstasy won't kill you!" or "You won't become an alcoholic with one drink."

Don't believe them. With drugs of any kind, and sex outside of marriage, there is no "just practicing." God's rules are like the soldier's parachute, a protection against unnecessary death.

The good news is: while we might still choose to sin and we might suffer the results of the sin we commit, God can and will forgive our sins.

Got the Answers?

When the Holy Spirit, who is truth, comes, he shall guide you into all truth. John 16:13, TLB.

How awake are you today? Can you figure out the answers to these puzzles? (Example: 7 D in a W would be 7 Days in a Week.)

1. 26 L of the A _____
2. 88 P K _____
3. 24 H in a D _____
4. 29 D in F in a L Y _____
5. 12 D of J _____
6. 4 Q in a G _____
7. 3 B M—S H T R _____
8. 40 D of R D F _____
9. 90 D in a R A _____
10. 11 P on a F T _____

Puzzles are fun when we do them just for play, but no one wants to play games with their lives. That's why God the Father sent the Holy Spirit to us, to give us the right answers to life's puzzles and to lead us into all the truth we need for salvation. And that's why you and I spend time getting to know Him well enough to hear His voice.

Answers: 1. 26 letters of the alphabet. **2.** 88 piano keys. **3.** 24 hours in a day. **4.** 29 days in February in a leap year. **5.** 12 disciples of Jesus. **6.** 4 quarts in a gallon. **7.** 3 blind mice—see how they run. **8.** 40 days of rain during Flood. **9.** 90 degrees in a right angle. **10.** 11 players on a football team.

3 October

Tumbling Walls

By faith the walls of Jericho fell. Hebrews 11:30, NIV.

Imagine living in a city that had a concrete wall going right down the middle. That's how people in Berlin, Germany, lived for 28 years. One morning Berliners were one city, and the next a wall was being built and soldiers with machine guns stood on guard to make certain no one tried to leave their side of the barrier.

If you were visiting your grandmother in the west part of the city and you lived in the east, you might not be able to go home again. You could live your whole life never meeting your uncles, aunts, and cousins who lived three miles away, on the other side of the hated wall.

On November 9, 1989, the wall came down, and the divided city was reunited. Some people thought the wall would stand forever; but God had other plans.

The Bible tells about another wall that crashed to the ground—Jericho. The soldiers on the walls laughed as the Israelites marched around the well-fortified city. But God was in control. No wall is too high, too thick. or too well-protected that God can't reduce it to rubble.

Got any walls in your life keeping you from reaching your goals? Tell God about them. He'll make history repeat itself.

Seeing Is Believing

We live by faith, not by sight. 2 Corinthians 5:7, NIV.

"Show me. I won't believe it until I see it."

"How do you know? How can you be sure?"

Mitch doubted everything. If he couldn't see it, for him it didn't exist. The first time he said he doubted God, I was stunned. I'd never met anyone who doubted there was a God. From when I was a small child, I knew there was a God. I talked with Him every day.

But my friend Mitch? No way. That is until he tried to replace a burned-out lightbulb—with wet hands. The resulting shock rattled him to his toenails. He couldn't let go until a friend unplugged the lamp from the wall unit.

Mitch had a new respect for electricity—something he couldn't see, but he definitely felt. From there, it wasn't much of a step to believe in the existence in the Creator who created electricity.

As for me, I have faith in God because I can see examples of His mighty power all around me, and I talk with Him every day. How about you? Will it take shock therapy for you to believe God exists? Or do you know Him so well that you have no doubts?

Smiley Face Day

A happy face means a glad heart; a sad face means a breaking heart. Proverbs 15:13, TLB.

When I was a kid, I used to play a game called bouncing smiles. I still play it. The object of the game is to bounce a smile to someone's face who is not smiling. You gain points when they smile back at you. You can play it in the mall, waiting in line at the grocery store or at the post office—anywhere you find people who look grouchy or sad. (You get extra points if you're in an airport where flights are being canceled.)

Today is officially Smiley Face Day, a day dedicated to good works and good cheer throughout the world. "Help Someone Smile" is the official theme of the day. Smiles are very simple to draw. Draw one on the top of your homework assignments, leave a few around for your folks to find, put them on all the thank-you notes you plan to write today.

The yellow smiley face, the international symbol of happiness and goodwill, was created by Harvey Ball of Worcester, Massachusetts, in 1963. So all of you Worcesterites, all of you Balls (my mother's maiden name was Ball), and all of you whom God has blessed beyond imagination, smile! And take the time to help someone else smile today as well.

Map Out Your Tongue

I'm determined to watch . . . [my] tongue so [it] won't land me in trouble. Psalm 39:1, Message.

Did you know that your tongue is as uniquely yours, just as your fingerprints and your DNA? It's true. Go ahead, stick out your tongue. Examine it in the mirror. Small organs, called taste buds, are located just beneath the surface of your tongue and at three places in your throat. They produce a mild chemical reaction that lets you know the difference between a lemon, an unripe persimmon, a chocolate bar, and a turnip—sweet, salty, sour, and bitter.

Test it for yourself. Make a map of your tongue and locate where each of the different taste buds are in your mouth. Remember you can get into serious trouble putting the wrong things into your mouth, but the Bible says you will get into greater trouble with what comes out of the mouth—words.

So watch that tongue of yours—don't let it get you into trouble by speaking at the wrong time, telling lies, or uttering unkind words. Watching your tongue can help keep you out of serious trouble!

A Night in Death Valley

Even when the way goes through Death Valley, I'm not afraid when you walk by my side. Psalm 23:4, Message.

The tiny yellow Volkswagen Beetle engine chugged, sputtered, and died. Ellen groaned and allowed the automobile to roll to the side of the road. A dramatic display of color filled the sky as the sun sank beneath the western horizon. *Should I try walking to the next town?* she wondered. "It can't be more than five miles ahead," she mumbled as she studied the state map. "No, my best bet is to stay with the car until someone comes along to help."

She'd considered stopping for the night in the last town. Now she wished she had as she found herself alone with a dead engine on an empty highway in California's Death Valley.

Ellen eyed the empty terrain outside the automobile—not a house, not a barn, not even a horse or sheep. She tried her cellular phone, but was out of range. Grabbing her jacket from the back seat, the young college student wadded it into a pillow and attempted to make herself comfortable until somebody came along. The words of Psalm 23 popped into her mind. She chuckled. "I'll bet there aren't too many, Lord, who really are walking with You through the actual valley of death."

(to be continued)

To the Rescue

When they call to me, I will answer them; when they are in trouble, I will be with them. Psalm 91:15, TEV.

Ellen slept fitfully until the headlights from an all-terrain vehicle filled the interior of her car with blinding light. Within seconds a heavily bearded face peered through the windshield at her. "What seems to be the trouble?" the stranger asked.

"My engine died."

"I can't hear you. Open the door."

She reached for the car door handle, then chose to roll her window down a few inches instead.

"If you'll get out of the car, I'll see what I can do."

Something inside Ellen told her to stay put. "I'd rather not. But if you could drive to the next gas station and have them send a tow truck, I would appreciate it."

The man frowned. Suddenly he aimed a revolver at her.

"Oh, dear God, help me," she whispered and closed her eyes.

One instant she saw the deadly weapon, and the next it was gone. She peered out the side window at two men wrestling on the ground. A gunshot echoed in the night, then a second man's eyes peered through the window. "Are you all right, ma'am?"

"Yes, thanks to you. What about the other man? Is he all right?"

(to be continued)

9 October

Armed Guard

For he will command his angels concerning you to guard you in all your ways. Psalm 91:11, NIV.

Don't worry about him. He won't bother you any longer," the second stranger assured her. Pointing to the cellular phone on the dashboard in front of her, he said, "Better call 911. This man needs medical attention."

"I tried, but I'm out of calling range."

He tipped his head to one side. "Try again."

She did as he said. Her call went through immediately. By the time she clicked off her cellular phone and glanced around to see what her rescuer was doing, he and his Harley-Davidson motorcycle were gone. Her mouth dropped open in surprise. She hadn't heard him leave. All she heard was a distant police siren.

Ellen was relieved when the police and the ambulance arrived. She told the two police officers what had happened. Her attacker would be all right. A bullet had grazed the side of his head. And he had passed out from fear.

As the paramedics loaded the wounded man into the ambulance, the officers looked around for dirt tracks of her rescuer or his bike. The sandy soil was completely undisturbed. One policeman suggested that there was no second man—that the wounded man accidentally shot himself with his own weapon. Tracks in the sand or not, Ellen knew better.

Of few Words

A wholesome tongue is a tree of life. Proverbs 15:4.

Airplane pioneers Orville and Wilbur Wright were famous for being untalkative. They especially hated making speeches. At a luncheon in the their honor, the toastmaster asked Wilbur to say a few words.

"There must be some mistake," the elder Wright stammered. "Orville is the one who does all the talking."

Then the toastmaster turned to Orville. Reluctantly Orville stood and announced, "Wilbur just made the speech," then sat down.

Words contain power to create and to destroy. I like to watch the television program *Who Wants to Be a Millionaire.* I am always struck with the power of words when Regis Philbin, the host, asks, "Is that your final answer?"

Presidents and prelates have argued over the meaning of "is." In the 2000 presidential elections every word the Supreme Court passed down was important. Every word you speak is important as well. Think about the words you speak:

Careless words	Gracious words
Cruel words	Joyous words
Bitter words	Timely words
Brutal words	Loving words

Whether you're a chatterbox like me or a nontalker like the Wright brothers, you have the words, and it's your choice how to choose to use them.

11 October

True Lies

Keep me from lying. Proverbs 30:8, TEV.

There's no such thing as true lies, right? Why say, "It's the honest truth?" All truth is honest, right?

Mason Locke Weems, alias Parson Weems, worked hard to make his lies true. By telling his tales again and again as he traveled around the early 13 states, his fables became "truth."

One of his most famous stories was about George Washington chopping down his father's cherry tree. And when asked if he did it, George admitted his mistake, for he couldn't tell a lie, but Mason could and did. When he got around to writing them down, his stories became extremely popular and were best-sellers from many years.

The famous storyteller Mark Twain (Samuel Clemens) once said of Locke's story about Washington, "Maybe George couldn't lie, but I can and I choose not to."

I like that. I too can lie, but I choose not to. Lying is a vicious habit that gets so strong one forgets which is truth and which is a lie. I wonder if that happened to old Mason Locke Weems.

The good news is, with God's help a liar can break the habit. Where once his or her words are dark with deception, God can make them as transparent as sunlight.

Winning by Losing

I will not deny my integrity. I will maintain my righteousness and never let go of it. Job 27:5, 6, NIV.

Integrity—what does it mean to you? Honesty on the playing field? in the classroom? at home? with friends?

Probably no man had a longer and more distinguished career in sports than Coach Amos Alonzo Stagg. For 42 years he was admired by students and graduates of the University of Chicago for his coaching skills and for being a man of integrity.

On one occasion Mr. Stagg's championship baseball team was defending its college title. The batter singled. When one of Stagg's men raced home with the winning run, the coach shouted, "Get back on third base. You cut it by a yard."

Frustrated, the runner protested. "The umpire didn't see me!"

"That doesn't make any difference!" Stagg roared. "Get back!"

Stagg's team lost the game, but for the young runner a battle of character was won. The player went on to become a giant in industry who became known as a man of integrity as well.

Talk About Embarrassing

Who can discern his errors? Forgive my hidden faults. Psalm 19:12, NIV.

People make mistakes. Take the one made by a flight attendant on a 747 bound for Europe. Before takeoff the pilot announced to the passengers in first class that the famous Charles A. Lindbergh was on board.

Lindbergh stood and nodded to his fellow passengers. When he sat down, he had trouble fastening his seat belt. A flight attendant graciously offered to help him with it, saying, "Is this your first crossing, Mr. Lindbergh?"

Imagine her embarrassment when she learned that Charles Lindbergh was the first man in history to fly solo from America to Europe.

On the death of President McKinley, Theodore Roosevelt succeeded him to the high office. A newspaper printer misspelled the word "oath." The resulting newspaper article read, "Surrounded by his Cabinet, Mr. Roosevelt took his simple bath as president of the United States."

Sometimes our mistakes are made in private, and no one knows but us and God. Sometimes we goof, and the whole world seems to know. Either way, God is gracious to forgive our errors and our sins. He wipes them away as if they'd never happened. Aren't you glad? I am.

Speaking of Errors

If a ruler's anger rises against you, do not leave your post; calmness can lay great errors to rest. Ecclesiastes 10:4, NIV.

Do you sometimes feel like a failure, always striking out? I do sometimes. Whenever I get down on myself, I remember that the best hitters in professional baseball have batting averages between .300 and .400. That means out of every 10 times up to bat, they hit safely three or four times.

Look at it another way. These great batters such as Sammy Sosa and Mark McGwire fail to hit more often than they hit. Time after time they step up to the plate and hit a grounder to an infielder or a fly ball to an outfielder or completely strike out.

Success isn't figured by averages. No one but you will remember the times you strike out in the early innings—if you hit a home run with the bases loaded in the bottom of the ninth.

When God and His angels take us on that extraterrestrial journey to His heavenly kingdom, your strikeouts, foul outs, and mess-ups will be forever forgotten. If you trust Him with your heart and life when you step up to bat or just sit on the bench, you're a part of God's winning team.

Don't Take Chances

Therefore, . . . be all the more eager to make your calling and election sure. For if you do, . . . you will receive a rich welcome into the eternal kingdom. 2 Peter 1:10, 11, NIV.

What are the chances that in 1906 six babies would be born aboard the German ship *Grosser Kurfurst:* one in first class, twins in second class, and triplets in third class? What are the chances that Robert Todd Lincoln would be present at Ford's Theater when his father, Abraham Lincoln, was assassinated, that he would be at the railroad station when President James Garfield was killed, and a few feet from President William McKinley at the Pan-American Exposition in Buffalo, New York, when McKinley was shot?

What are the chances? Believe it or not, the coincidences are true.

Some people think living forever in a perfect world is unbelievable too. But believe it or not, heaven is a reality for those who choose to follow Jesus. No one will be in heaven by accident. That's why Peter, a friend of Jesus, wrote, "Make your calling . . . sure." Don't take chances on where you'll spend your eternity. Ask God and He will teach you the way of salvation. He wants you there even more than you might want to be there, if you can imagine such a thing.

Ask Yourself

Many a man claims to have unfailing love, but a faithful man who can find? Proverbs 20:6, NIV.

If you found a wallet with $1,000 in it, would you give it to the owner if you were sure no one would ever know you found it?

2. If the bus driver failed to collect your fare, would you remind them?

3. If there were no locks on any house, store, or bank, would you take anything if you knew no one would find out?

4. If you had to live with someone like you for the rest of your life, would you be happy?

5. Your friends are waiting outside, and Fido begs for water—will you take the time to fill his bowl?

Simple questions with yes and no answers. How did you do? What you and I do in private, when no one's looking, reveals the real you, the real me.

Many people say, "It's OK if you don't get caught." Not so. Honesty, integrity, kindness, cheerfulness, and faithfulness are the traits of character God sees and rewards.

17 October

Friendly Encounter

He who is kind to the poor lends to the Lord, and he will reward him for what he has done. Proverbs 19:17, NIV.

When most people hear the name Jesse James, they think, *Outlaw! Thief! Bandit!* But like most people, the infamous raider of the 1800s was more complex than that.

The story is told about H. C. Wantland, a Methodist minister traveling through his area of ministry (called a parish) in Missouri. The sun was setting on the horizon when Jesse James rode up beside his buggy.

"Hello there, Jesse," the minister called.

"What are you doing out here?" the bandit asked.

"Collecting money for the poor," the minister admitted.

"Got much on you?"

"About $600."

Jesse started in surprise. "Six hundred dollars is a lot of money, Preacher!"

"Yes, it is, Jesse."

The bandit frowned. "Don't you know better than to carry that much cash on you? Someone is liable to rob you."

"That's true," the minister admitted.

"You're lucky I came along when I did. I'll see you get home safely, Preacher."

Even such a thief as Jesse James wasn't all bad all the time. Only God can judge a person's heart for good or evil.

Person's Day

There is neither Jew nor Greek, slave nor free, male nor female, for you are all one in Christ Jesus. Galatians 3:28, NIV.

Who's smarter—boys or girls? Obviously, girls! Before you guys blow a fuse, remember, I am female! So of course I would say females are smarter. And I know that if you're male, you believe males are smarter. That's OK. The truth is, there are an equal number of brilliant males and females.

That's why when I discovered that Canada is celebrating Person's Day today, I had to write about it. Person's Day celebrates the anniversary of the 1929 ruling that declared women to be "persons" in Canada. (It took the lawmakers that long to figure that out?)

Prior to the ruling, English common law declared that women were persons in matters of pains and penalties, but not persons in matters of rights and privileges. In 1929 five Alberta women led by Emily Murphy took the law to court to have it overturned. The government was so pleased with Mrs. Murphy's actions that it took them 50 years to congratulate her for her outstanding service.

Two thousand years ago the apostle Paul settled the question. When it comes to our standing with Jesus, there is no male or female. We are equal in Him.

19 October

The Orphan Train

I will not leave you as orphans; I will come to you. John 14:18, NIV.

Johnny hid behind a wooden crate in a cluttered alleyway of New York City. He hated stealing sausages from the corner grocer, but he had to feed his little sister. No one else would.

Like a flash, he darted past an ice wagon and across the busy street. Up the garbage-strewn stairs to the third floor he bounded, then burst into the room he and Sarah called home. He screeched to a stop at seeing two strangers standing in the middle of the room. One, a woman, was holding Sarah in her arms.

"Johnny, don't be afraid." The man grabbed the boy by the collar. "Mrs. Simms and I are here to help you now that your mother died. Do you know where your father is? Do you have any family at all?"

Johnny shook his head.

"You need someone to take care of you," Mr. Simms spoke with authority.

"I take good care of Sarah, don't I?" Johnny eyed his little sister who cowered at the fierceness in her brother's voice.

"I know you try, Johnny, but you need help." The woman smiled. "Would you like to take a train ride out West where a family will adopt you and your sister? You'd have a real family again."

(to be continued)

302

Alone, but Never Forgotten

Because of your great compassion you did not abandon them in the desert. Nehemiah 9:19, NIV.

Johnny and Sarah are real children who became part of the more than 150,000 homeless children and poor families transported west between 1854 and 1929 on the orphan train. The children's aid societies of Boston, New York City, and Chicago arranged with Midwestern families to take the children under contract agreement to pay the children's fare.

Some children were adopted into loving families; others, including many unwanted babies, became indentured servants, working for years for the host family to pay off the cost of their train ticket and care.

Johnny and Sarah were two of the lucky ones, adopted by a loving farm family in Kansas.

Every year the survivors and descendants of survivors attend an orphan train reunion in Fayetteville, Arkansas. Similar reunions are held in the other states where children were shipped.

While accurate records of these children's placements on this earth were not kept, God never lost track of these children. No child or adult ever born is so unimportant that God doesn't record every detail of their life. And someday soon they'll attend a grand reunion that will be out of this world!

Keeping a Promise

I will come again. John 14:3.

On March 12, 1942, the war in the Pacific wasn't going well for the Allied troops. American general Douglas MacArthur received orders to abandon the Philippines to the invading Japanese Army. Before leaving the islands, General MacArthur promised the people, "I shall return." His words resounded over the shortwave radio and into the terrified hearts of those he had to leave behind.

On October 20, 1944, after U.S. planes bombed the Japanese stronghold in the north, four divisions of American soldiers landed on Leyte, a small island in the north. After a few hours of battle General MacArthur stepped on Philippine soil, thus fulfilling his promise to return to free the citizens of the Philippine Islands from the Japanese Army. That was World War II.

A much greater war has been raging since before the Garden of Eden, a war that was won on the hill of Mount Calvary.

Two thousand years ago, when Jesus returned to heaven, He promised His followers, "I will return." One day I know He will return to keep His promise too. When He does, He will not only liberate the people of the Philippine Islands. The King of the universe will free all those on Planet Earth who love Him, regardless of their nationality, color, or heritage. Aren't you glad He keeps His word?

Duking It Out

Why do you look for the living among the dead? He is not here; he has risen! Luke 24:5,6, NIV.

The English Duke of Wellington fought Napoleon Bonaparte at the Battle of Waterloo, one of the most significant battles in history.

The news of the outcome of the battle came by sailing ship to the south coast of England and was carried overland by semaphore flags to the top of Winchester Cathedral and on into London. The citizens of London waited as the semaphore spelled out the words, "W-E-L-L-I-N-G-T-O-N D-E-F-E-A-T-E-D."

Suddenly a dense fog blocked the view. The uncompleted message was forwarded to London. The people of London sank into despair. They rushed to their homes, preparing for the certain enemy invasion of their country.

After a few hours the fog lifted, and the rest of the message was waved through. "W-E-L-L-I-N-G-T-O-N D-E-F-E-A-T-E-D T-H-E E-N-E-M-Y." Imagine how relieved the citizens of London were to learn the truth about the battle.

Two thousand years ago, as Jesus' dead body was placed in the borrowed tomb, His friends and family read the message "J-E-S-U-S D-E-F-E-A-T-E-D." Then the fog of discouragement fell over His disciples. On Sunday morning the fog lifted, revealing the rest of the story. "J-E-S-U-S D-E-F-E-A-T-E-D D-E-A-T-H!"

23 October

The Eyes Have It

Whether he is a sinner or not, I don't know. One thing I do know. I was blind but now I see! John 9:25, NIV.

No matter how great your eyesight might be, you have a blind spot. This is the point where the nerve endings inside the back of your eyeball connect with the optic nerve that conveys light images to your brain. There is one point where there are no light-sensitive nerve endings—that's your blind spot.

Try it for yourself. Note the cross and the dot on the bottom of this page. Close your left eye and hold this page before your right eye. Fix your gaze on the cross and move the book toward you and away from you. When you find the distance at which the dot disappears, you will have found your blind spot.

For God's kids, the cross of Jesus blocks out different colors, nationalities, ages, sizes, or abilities in people and helps us see everyone as God sees them.

✚ ●

One World

And in the days of these kings shall the God of heaven set up a kingdom, which shall never be destroyed. Daniel 2:44.

Have you ever wondered why so much of recorded history is about wars and battles? Who beat whom and what king defeated what ruler? Why can't people get along enough to live peacefully in one world? You guessed it—the sin of greed.

King Nebuchadnezzar tried to rule all people; so did Alexander the Great (what was so great about him?); as did the caesars in Christ's day; Charlemagne and Louis XIV, too. Five-foot-two-inch Napoleon tried, but the Duke of Wellington ended those dreams of a world empire.

In 1914 Kaiser Wilhelm had the same idea, a world controlled by him through force. Two days after the news of the kaiser's defeat came through, a corporal left a German hospital with a feverish desire to rule the world—Adolf Hitler.

Since Hitler dozens more greedy people have been determined to rule their own little corner of the world through force. If they'd read God's book, these people would have known their attempts were futile. They could have saved themselves and millions of others the pain of war.

One day King Jesus will rule over His people, not by the force of bullets and bombs, but through the power of eternal love.

25 October

God's Goatherd

Now Samuel did not yet know the Lord, neither was the word of the Lord yet revealed unto Him. 1 Samuel 3:7.

'm just a kid," you might say. "I need to grow up before God can use me." Not true. A young Bedouin goatherd boy was throwing stones at various targets in the hills along the Dead Sea while searching for his lost goat. He threw a stone in a cave and heard something break. When he checked it out, he discovered he'd broken a pottery vase. Inside the vase were tightly rolled 2,000-year-old parchment scrolls—handwritten copies of the Bible.

Other caves in the area yielded thousands of fragments of manuscripts from the Old Testament. We had many copies of the New Testament in Hebrew and Greek, including one produced within 30 years of the New Testament writers themselves. But that was not true of the Old Testament books until the discovery of the Dead Sea scrolls.

The Isaiah scroll, inscribed on 17 sheets of leather sewn together, was intact from the first verse to the last, matching the book of Isaiah in your Bible and mine.

Just as He used young Samuel to give His Word to Eli, God used a stone and a young Bedouin boy to prove His Word to you and me.

A Christian Bounty

And thine ears shall hear a word behind thee, saying, This is the way, walk ye in it. Isaiah 30:21.

utineers on early sailing ships faced death should they fail. So once Fletcher Christian, John Adams, and the others decided to commandeer the *Bounty* from Captain Bligh, they had to succeed.

Setting the captain adrift in a small boat with 18 loyal sailors, the mutineers, along with several Tahitians, sailed to a remote uninhabited island in the South Pacific called Pitcairn. They unloaded the ship's cargo, then burned the vessel so no one could escape the island to tell of the fugitives' whereabouts.

The fugitives celebrated their escape with drunken orgies. Fights broke out and people were killed. At last only one of the mutineers—John Adams—was left. Surrounded by the children of the fugitives, John felt responsible for their lives.

While taking stock of their provisions, John found a Bible in the bottom of one of the ship's sea chests. He read it, then read it to the children. The former mutineer built a small church and a school. Today every citizen on Pitcairn Island is a Christian because of the life-changing power of God's Word. Travelers on passing ships marvel that there are no bars and no jails on the island. None are needed in a country where everyone loves God.

27 October

Sing, Baby, Sing!

Raise God from the earth, you sea dragons, you fathomless ocean depths. . . . Praise from all who love God! Psalm 148:7-14, Message.

In the water off Maui, Jim Darling drags a hydrophone beneath his boat to record the concert of a giant humpback whale performing 40 feet below the surface. The whale's song is so loud that earphones aren't needed. Bass rumbles reverberate through the boat's hull and rise from the waves like the lowest octave from a cathedral pipe organ. Plaintive moans and glissandos, like air squealing out of a balloon when you stretch the neck tight follow.

The notes build into phrases and repeated themes, lasting up to 30 minutes. Scientists have learned that all humpbacks in a region sing the same song, a song that constantly evolves as it is produced.

Scuba divers report that in the water they not only hear the whale's voice but feel it inside their heads and bones. "At 30 feet," one diver claims, "I was totally immersed—dunked, drenched—in humpback music. The sea quivered with it."

Scientists may not understand what the intricate arias are about, but I do. David said that all creation praises God. So sing, baby humpback. Together you and I will sing our praises to God, our Creator!

A Brilliant Fool

Of what use is money in the hand of a fool? Proverbs 17:16, NIV.

He looks funny, Mama." The 7-year-old boy pointed at the man with the exceptionally long arms playing the violin.

"Shh," mother scolded. "That's Niccolò Paganini, the greatest violinist of all time!"

Born on October 27, 1782, in Genoa, Italy, Niccolò's legendary long arms probably contributed to his unique skills as a performer. The fiddler quickly became popular throughout Europe, and very rich.

When the 58-year-old virtuoso died in Nice, France, he died penniless. His last years he lived in abject poverty, embarrassed by his huge debts. Did he spend his great wealth on food, houses, fast horses, or expensive clothes? No, the genius on the violin gambled away his fortune.

No one likes to think of himself as a fool. Yet, as poor Niccolò, many learn too late that a fool never has so much money he can afford to waste it at a slot machine or on a sweepstakes ticket. As the addiction of alcohol or tobacco, gambling controls the fool. It's never the other way around—even for a brilliant fool.

Going to the Promised Land

I have never seen the righteous forsaken or their children begging for bread. Psalm 37:25, NIV.

We're going to California," Anna breathed to herself as the farm wagon, loaded with all her family's earthly possession rolled across the prairie. "We're actually going to California!"

In April 1846 Anna and her husband took their place in the 87-member wagon train of immigrants, families, and businessmen leaving Springfield, Illinois, to begin their new life in a new land.

Brothers George and Jacob Donner and their partner James Reed eagerly led the people across the prairie. The caravan experienced the usual delays on the westward trail—illnesses, breakdowns, and Indian attacks.

Winter weather trapped them in a pass in the Sierra Nevadas. Deep snows prevented them from hunting or fishing for food. Their supplies ran out. Their numbers dwindled to 48 by journey's end on April 27, 1847. Later the world discovered they'd survived by eating their dead.

What would you have done if you'd been in the Donner party? What would I do? I don't know. But I do know you and I are "journeying" to a promised land greater than California. Along the way, we'll have hard times when the only way to survive seems to be to go against God's commands. Today's promise gives us faith to withstand the most beguiling temptation.

The Color of Your Sky

There will be no more night. They will not need the light of a lamp or the light of the sun, for the Lord God will give them light.
Revelation 22:5, NIV.

What color is your sky? Probably the same as mine since everyone on Planet Earth shares the same sky. Of course, if you live in such big cities as Denver or Los Angeles, you may wake up to brown smoggy skies. Some mornings in Seattle or Buffalo the skies may be foggy gray.

However, a cerulean blue sky with puffy white clouds is earth's signature sky and exists nowhere else. Did you know the skies on other planets aren't typically blue as ours are? Each planet has its own particular sky color.

Mars's sky is vermilion orange, Uranus's is blue-green, as is Neptune's. Mercury's sky is black, as is the moon's. Jupiter's is blue-black because of ammonia ice particles in the atmosphere.

Interesting, huh? What about heaven? Blue like the earth's? Or golden? Or shimmery silver? Or pearlized? Whatever color its sky, I know I want to be there and see it for myself. How about you?

31 October

Gates of Hell

We have examined this, and it is true. So hear it and apply it to yourself. Job 5:27 NIV.

Just what do you know about Halloween? Here's a few facts that can curl the straightest of hair, or make it stand on end.

Cannaught, England, claims to have the "gates of hell." And on Halloween people throughout history have believed Satan is allowed to open these gates to free his imps.

Remember the angels expelled from heaven with Lucifer? According to legend, these imps take the form of black cats, ravens, and black goats—all sacred symbols to people who believe in witchcraft and who race about the countryside sacrificing small children and animals to their god—Satan. Supposedly the imps amuse themselves by carrying off people's garden gates, ringing doorbells, and tapping on people's windows—hence today's trick or treat.

Jack-o'-lanterns were to scare off demons. Dressing in costumes was the way the people of the Middle Ages kept the demons from recognizing them.

Halloween wasn't a game then and isn't now! Jack-o'-lanterns and weird costumes don't protect from evil forces. Messing around with demons can be dangerous to a Christian's spiritual health. The wise child of God steers clear of anything connected with the father of lies.

Giving Thanks

Give thanks in all circumstances, for this is God's will for you in Christ Jesus. 1 Thessalonians 5:18, NIV.

I like the story of an optimistic preacher from Florida who was assigned his first church, in Wisconsin. He began his prayer every Sabbath morning with, "I thank You, God, for the weather."

On an icy, windy, bitter cold Sabbath in January with a $-20°F$ wind chill factor, the church's furnace died. As the few people who managed to make it to church shivered in the cold, they wondered if the young minister would be able to pray his positive prayer.

On cue the young man, bundled in overcoat, heavy boots, a hat, wool scarf, and fur-lined gloves took his place behind the pulpit. The people leaned forward to listen as the man closed his eyes and bowed his head to pray. "Dear Father, we thank You that You send us so few Sabbaths like today."

The preacher had discovered at a young age the single most important secret to success and happiness—give thanks in everything.

If you want to enjoy success in this world and in the next, cultivate an attitude of gratitude.

His First Kill

Don't be afraid of these who want to murder you. They can only kill the body; they have no power over your souls. Luke 12:4, TLB.

ollowing boot camp, Rich Luttrell, a puny 18-year-old kid from Chicago's housing projects, found himself with two new pairs of boots, a new pair of shoes, and brand-new clothes—all at the same time. But he also found himself a member of the 101st Airborne First Brigade, trained to fight like guerrillas—night ambushes, search and destroy.

Dropped into the thick of war in Vietnam, Rich wondered, *What am I doing here? This is a big mistake.*

One hot sultry day, as he tramped through the jungle's tangled undergrowth, he had no idea his enemy was but a few feet away. Out of the corner of his right eye he suddenly saw a North Vietnamese soldier leaning over an AK-47. Rich was in his enemy's gunsight.

Fear flooded through Rich. It was kill or be killed. The American soldier turned and looked his enemy full in the face, then pulled the trigger. The North Vietnamese soldier slumped to the ground.

Stunned, Rich realized he'd actually killed a man, rather than having been killed. With the adrenaline rush over, the young soldier's legs felt like rubber.

(to be continued)

A Black-and-White Photograph

Come to me, all you who are weary and burdened, and I will give you rest. Matthew 11:28, NIV.

Rich watched in horror as his buddies ransacked the dead soldier's pockets. From the dead man's wallet a postage-stamp-sized piece of paper fell to the ground. Rich picked it up. It was a photograph of the dead soldier and a little girl. Rich knew he'd killed some little girl's father. When the platoon moved out, Rich stuck the photo in his own wallet.

At the end of his tour of duty Rich came home with a caseful of medals and married his hometown sweetheart. Of all the horrors of war he'd seen, that little girl's face haunted him most. Sometimes he wished he'd never taken that picture home with him.

More than 20 years after his return from Vietnam, Rich and his wife decided to visit the Vietnam Veterans Memorial in Washington, D.C. At the hotel, before going to the memorial, he scribbled out a note to the dead Vietnamese soldier in which he asked forgiveness for taking the man's life.

The next day he placed the letter and the photograph at the foot of the memorial. As he did, the load of guilt he'd been carrying lifted from his shoulders. He felt great. He felt free!

(to be continued)

Photo Power

Let the peace of Christ rule in your hearts. Colossians 3:15, NIV.

R ich Luttrell thought he'd gotten rid of the photograph. He had, until a friend showed him page 53 in the book *Offerings at the Wall*. There, with his letter of apology, was the photograph that had haunted him for so long.

The wall's curator, Druery Felton, had found the photo and Rich's apology. The photograph disturbed him too. He used the letter and picture during exhibits of the Wall to teach new generations about wars and what fighting did to people. Later they were included in *Offerings at the Wall*.

A copy of the book found its way to Illinois state representative Ron Stephens, who recognized his good friend Rich Luttrell's name. When Ron showed the photo to Rich, Rich broke into tears. It was as if the little girl were accusing him of abandoning her.

"What do you want from me?" he cried.

Getting the original picture back from Druery Felton, Rich decided he would never again find peace until he found the little girl in the photograph. But how would he do that? Rich didn't know her name, where she lived, or even if she were alive.

(to be continued)

In the Hands of Angels

My angel will go ahead of you. Exodus 23:23, NIV.

Rich Luttrell contacted a newspaper reporter in St. Louis with his story. When the story made the front page of the St. Louis *Post-Dispatch,* Rich stuck it in a letter to the Vietnamese ambassador to Washington, D.C. He explained to the ambassador that he would like to locate the girl and her family. With nearly 80 million people in Vietnam, Rich's chances were almost nil.

The ambassador forwarded the article containing the photograph to Hanoi, the capital of Vietnam. There a newspaper editor printed the photo and the story, asking, "Does anyone know these people?"

A subscriber to the paper decided to send his mother a care package. He wrapped the gift in the newspaper containing the photo and sent it to the rural village where his mother lived. Recognizing the photograph, the woman took the paper to a tiny hamlet down the road. "This is your father," she told the soldier's family. For 30 years the man's family had known him to be MIA—missing in action.

Rich Luttrell flew to Vietnam and returned the only existing photograph of the man to Lan, the little girl, now a 40-year-old woman. To the soldier's family, it was as if their loved one had finally come home. Rich felt only joy, for he could finally forgive himself.

6 November

Young King Tut

By faith Moses . . . refused to be known as the son of Pharaoh's daughter. He chose to be mistreated along with the people of God rather than to enjoy the pleasures of sin for a short time. Hebrews 11:24, 25, NIV.

The pyramids of Egypt held the bodies of Egyptian royalty and their wealth. Over the years grave robbers stripped the tombs of their riches, all except one.

One tomb was so carefully hidden it remained untouched for more than 3,000 years—the tomb of the boy ruler Tutankhamen, King Tut. Mummified around 1340 B.C., the young man's face was covered with a golden mask; his body was decorated with a golden collar, belt, bracelets, and anklets; his fingers and toes bore gold shields. With the gold on his body, King Tut's solid gold coffin weighed about 250 pounds.

The coffin was protected by two gold-plated caskets placed within a stone sarcophagus surrounded by four golden-walled shrines, one as big as a bedroom. All that gold and the boy king never got to enjoy it. For King Tut the season of fabulous wealth ended with his last breath.

From today's text we can surmise that Moses knew something that the pharaohs of Egypt didn't. Do you know his secret?

(to be continued)

forward Thinking

He [Moses] regarded disgrace for the sake of Christ as of greater value than the treasures of Egypt, because he was looking ahead to his reward. Hebrews 11:26, NIV.

Wow! Talk about riches! Makes Bill Gates look like a pauper. This week, in 1922, archaeologists uncovered the king's fabulous tomb. Along with the incredible wealth buried with the king's body, there were other rooms in which they found golden beds, thrones, chests, chariots, figures, idols, even toys.

Just think! All that wealth could have belonged to Moses. If Moses had stayed in Egypt and become pharaoh he could have been mummified and surrounded by a hoard of gold when he died. But his story didn't end there.

Soon after Moses died his grave was robbed—not of a fabulous fortune in gold or jewels, but of Moses himself. Jesus, the Creator of all, raised His faithful servant Moses to life eternal. Moses made a wise choice, don't you agree? After all, a casket is still a casket, whether it's made of gold or pine. And golden-lined burial shrines house the bones of dead people while a live Moses walks heaven's streets of gold.

The outcome for you can be the same—eternal life—if you make the wiser choice.

8 November

X-ray Day

My frame was not hidden from you when I was made in the secret place. When I was woven together in the depths of the earth, your eyes saw my unformed body. Psalm 139:15, 16, NIV.

Recently I had my picture taken. No one said "Say cheese" or "Smile for the birdie." My photo wasn't taken with my husband's hand-held camera, but with a highly technical camera that sees through skin and fat, right to the bone. After I fell off my bike, I had to have my leg X-rayed to be sure I hadn't broken a bone.

People have X-rays taken all the time. It doesn't hurt and it's no big deal, right? Yes and no. Before November 8, 1895, having an X-ray was unheard-of. Thanks to physicist Wilhelm Conrad Roentgen, my doctor can look at my X-ray negatives and see what bone needs fixing without slicing into my leg to check it out. I like that, believe me.

But God can go one better than the best X-ray machines. He sees your inmost being—the person you hide from others. He saw you before you were born. You are not an accident. He ordained your days before you were born. To Him, there is nothing unimportant about you—absolutely nothing!

Music Makers

Sing and make music in your heart to the Lord. Ephesians 5:19, NIV.

My daddy couldn't sing—not a note! With much coaxing I could sometimes get him to croak, "Sweet A-de-line . . ." (That was the first line to a song popular when he was a kid.) But those moments were rare.

Now, my mother, my sister Connie, and I loved to sing—anyplace, anytime. We sang around the piano on Friday evenings; we sang in church on Sabbath; we loved to sing. And Daddy's face would beam with pride and enjoyment whenever we did.

At church one Sabbath, a visiting pastor sang "The Love of God." I didn't realize how much my father wished he could sing until on the way home he said, "When I get to heaven I'm going to sing in a special choir. There'll be 1,000 sopranos, 1,000 altos, 1,000 tenors, and me. I'll sing bass." And I plan to be front row center when he does.

I wonder if my dad realized that, as he went through his day painting houses and praising God, he was singing and making music in his heart to God—even when no human could hear him.

How about you? When you sing and make music to God, do you sing soprano, alto, tenor, bass . . . or praise Him with your silence?

Music of the Spheres

*"Where were you when I laid the foundations of the earth? . . .
Who laid its cornerstone as the morning stars sang together and
all the angels shouted for joy?" Job 38:4-7, TLB.*

I love watching the stars on the desert at night. From horizon
to horizon, bright stars, blinking stars, shooting stars, planets, and satellites seem so close I want to reach up and
catch one for my very own.

OK, I know some stars are actually planets bigger than our
sun. And I know they're flaming balls of fire that would reduce
me to ashes in an instant. But I think the poet in me imagines
them to be more like fireflies.

Imagine the stars singing together. What song of praise do
they sing? Will we hear them sing when our ears are endowed
with exceptional hearing in heaven?

NASA tells us that outer space is totally silent. Have you
ever been in a place so silent that your ears ring? I have—in
the New Mexican desert. It's as if God is standing right beside
me. A walk in the snow can produce the same reaction.

At silent times like these I can feel God's presence. Just as
God loves our music and laughter, He comes to us in our silence,
too. Find a quiet spot today and invite God to enjoy it with you.
He's never too busy to spend time with His kids, you know.

Good Advice

The way of a fool seem right to him, but a wise man listens to advice. Proverbs 12:15, NIV.

Advice comes from many different sources—some good, some not so good. Here's a few pieces of good advice off the Internet:

1. Letting the cat out of the bag is a whole lot easier than putting it back inside.

2. If you find yourself in a hole, stop digging.

3. If you imagine yourself to be a person of influence, try ordering around someone else's dog.

4. When you give a lesson in meanness to a critter or a person, don't be surprised if they learn the lesson.

5. The quickest way to double your money is to fold it over and put it in your pocket.

The book of Proverbs has lots of good advice that is as fresh and new as anything you'd find off the Internet. It never grows old, because it comes from God. Can you find five Scripture metaphors (word pictures) that give similarly wise advice? For example, see Proverbs 20:17.

Great Dads

Let's have a feast and celebrate. For this son of mine was dead and is alive again. Luke 15:23, 24, NIV.

In Greece a man and his son were sleeping in their house one night when an earthquake hit, reducing the walls to rubble. With the next tremor the building's main support beam groaned and cracked. Thinking quickly, the father reached up and stopped its fall just short of his son's head. With super-human effort the man supported the heavy wooden beam for 24 hours.

Rescuers dug them from the rubble and rushed them to the hospital. The boy lived; the father died. He had given his life to save his son.

Sometimes boys and girls think that while Jesus loves them, maybe God the Father doesn't love all that much. Maybe Jesus has to beg His Father to be kind to us. Not so.

God the Father's love is just as strong as Jesus' love. While God the Father would have done everything possible to save Jesus from dying on the cross, He loved us too much to stop Him. It took a God-power far beyond any power we can imagine to watch His Son die. Do you understand it? I don't either. But I thank Him for it every day I live and breathe. How about you?

Hearing God's Voice

The sheep listen to his voice. He [the shepherd] calls his own sheep by name and leads them out. John 10:3, NIV.

Hi, boys and girls, moms and dads, grandmas and grandpas, kitty cats and puppy dogs, pet goldfish and gerbils, welcome to *The Family Hour.*" As old as I am, I still don't understand how radio waves work. I can turn a knob in my Chevy while driving 60 miles per hour 100 miles from home and hear my own voice being transmitted from radio station KARM in Visalia, where I host an evening program called *The Family Hour.* That's weird!

What's weirder still is knowing that everywhere I go thousands of sound waves blast my ears carrying all kinds of messages. But I hear certain radio waves only if I have a radio receiver tuned to the right station. It is a mystery to me, no matter how often my scientist husband explains it.

Understand it or not, I especially appreciate those waves during the hour's drive home from the Fresno airport late at night. I turn on the radio to KARM and hear the familiar voices of Christian music. It's as if God's guiding me home.

Jesus called me His sheep, listening for His voice. And it is that voice that will guide me to my eternal home.

Life-giving Blood!

With your blood you purchased men for God. Revelation 5:9, NIV.

Four-year-old Brenda had a rare blood type. She would die without a blood transfusion. When it was discovered that her 6-year-old brother, Sam, had the same blood type, his mother and the doctors asked him if he'd be willing to give blood for his sister. The boy thought a moment and agreed.

The nurse placed Sam on a gurney next to his sister's bed and prepared the needle for his arm. A tear trickled down the boy's cheek as he asked, "How long does it take to die?"

Thinking he was talking about losing his sister, the nurse asked, "Die? Why do you ask?"

"I just wanted to know when I would die."

The nurse was stunned. "You're not going to die, Sam; I promise."

The boy had thought that he would need to die to save his sister's life.

November 14, 1666, was an incredible day in history. This was the day the first successful blood transfusion was made. If you or anyone you love has ever had a blood transfusion, you have cause to celebrate. Actually, we all have reason to celebrate the day Jesus gave His blood to give us life.

Tell Me Why

Be ready always to give an answer to every man that asketh you a reason of the hope that is in you. 1 Peter 3:15.

There are lots of questions to which I don't have answers. Here are a few of them:

1. Why do drugstores make the sick walk to the back of the store to get their prescriptions while healthy people can buy cigarettes at the front counter?

2. Why do we leave cars worth thousands of dollars in the driveway so we can store useless junk in the garage?

3. Why do banks have drive-up ATM machines with braille lettering?

4. Why do people order double cheeseburgers, large fries, and a diet Coke?

5. Why can the pizza deliveryperson get to my house faster than an ambulance driver?

Silly questions? Perhaps. Definitely questions to which we don't need to know the answers (if there are any). But there are questions—eternal questions—God didn't leave us to wondering about. Who am I? Who loves me more than life itself? Can I be forgiven? Where am I going? God gave us definite answers to these questions and so many more in His Word. Can you think of more?

16 November

In Need of Food

Blessed is he who is kind to the needy. Proverbs 14:21, NIV.

Flying to a speaking engagement in North Dakota, I had to change planes. Our plane had been grounded in another city because of bad weather. We'd been warned that when it landed, we would board and take off as quickly as possible.

I hadn't eaten since breakfast and was getting mighty hungry. The small waiting area had no eating facilities or snack bars, only vending machines that took change and dollar bills. I had no bills smaller than a five.

Not daring to run to the main terminal to get some food, I asked the ticket agent if she could give me change. She couldn't. I returned to my seat.

My stomach growled, and my head felt dizzy. Knowing I have diabetes, I should have brought snacks along with me, but I didn't. What should I do? I was too embarrassed to ask any of my fellow passengers for help. But I knew I had to do something.

In desperation, I pulled out my money and walked over to a man reading a newspaper and asked if he could change a five. He shook his head and buried himself deeper in the paper. I asked a second—same answer. Neither bothered to check his wallet or even to glance up at me.

(to be continued)

A Handful of Quarters

Live generously. Matthew 5:42, Message.

Yesterday you left me in the airport with dropping blood sugar, without food, and with no bills smaller than a five. I was desperate. Embarrassed at being rejected by two men already, I wondered, *Whom should I ask next?* As I glanced around the small waiting area, people averted my gaze, as if embarrassed for me. I felt like a panhandler on a San Francisco street corner.

Gathering up my courage once more, I walked up to a rather disheveled middle-aged woman surrounded by luggage and shopping bags and reading the supermarket tabloid *The Enquirer.*

"Ma'am . . ." I cleared my suddenly parched throat. "Do you have change for a five? I need change for the vending machines."

Immediately she dug in her bag, drew out a bulging change purse, and dumped the contents in my hand. There must have been $10 worth of quarters glistening in my hand.

"Wait. I need only 20 of these," I protested.

"Nonsense."

"Well, thank you," I stammered. "You are so kind."

"Just pass it on to someone else." She smiled and returned to her newspaper.

(to be continued)

A Pocketful of Gratitude

Freely you have received, freely give. Matthew 10:8, NIV.

I thanked the woman profusely, then hurried to the vending machines for a can of lemonade and two bags of trail mix. Just then the gate attendant called my flight.

By the time we landed in Bismarck the shops were closed, and my ride to the academy where I would speak had given up and gone home. I contacted the appropriate people, then sat down in the deserted airport lobby to wait.

I'd barely arranged my luggage when a young woman carrying a crying baby in one arm and holding the hand of a tearful 4-year-old by her side came up to me. "Ma'am, sorry to bother you, but my plane was late and I need to call my husband, but I don't have any money. You wouldn't have a quarter or two I could borrow?"

I smiled as tears filled my eyes. "Did you come in on the last flight too?" I asked as I pawed through my purse for my wallet.

"Yes. It's going to take my husband an hour to drive back to get us," she confided, but not before her daughter whined, "Mommy, I'm so hungry."

"Shh," she whispered. "Not now. Daddy will bring something from home."

I dumped the remaining quarters into the surprised woman's hand. I cut off her protests with "There are food vending machines at the end of the hall."

An Address to Remember

Comfort one another with these words. 1 Thessalonians 4:18.

On November 19, 1863, an event was held to memorialize dead Americans who'd given their lives in battle. The main speaker was so unpopular, he hadn't been invited to the festivities. But since Abe was president, the officials reluctantly agreed to permit him to speak. So on the train to Gettysburg, Pennsylvania, President Abraham Lincoln scribbled a few words on the back of an envelope, or so legend has it.

The men who'd been asked to speak droned on for hours, in eloquent and impressive vocabulary. Today no one remembers what they said. Finally the platform official introduced Mr. Lincoln to the crowd of 2,000. The tall angular man rose to his feet, strode to the podium, and delivered a speech that would resonate throughout history.

"Fourscore and seven years ago our fathers brought forth on this continent, a new nation . . . dedicated to the proposition that all men are created equal." It was a message that would cheer the heart of every American for generations to come.

A message that brings cheer to the heart of every Christian is found in 1 Thessalonians 4:16-18. See if those words don't cheer your heart as well.

Tongue Twisters

Vicious wolves are going to . . . rip into this flock, men from your own ranks twisting words so as to seduce disciples into following them instead of Jesus. Acts 20:29, 30, Message.

As I've already told you, I love the sound of words—words that tantalize your tongue and tickle your mind. See how fast you can read aloud the following:

1. Swan swam over the sea. Swim, swan, swim! Swan swum back again. Well-swum swan.

2. Slim sly Sam stole, then sold, old Otto's old oily auto in the early hours.

3. Surely sheep shouldn't sleep in a shack; sheep should surely sleep in a shed.

4. Two three-toed toads and two two-toed toads talked to a three-toed tree.

5. I saw Esau kissing Katie Custer. I saw Esau, he saw me, and she saw I saw Esau.

We laugh when word twisters twist our tongues, but there's nothing funny about people who try to twist our minds, to mix us up regarding Jesus. In today's text the apostle Paul warned about such people. He likens them to vicious wolves ripping into a flock of sheep. The only protection we have against such individuals is to study the Word of God.

A Sense of Direction

I know the one in whom I trust, and I am sure that he is able to safely guard all that I have given him until the day of his return. 2 Timothy 1:12, TLB.

My husband, daughters, and I had stopped at a restaurant on our way home to Wisconsin from visiting Grandma's house in upstate New York. Night had fallen by the time we finished our meal and once again loaded into the car to continue our journey toward home.

My husband had barely turned onto the main highway when 3-year-old Rhonda asked, "Are we going back to Grandma's house?"

"No, honey," he called over his shoulder.

"Yes, we are," she assured us.

The little girl was right. In the dark, he'd turned east instead of west. Something in the child's brain told her we were heading back in the direction from which we'd come.

Scientists say some people's brains have a stronger electrical field than others have. Rhonda's sense of direction is very strong. Without a compass, she can always point out which way is north, south, east, or west.

Knowing which way to go physically is great, but knowing which way to go spiritually is greatest of all. And that's available to all of God's children for the asking.

An Unusual Tale

Have you never read, "From the lips of children and infants you have ordained praise"? Matthew 21:16, NIV.

This news story is reported to be true. An atheist couple had a child. The girl was never told about Jesus. One night the 5-year-old watched in horror as her father, in the middle of an argument, shot the woman, then himself.

The girl was placed in a Christian foster home. During her first visit to church, the teacher, not knowing anything about the child's background, held up a picture of Jesus and asked, "Does anyone know who this is?"

The little girl raised her hand excitedly. "I do! That's the Man who was holding me the night my parents died."

This story doesn't surprise me. For my Bible tells of how much my Jesus loved kids. When He was here on earth, He loved having the children climb onto His lap while He told His stories. For that matter, when the disciples tried to shoo them away, He said, "No! Don't stop them from coming to Me. My kingdom is made up of little children. You must become one to enter it."

Some grown-ups have a hard time trusting God to take care of them. One way not to lose that childlike trust is to remember to thank Him for everything He does for you.

Funny, Isn't It?

Don't be afraid; just believe. Mark 5:36, NIV.

Funny, isn't it, how people believe what the newspapers say, but question what the Bible tells them?

Funny how some say they believe in God, but follow Satan.

Funny how some people laugh at dirty jokes, but feel uncomfortable if anyone talks about God.

Funny how others seem all fired up about God on Sabbath, but curse and swear, taking His name in vain, during the week.

Funny, isn't it, that we sometimes worry more about what our friends think of us than what God thinks of us?

Funny how we gripe about eating the squash mom made for supper but not about other kids who will be thankful just to have a hot meal on Thanksgiving Day.

Funny how we worry that we're not wearing the latest jeans jacket or Old Navy sweatshirt, but don't give a thought to the kids who have to skip school on extra-cold days because they don't have a warm enough coat to wear.

Funny, isn't it? Or is it?

To "just believe," as Jesus said to do in today's verse, changes everything. Look back over the list of "Funny, isn't its" and consider how faith and complete trust in God would give you a new perspective.

D. B. Cooper

I have seen a wicked . . . man flourishing like a green tree in its native soil, but he soon passed away and was no more; though I looked for him he could not be found. Psalm 37:35, 36, NIV.

His plane ticket identified him as D. B. Cooper. No one knows if that was his real name. On November 25, 1971, a middle-aged man held up a Northwest Airlines 727 jetliner. That's right, just like the train robberies of Butch Cassidy and the Sundance Kid in the 1800s. On a flight from Portland to Seattle, Cooper ordered the plane to land, collected $200,000 from the passengers, and got four parachutes. The crew then flew him south, where he leaped from the plane into the Cascade Mountain wilderness of Washington State.

Massive hunts turned up nothing—no man, no parachute, no money. It wasn't until 1980 that two boys found several thousand dollars floating in one of the tributaries of the Columbia River. The cash was traced to the stolen money. Did D. B. Cooper live to enjoy his purloined wealth? Did he die in his dangerous jump?

What does it matter? Sometimes God's children envy the wicked's success—their money, their houses and lands—but forget that they have their reward. This world's all they'll get while those who love God will live forever surrounded by more riches than D. B. Cooper could ever have imagined. What's $200,000 compared to that?

The Lie Detector

Better to be poor than a liar. Proverbs 19:22, NIV.

The police in Radnor, Pennsylvania, arrested a man for robbing an all-night gas station. While interrogating the suspect, they placed a metal colander on his head and connected it with wires to a photocopy machine. The message "He's lying" was placed in the copier. The police pushed the copy button each time they thought the man was lying. Believing the "lie detector" was working, the suspect confessed. There's no doubt the man wasn't the smartest liar the world has ever seen.

Whenever I'm tempted to protect myself by lying, I remember a story Corrie ten Boom told in her book *The Hiding Place*. She and her family hid Jewish people in their home during World War II. One time when soldiers charged into their home rounding up workers for the munitions factory and asked where Corrie's nephews were, her niece said, "Why, they're under the table."

The soldiers searched everywhere else in the house and found nothing. Thinking the girl was being sarcastic, they left without ever looking under the cloth-covered table, where the young men were hiding.

God has a thousand ways to care for us. I doubt that any of those ways include lying. What do you think?

26 November

Search for freedom?

I run in the path of your commands, for you have set my heart free. Psalm 119:32, NIV.

Isabella Van Wagener was convinced that Congress should form a "Negro state" on public lands in the West. She petitioned her congressmen. She visited the Capitol. She talked with everyone who would listen, but to no avail.

Isabella, better known as Sojourner Truth, spent her life fighting for freedom. For her, freedom was everything. The former slave had been sold four times before she escaped to freedom along the Underground Railroad.

Once slavery was abolished in the United States, Sojourner became a champion of women's rights. She traveled by horse and buggy, train, or stagecoach from town to town in the eastern United States, preaching freedom and fairness for all.

While her body was free, her true freedom came when she met Jesus Christ. That's when her heart was set free—set free of all the anger and hate for what White people had done to her.

Sojourner's message broadened to proclaim the good news of salvation in Jesus. Wherever the feisty little woman went, people learned of the gospel of freedom.

Happy Thanksgiving

Come before him with thankful hearts. Let us sing him psalms of praise. Psalm 95:2, TLB.

S o you think the Thanksgiving holiday has been around since the time of the Pilgrims? Not true. It took the efforts of three presidents and an act of Congress to get the entire country to give thanks on the same date.

More than 150 years after the Pilgrims celebrated the first Thanksgiving with Native Americans, someone suggested to President Washington that the event be turned into a national holiday.

Old George thought it was a good idea and declared that in the new United States there should be a Thanksgiving holiday in the month of November. But it wasn't until 1863, at the height of the American Civil War, that President Lincoln made Thanksgiving an official national holiday to be celebrated the last Thursday of November.

In 1939 President Franklin D. Roosevelt moved it forward one week so as to allow for more shopping days before Christmas. It took Congress, in 1941, to make the fourth Thursday of November Thanksgiving officially.

While celebrating a day of gratitude and thanksgiving as a country is good, making every day a day of praise and thanksgiving pleases God even more.

341

Praise Your Way

Accept, O Lord, the willing praise of my mouth. Psalm 119:108, NIV.

Leaving gratitude and praise out of your prayers to God is like giving a friend a vegeburger sandwich without the vegeburger. You include the bread, the lettuce, the tomato slices, the pickles, the onion slice, the ketchup, and the mayonnaise, but forget to include the vegeburger. Silly, huh?

A friend of mine, working at a food counter in a bus station, would for fun assemble hamburgers with everything on it but the meat. Instead of placing the burger in the bun along with the lettuce, tomato, cheese, onion, and ketchup, she would wrap it separately and place it under the wrapped sandwich.

Imagine the surprise of finding your burger after you finished eating your sandwich. Probably most people didn't even miss the burger, what with all the other flavors fighting for their attention.

But what's a vegeburger sandwich without the burger?

Sometimes we stuff our prayers with so many things and forget the best part of praying—the praise. Does God miss the praise? Yes. Will He listen to a thankless prayer? Yes, but our Creator finds our prayers much more satisfying and "tasty" when they include our genuine praise and gratitude.

Alphabet Praise

Thank God! He deserves your thanks. His love never quits.
Psalm 136:1, Message.

I have a game for you to play. Open your Bible to Psalm 136.
You will see a phrase repeated again and again: "His love endures forever" or "His love never quits." Means the same
thing, right?

With friends or with family members, go through the alphabet naming things for which you are thankful without repeating what anyone before you said. The only other rule is
that you must follow each item with the words "His love never
quits!" (Example: "I thank God for air; His love never quits!")

To do the praise alphabet alone, write as many things for
which you are thankful that begin with each letter—remembering to repeat the phrase "His love never quits" after each word.

> A—His love never quits!
> B—His love never quits!
> C—His love never quits!
> Etc.

30 November

Do-It-Yourself Brain Surgery

Create in me a new, clean heart, O God, filled with clean thoughts and right desires. Psalm 51:10, TLB.

In Ohio an unidentified man in his late 20s walked into a police station with a nine-inch wire protruding from his forehead. He calmly asked the desk sergeant to give him an X-ray to help him find his brain, which he claimed had been stolen. Using a Black and Decker power drill, the poor man had drilled a six-inch hole in his own skull and stuck a wire into it, trying to find the missing brain.

The police rushed him to the nearest emergency room, then on to a psychiatric hospital for evaluation. Is this something you would do? I hope not. Would the man have been any less delusional if he tried to perform open-heart surgery? Probably not.

Brain and heart surgeons study for many years to learn how to operate on a human being. And they certainly would not consider slicing into their own bodies, no matter how much they knew about the workings of the brain and heart.

When it comes to getting rid of sin, some people think they must perform "do-it-yourself" surgery in order to get a new heart. Jesus is the Master Surgeon who removes my selfish, dirty, sinful heart and puts a brand-spanking-new heart in its place.

family Reunion

God blessed them and said to them, . . . "Rule over the fish of the sea and the birds of the air and over every living creature that moves on the ground." Genesis 1:28, NIV.

Koko the gorilla can sign more than 500 words, and he "chats" on the Internet. Alex the parrot can identify 100 different objects, seven colors, and five shapes. He can count to six and speak in meaningful sentences. Michael the gorilla loves Luciano Pavarotti and refuses to go outside whenever the Italian tenor is on TV. Flint the chimp died of a broken heart after his mother died.

Animals have feelings and intellects far more extensive than humans know, but that doesn't make any of them my cousin or my great-great-great-grandfather as some scientists would have me believe. Buddy Houtaling, a Christian singer-songwriter, calls a trip to the zoo a visit, not a family reunion.

Believing that God made humans in His image and not through millions of years of evolution makes all the difference in our behavior. If we evolved from animals, we can't feel guilty for our sins. We're just acting like our ancestors, right? But if we believe we are made in God's image, then we have a reason to live up to our "family name," a reason to behave like our Dad.

Let's Laugh

There is a time for everything . . . a time to weep and a time to laugh. Ecclesiastes 3:1-4, NIV.

I love to laugh. Sometimes I laugh at the right time; and try as I might to prevent it, sometimes I laugh at the wrong time. God's Word says that there is a time to laugh and there is a time to refrain from laughing.

If an elder in church says, "Turn over in your hymnal . . ." (Can you imagine turning over in your hymnal as you would in bed?), or if he asks us to pray for the people sick in our bulletin (Eww! Gross!), I laugh.

I cringe when I remember the time I mistook a stranger in the next stall in a women's restroom for my daughter, and I stomped on her sneaker. When I tried to apologize, I couldn't control my embarrassed laughter—bad timing.

While there are times laughter is inappropriate, there are three situations in which laughter is downright dangerous for the child of God. Laughing at another person's disability or misfortune; poking fun at God or at something sacred; and laughing at sin—our own or others'—hurts God's heart and turns our own hearts cold.

Where Is Santa Claus?

Reality . . . is found in Christ. Colossians 2:17, NIV.

Is there a real Santa Claus? Yes! There is a town called Santa Claus, Indiana. It is the only Santa Claus post office in the world. Each year since 1914, between November 15 and December 20, 500,000 pieces of mail are hand-stamped by the town's postmaster and a volunteer staff. The town of Santa Claus has streets named Silver Bell Terrace, Candy Cane Lane, Reindeer Circle, and Prance Drive.

I love Christmas, but not for the fictional Santa and his flying reindeer. As a kid, I never believed in him. Too many elements of the story were illogical. I got in trouble with the mothers in the neighborhood when I told my friends Santa wasn't real.

Besides, I knew the real story of Christmas, about a Baby born in a manger who would change my life forever. While Jesus sees me when I'm bad or good, He loves me and forgives me when I ask. He doesn't just ride off to the North Pole to make next year's presents; He stays by my side, loving me and guiding me through good times and bad. And when He comes back, it won't be down my chimney, but in a sky full of angels for the entire world to see—a reality that's out of this world!

A Civil War Christmas

[Add] to godliness, brotherly kindness; and to brotherly kindness, love. 2 Peter 1:7, NIV.

Christmas 1864 wasn't an easy time for the soldiers embroiled in the Civil War. Tired, sick, hungry, all any of them wanted to do was go home and be with their families, regardless of which side they were on.

And as with any war, the civilians suffered too. Following Union Major General William T. Sherman's capture of Savannah, Georgia, 90 Northern soldiers and their captain felt sorry for the Southern people struggling to survive after the attack. Their pantries, livestock, and homes had been ransacked by the advancing army.

The victorious soldiers decided to play Santa. On Christmas Day they strapped tree-branch antlers to the heads of their mules, filled their wagons with food and distributed it to the starving women and children living in the ravaged countryside.

While the men couldn't undo the terrible results of war, they could and did ease the pain and hunger of a few.

Spinning Planets

God stretches out heaven over empty space, and hangs the earth upon nothing. Job 26:7, TLB.

For NASA space engineers, aiming a spacecraft to land on Mars or meet up with a particular comet or asteroid is more difficult than you may think. Not only are Earth and the target moving in different orbits around the sun, but the Earth itself is spinning at about 1,000 miles per hour.

Imagine doing the following experiment:

1. Collect several tennis or golf balls in a bucket or basket. Take the basket of balls and a second container, such as a laundry basket or wastebasket, to the nearest playground that has a merry-go-round, the kind you hop on and ride.

2. Place the empty basket on the ground 9 to 12 feet from the merry-go-round, then try to make the basket from the still merry-go-round. Easy.

3. Now, spin around on the merry-go-round and toss the balls into the empty basket.

4. Now imagine the target is on another spinning merry-go-round on the other side of the playground. A little more difficult, huh?

But not for our Creator-God. In or out of this world "He spake, and it was done; he commanded, and it stood fast" (Psalm 33:9).

349

6 December

A Very Pickle Christmas

Never get a lazy man to do something for you; he will be an irritant as vinegar on your teeth or smoke in your eyes. Proverbs 10:26, TEV.

The traditions of mistletoe, eggnog, and candy canes we associate with Christmas, but pickles? In Berrien County, Michigan, Christmastime means pickle time.

Each December the village of Berrien Springs holds a Christmas Pickle Festival. This tradition started with a blown-glass pickle ornament pioneer families would hide on their Christmas tree for the children to find on Christmas morning. According to the legend that springs from the 1930s, the first one to find the ornament received an extra gift.

A very pickle Christmas may seem kind of silly at first. But think about it. Pickles don't grow ready-to-eat in their brine. It takes work to make a good pickle. A basket of pickle-cukes, a room to clean, a school project to do—if you've ever had a friend who's suppose to help you with a task and left you all the work, it sets your teeth on edge just as a mouthful of vinegar would.

The wisdom from the book of Proverbs is as accurate today as it was back when King Solomon was growing up in his father David's royal court. God's Word doesn't grow old with time.

A Day of Infamy

While people are saying, "Peace and safety," destruction will come on them suddenly, . . . and they will not escape. 1 Thessalonians 5:3, NIV.

Early Sunday morning, December 7, 1941, an enlisted man in Honolulu, Hawaii, was practicing with radar equipment, hoping to learn how to operate the system, when he detected incoming planes 132 miles west of the islands. When he reported it to his superior officers, they laughed at his overactive imagination. There was no threat in that area of the world. Hitler was in Europe, and the Japanese were in the midst of negotiations with the president in Washington.

By 8:00 a.m. the people of the United States knew the meaning of today's text. The surprise attack sank more than 15 U.S. ships, destroyed more than 180 planes, and killed or wounded 3,000 people. President Roosevelt declared that December 7, 1941, would go down in history as a "date which will live in infamy." America was at war.

There's never been a time in this world's history when the threat of war was totally erased. Yet despite mad dictators and kings, renegade rulers and despots, hideous crime and violence, we can be certain of God's promises and His presence. I like that, don't you?

8 December

Confusing Names

Say to the Israelites, "The Lord, the God of your fathers—the God of Abraham, the God of Isaac and the God of Jacob—has sent me to you." This is my name forever, the name by which I am to be remembered from generation to generation. Exodus 3:15, NIV.

If I invited the following people to a party, how many guests did I invite? Martin Clifford, Harry Clifton, Clifford Clive, Sir Alan Cobram, Owen Conquest, Gordon Conway, Harry Dorian, Frank Drakem, Freeman Fox, Hamilton Greening, Cecil Herber, Prosper Howard, Robert Jennings, Gillingham Jones, T. Harcourt Llewelyn, Clifford Owen, Ralph Redway, Ridley Redway, Frank Richards, Hilda Richards, Raleigh Robbins, Robert Rogers, Eric Stanhope, Robert Stanley, Nigel Wallace, and Talbot Wynard.

Actually, only one besides me would be attending the party, because all the names listed are the same person, an author named Charles Harold St. John Hamilton. For some reason Mr. Hamilton chooses to write under each of the above pen names.

Confusing to be one person one day and another person another day, don't you think? We live in a world of change, including people's names. Aren't you glad we can depend on God to be the same, yesterday, today, and forever? I am.

∏ames and Places

I saw the Holy City, the new Jerusalem, coming down out of heaven from God. . . . It had a great, high wall with twelve gates . . . The foundations of the city were decorated with every kind of precious stone. The first foundation was jasper, the second sapphire, the third chalcedony, the fourth emerald, the fifth sardonyx, the sixth carnelian, the seventh chrysolite, the eighth beryl, the ninth topaz, the tenth chrysoprase, the eleventh jacinth, and the twelfth amethyst. The twelve gates were twelve pearls. . . . The street was of pure gold, like transparent glass. Revelation 21:2-21, NIV.

ince I was little, I have loved maps, because I like to travel. When I read the names of many of America's towns and cities, I get instant pictures in my mind. New York City: skyscrapers, subways, and lots of people. Los Angeles: palm trees, sunny beaches, and movie stars. San Francisco: cable cars, cotton candy colored houses built on steep hills. Biloxi, Mississippi: fishing boats and lazy, steamy afternoons.

Imagine what these places look like: Lick Skillet, Texas; Gouge Eye, California; Curtin, Oregon; Stumpy Point, North Carolina. Or Los Banos, California (which means bathroom).

The Bible gives us vivid word pictures of what heaven is like. It's a place I don't intend only to visit, but to live there in a mansion prepared for me by God Himself. How about you?

Either on paper or in your mind, draw a picture of God's heavenly city from today's description. (Your dictionary will have descriptions of some of the jewels you might not recognize.)

America's Christmas Tree

Blessed forever are all who . . . have the right . . . to eat the fruit from the Tree of Life. Revelation 22:14, TLB.

What a wonderful Christmas tree this would be," a little girl remarked as she stood beside the massive General Grant tree in what was then called General Grant National Park. Charles E. Lee of Sanger, California, heard the little girl's remark and presented the idea to President Calvin Coolidge, who in turn designated the General Grant tree to be the nation's Christmas Tree in 1926. Each year since, a Christmas celebration is held and a wreath is laid at the base of the giant evergreen.

A Sanger native who took part in the first ceremony returned recently to give the Christmas message. Jasper G. Havens, a minister in Idaho, recalled the cold trip of 1926 his family made in their Model-T Ford.

I've never attended the Christmas celebration, even though I live less than 50 miles from the tree. The roads are snowy, and it's frightfully cold up in the mountains. But there's an-out-of-this-world celebration that I don't want to miss for any reason. It will be held around another tree—heaven's "ever green" tree of life. That's one celebration none of us want to miss. And God promises us we don't have to, unless we choose not to be there.

Running With the Bulls

I am now giving you the choice between life and death, . . . and I will call heaven and earth to witness the choice you make. Choose life. Deuteronomy 30:19, TEV.

I've heard of people doing stupid things, but each year in a small Spanish city bulls run loose down the middle of the streets. To prove their bravery, grown men risk their lives to run with these terrified, stampeding creatures.

On December 11, 1846, one of the most unusual battles in military history occurred. A battalion of U.S. soldiers, camping along the San Pedro River in Arizona, were attacked by a herd of wild, longhorn bulls. After 45 minutes of battle, men and mules were injured; wagons were damaged. Several of the bulls had to be shot and killed.

It's one thing to defend yourself against a herd of marauding bulls, but quite another to risk your life to "prove" you're tough or cool. Nothing good is ever proved by doing something dangerous, whether it be playing "chicken" on the highway, chugging alcohol, or having sex before marriage.

On the contrary, it takes a strong man to make a wise choice when those around him are acting stupid. It takes a courageous woman to refuse to risk her life and her future by saying no to friends who don't seem to be smart enough to see past the thrill of the moment.

Conner's Sneakers

Consider the lilies how they grow: they toil not, they spin not; and yet I say unto you, that Solomon in all his glory was not arrayed like one of these. Luke 12:27.

You don't understand, Mama; I need those Nikes!" Conner's lower lip protruded almost far enough to trip over. "I've got to have a pair. All the kids have 'em."

Life had changed since Conner's dad left him and his mom. Where there'd been money for most of the 11-year-old's wants, now there was none. And Conner didn't like the change one little bit.

On December 12, 1851, a former U.S. ambassador to Mexico died. Can you figure out what an ambassador has to do with Conner's designer sneakers? Read on!

Joel Roberts Poinsett returned to the United States from Mexico with what has become part of our Christmas traditions. By now I'm sure you've guessed what it is—the Christmas poinsettia plant.

Whether poinsettias, lilies, dandelions—flowers don't worry if their colors are bright. They don't throw a tizzy fit if another plant's blossoms are bigger than theirs.

During the holiday season, when stores spend millions of dollars to plant discontent and greed in your heart, remember the poinsettia and relax. Just as God clothes the radiant poinsettia, He will meet your needs, too.

Home, Sweet Home

He stops wars all over the world; he breaks bows, destroys spears, and sets shields on fire. Psalm 46:9, TEV.

After the Battle of Fredericksburg, one of the bloodiest battles during the Civil War, 10,000 Federal troops and 70,000 Confederates were camped on opposite sides of the Rappahannock River in Virginia. More than 12,000 Federals had been killed or wounded; Confederates lost about 5,000. Thoughts of hate and murder filled the minds of the soldiers on both sides of the river.

At twilight the regimental bands on both sides began their customary evening concerts that, while bivouacked close to one another, became "the battle of the bands."

On this particular night a Federal band played John Howard Payne's "Home, Sweet Home." Then the Confederate bands took up the strain. One after another, the regimental bands of both armies joined in. Books were closed, pens laid aside, games of tag stopped, playing cards drifted to the ground as everyone stopped to listen. Both sides began singing.

At the end of the song the soldiers cheered wildly, jumping up and down and throwing their hats into the air. Mr. Payne's song halted bitterness and hatred between the armies. If there hadn't been a river between them, the war would have ended on the spot.

One day God's song of victory will forever end the battles humans fight. That's a song I look forward to singing. How about you?

14 December

An Empty Shoe Box

He will always make you rich enough to be generous at all times, so that many will thank God for your gifts which they receive from us. 2 Corinthians 9:11, TEV.

Wow! Read that again! "Always . . . rich enough to be generous." I like that! There's no limit to the good deeds you can do at Christmas time, from Toys for Tots to Coats for Kids to food for the rescue mission in your town. You may think, *I'm just a kid; I can't do anything.*

By now, I hope you realize that the "I'm just a kid" excuse is no excuse at all. There is always someone God's kids can help. Try this idea on for size:

Got an empty shoe box? Begin next Christmas's project today with Operation Christmas Child. Throughout the year buy small toys such as jacks or a jump rope, toiletries such as a new toothbrush or comb or hand mirror, maybe a flashlight or a stuffed animal, and place them in your shoe box. When it's full, start another.

In 1999 Operation Christmas Child delivered more than 3 million shoe box gifts to suffering children in 60 countries. Simple and fun . . . but then giving to others is always fun.

Operation Christmas Child may not be for you, but God has a thousand ways for you to help others, regardless of your age or situation.

The Great Snowball Battle

War and its miseries are decreed from that time to the very end. Daniel 9:26, TLB.

The winter of 1863-1864 was brutally cold and bleak. All the Southern soldiers camped outside Dalton, Georgia, could do was to gather wood and try to keep warm between meals.

Separating the Georgian soldiers from the Tennessean troops was a huge ravine. One morning the soldiers awoke to a world covered with a foot or more of snow.

The battle started with a few friendly snowballs tossed between the Tennessee men, then grew into a war between entire companies. Before long the Tennesseans squared off for battle against the Georgians on the other side of the ravine. Five thousand men participated.

Local citizens gathered to watch as hundreds of snowballs filled the air, with men stumbling and tripping over one another to avoid being hit. Finally the Tennesseans broke through the Georgians' line, and the Tennessean colonel ordered his men back to their own camp. Black eyes, bruises, and broken arms were the only casualties.

There will be wars until Jesus returns, but wouldn't it be neat if grown-ups, kids, and nations alike could settle their differences with snowballs instead of bullets?

More About Home

Trust Me. There is plenty of room for you in my Father's home.
John 14:1, Message.

r. and Mrs. Abraham Lincoln invited Italian singer Adelina Patti to the White House in 1862. The president's aides hoped the woman's singing would ease the president's and his wife's grief after the death of their 11-year-old son, Willie.

Miss Patti sang her repertoire of songs, ending with "The Last Rose of Summer," one of the saddest songs of the day. Her last song left Mary Lincoln in tears, and the president covering his face with his hands. While trying to think of a happy song to sing, the president asked her to sing Payne's "Home, Sweet Home."

"'Mid pleasures and palaces though we may roam, be it ever so humble, there's no place like home." The promise of one day going home to live with God forever and to see their precious son comforted the grieving parents.

When Jesus says, "Trust me," He means it. From a tar paper shack beside the railroad track to the presidential White House on Pennsylvania Avenue, Jesus' promise to return and take us "home" to live with Him forever brings an out-of-this-world peace and joy to all God's children at any time of year.

Doubtless in Ohio

If any of you lack wisdom, he should ask of God. . . . But when he asks, he must believe and not doubt. James 1:5, 6, NIV.

In the late 1870s a church held a conference in Indiana. The president of the college where they were meeting had a scientific background. When he spoke, he said, "I believe we are living in a very exciting age."

The bishop of the church said, "What do you see?"

The college president answered, "I believe we are coming to a time when we will see men flying through the air like birds."

To which the bishop grunted in disbelief, "This is heresy! Blasphemy! Flight is reserved for angels. We will have no such talk at this meeting!" After the conference, Bishop Wright went home to his sons, Orville and Wilbur.

On December 17, 1903, at 10:35 a.m., Orville took off into a 27-mile-per-hour wind. He flew for 120 feet for 12 seconds.

Not everyone was impressed. When they wired their sister Katherine of their success, she told the local newspaper editor, who replied, "Isn't it nice they'll be home for Christmas?"

How many dreams fail because someone said something couldn't or shouldn't be done? What dreams do you have that seem impossible? No doubt, God turns impossibilities into possibilities if we trust Him.

Angels' Inn Disguised

Remember to welcome strangers in your homes. There are some who did that and welcomed angels without knowing it. Hebrews 13:2, TEV.

With a week's leave from the Marine Corps, Lance and his wife, Linda, headed home to Seattle for Christmas, a 1,000-mile, 24-hour drive from their home in California. Four hundred miles into their trip their car quit running in the tiny town of Avalon, California.

With nothing else to do, the couple walked to a nearby lighted church, where they were welcomed by a friendly woman. When she learned their predicament, she insisted they come home with her and her husband. For two days they treated Lance and Linda like family.

When the money wired from Lance and Linda's family got lost, their hosts paid the car repair bill. "Repay us when you can," they said. "We want you home for Christmas."

Overcome with gratitude, Linda blurted, "I don't know how to thank you. You've been like angels!"

To which their host replied, "The Bible tells us to entertain strangers, so to us, you're the angels."

Linda and Lance made it home to Washington and on the return trip to their home in southern California repaid their bill. The couple will always remember the time they stayed at the "Angels' Inn" disguised.

War of the Worlds

Fear not, for I have redeemed you; I have called you by name; you are mine. Isaiah 43:1, NIV.

Rhea, come hear this!" Ned turned up the volume on the radio.

His wife paused at the door to the parlor. "What is it?"

"You're not going to believe this!" Ned, his face ashen, leaned forward in his winged-back upholstered chair to hear the words of the announcer more clearly.

"We're being invaded?" Rhea asked in an excited whisper.

He nodded. "By Martians . . ." His words drifted off at the sound of frightened voices coming from the floor model mahogany Philco radio. Rhea sat down on the footstool in front of the radio. In horror the couple listened to the newscast describing a Martian invasion of New Jersey.

Ned and Rhea, as thousands of other Americans, had tuned in late to a radio drama of H. G. Wells's famous novel, *War of the Worlds,* performed by Orson Welles and the Mercury players. The simulated news bulletin of October 30, 1938, sounded so real that people everywhere panicked.

One day the world will be invaded not by Martians, but by God's mighty angels and His Son, Jesus. Many people will panic at the sight of His coming. But for God's children, that day will be cause for celebration, not fear.

363

Happy Birthday, Jesus

The Savior—yes, the Messiah, the Lord—has been born tonight in Bethlehem! Luke 2:11, TLB.

The congregation gathered at the church for the annual Christmas program. Upon entering the sanctuary, each worshipper was given a candle, which the ushers lit as the lights were dimmed.

Suddenly in the dark, with only candles glowing, a 5-year-old girl began to sing, "Happy birthday to you . . ." A chuckle passed through the room. On the second line of the song others joined her. By the end of the simple song everyone was singing full voice.

Experts say "Happy Birthday" is the most sung song in the world. I can't think of a more appropriate time for the song to be sung than at Christmas, to celebrate our Savior's birth, which makes all the other joys of Christmas possible.

Friends of mine celebrate an interesting tradition at their home. On Christmas morning they set a special place for Jesus at their table, complete with homemade birthday cards and presents. (The gifts are things appropriate to give to "needing people in the community.") They have a cake and candles and sing "Happy birthday, Jesus." What a way to begin Christmas Day and to help the youngest to the oldest in the family to remember that Jesus is the reason for the season.

Miracles or Not

You are the God who performs miracles; you display your power among the peoples. Psalm 77:14, NIV.

The genius physicist Albert Einstein once said, "There are two ways to live life. One is as though nothing were a miracle; the other is as though everything is a miracle."

I know Katie would agree. Katie was driving home from work on a country road when a raccoon darted in front of her car. She swerved onto the shoulder of the road to avoid it. After her steering wheel locked, she slammed on the brakes and prayed, "God, help me!" She passed out as her car crashed into a tree.

When she awoke, Katie smelled gasoline and smoke, then saw a kind-faced man peering in the front passenger window. With little effort he opened the mangled door, undid Katie's seat belt, and scooped her into his arms. He set her on the ground several feet away from the wrecked car.

The next thing she knew, paramedics were loading her into an ambulance. When she insisted on thanking the man who'd helped her, the paramedic asked, "What man? When we got here, you were lying on the ground—alone."

Searches to find the gentle stranger failed. But Katie will never forget the "guardian angel" who saved her life.

22 December

Christmas Greetings!

All who are with me send you greetings. Give our greetings to our friends in the faith. God's grace be with you all. Titus 3:15, TEV.

When I was a preschooler, I enjoyed "organizing" the family's Christmas cards into categories: a stack for the trees and candles; one for the Santas and reindeer; one for the Nativity scenes (which included the Magi and the shepherds); one for the snow scenes; and one for the leftover boring ones that were too adult for me to appreciate.

I still love getting Christmas cards and letters (and now e-mail messages) from my friends and family members who live too far away to see. It's fun to learn what's happening in their lives.

Christmas cards go back to 1843 when Londoner Sir Henry Cole commissioned an artist to make 1,000 cards for him to give to his friends. Within 20 years Cole's idea became a Christmas custom.

The apostle Paul spent his days in a Roman prison writing letters to his friends and to his Christian family. A friend of mine combines Paul's letters with Cole's Christmas cards by including with each card appropriate messages from God's Word.

A good idea, huh? What creative way can you share the love of Jesus with your distant friends and family this Christmas season?

A New Song

He taught me how to sing the latest God-song, a praise song to our God. Psalm 40:3, Message.

Franz Gruber watched the snowflakes outside the small church in Oberndorf, Austria, on the night of the annual Christmas program. Behind him the church organ sat broken. "How will the children's choir sing the old carols without accompaniment?" he asked the church's priest.

"We could teach them a new song," the priest suggested as he placed in Franz's hands a copy of a poem he'd written earlier in the afternoon.

Franz silently read the words. "Father Josef," he said, "the words sing themselves. I'm going home to write down the melody before it slips from my mind."

That evening Franz Gruber, Father Josef Mohr, and the children's choir sang the words to what would become the world's best loved Christmas carol, "Silent Night."

If the organ hadn't broken down on that snowy day in 1818, the simple and elegant carol may never have been written.

God promises to give each of us a new song to sing. Sometimes, as with Franz Gruber and Josef Mohr, it takes an apparent tragedy before we stop to listen and appreciate that song. And sometimes the song just comes when we need a song to sing.

Message Out of This World!

And God called the dry land Earth; and the gathering together of the waters called He seas: and God saw it was good. Genesis 1:9, 10, TLB.

On December 24, 1968, a message was broadcast from the crew of *Apollo 8* as the craft appeared on the other side of the moon. They had successfully circled the back side of the moon. Once communications had been reestablished, the NASA controllers and millions of people around the world heard the three astronauts aboard the *Apollo* read the creation story from Genesis. The effect was overpowering as Frank Borman, the commander of the craft, read the last verses of today's text. "'. . . and God saw that it was good.'" He paused, then concluded, "And from the crew of *Apollo 8,* we close with good night, good luck, a Merry Christmas, and God bless all of you—all of you on the good earth."

It had been a chaotic year for America. Martin Luther King, Jr., and Robert Kennedy had been killed. Riots tore apart the nation's cities. And Americans were bitterly divided over the Vietnam War.

That night Apollo's message became the second most important message received from out of this world. The most important message came on Christmas morning 2,000 years ago when the Creator of the universe became a human baby to demonstrate His love for you and me.

Merry Christmas

The shepherds returned, glorifying and praising God for all the things they had heard and seen, which were just as they had been told. Luke 2:20, NIV.

Eight-year-old Kyle was chosen to play the role of the innkeeper for the school Christmas play. It bothered him every time he had to turn Mary and Joseph away from his door.

On the night of the performance, poor Kyle couldn't stand it any longer. Kyle opened the door at Joseph's knock. He paused after Joseph recited his lines, requesting lodging for the night.

Thinking the innkeeper had forgotten his line, the audience held their breath until Kyle began to speak. "I'm sorry, but there's no room in my inn." Before Joseph could turn away from the door, Kyle added, "But you and your wife can come in for chocolate milk and cookies if you'd like."

If you lived in Palestine at the time of Jesus' birth, where would you fit into the Christmas story? Would you be a shepherd? The innkeeper? King Herod? One of the Magi? Another traveler looking for a place to sleep? Or one of the citizens of Bethlehem inconvenienced by the swarm of strangers invading your town?

Think about it. I pray I would be either one of the Magi or a shepherd, waiting and watching for their Savior's arrival. How about you?

26 December

National Whiner's Day

I know what it is to be in need, and I know what it is to have plenty. I have learned the secret of being content in any and every situation. Philippians 4:12, NIV.

Believe it or not, today is National Whiner's Day, a day dedicated to whiners who return Christmas gifts and demand lots of attention. I think the day must have been inspired by a salesclerk in a department store, don't you?

My daughter Kelli worked at Macy's one holiday season, and you wouldn't believe the number of grouchy, dishonest, and nasty people she had to serve.

The purpose of National Whiner's Day is to encourage people to be happy with what they have instead of whining over what they don't have. So you didn't get the latest Nintendo game, or your grandmother gave you another ugly sweater for Christmas. The apostle Paul was in a nasty prison cell when he wrote his encouraging letter to the Philippians. He might have appreciated your grandmother's hand-knitted sweater.

Remember, there's always something for which to be thankful, and there's always someone who's worse off than you.

Ready or Not

Remember, then, what you were taught. . . . If you do not wake up, I will come upon you like a thief, and you will not even know the time when I will come. Revelation 3:3, TEV.

In the months leading up to Christmas 1776, the War of Independence was not going well for General Washington and his troops. Morale was low, and Washington feared that most of his army would quit and go home. So he came up with a plan to cross the Delaware River into New Jersey on Christmas night and surprise-attack the British, who would be groggy after their Christmas celebrations.

A Loyalist farmer who lived alongside the Delaware River spotted the first of the flat-bottomed boats carrying Washington's 2,400 men. He hurried to warn Colonel Rall, the Hessian commander. When he wasn't allowed to talk to the colonel, the farmer scribbled his warning on a piece of paper and gave it to a corporal who rushed it to the colonel's tent, where the colonel and several other officers were playing cards.

Enjoying a winning streak, Rall slipped the note into his vest pocket, planning to read it later. As a result, Washington's army surprised and defeated the British.

Jesus promises in His Word that He will return. If we put off reading His message, His coming will be like a thief in the night instead of an event to celebrate.

28 December

Poor Richard's Bad Advice

Listen to advice and accept instruction, and in the end you will be wise. Proverbs 19:20, NIV.

The first edition of *Poor Richard's Almanack,* by Richard Saunders, was published on December 28, 1732. Benjamin Franklin chose to publish the almanac under a pseudonym, fearing it might appear unseemly for a statesman like himself to write advice for the "common man." The project was so successful, he wrote one every year for 25 years.

Several of his nuggets of wisdom became so well known that later generations thought they came from the Bible. One of these is "God helps them that help themselves." The truth is God doesn't help those who help themselves; God helps those who help others. Which goes to show you that even a wise old statesman like Benjamin Franklin didn't have all the answers.

You and I can be even wiser than Ben if we go to the source of wisdom, God's Word—the Bible.

Hold On!

Let us hold on firmly to the hope we profess, because we can trust God to keep his promise. Hebrews 10:23, TEV.

Chris ambled along the turbulent river swollen from the melting snows of an unexpected midwinter thaw. His thoughts were of a history exam he'd flunked on Friday until he spotted a broken tree trunk stretching out over much of the river. Always one for a challenge, the 13-year-old hopped up on the log and balanced his way along the slippery bark surface to the spot where the log divided into a series of branches.

Suddenly the branch on which he was standing broke, sending him into the raging waters. Chris shouted for help as the river's swift current swept him downstream. He grabbed for tree limbs, but nothing slowed his wild ride downriver.

Eventually Chris grabbed hold of a tree branch lodged in a small clump of debris gathered around a large rock. It held.

An out-of-work logger walking his dog spotted Chris and shouted, "Hold on! I'll be right back!"

Hold on, Chris thought, his fingers aching from the cold. *Oh, dear God, help me to hold on!*

(to be continued)

30 December

I'll Be Back

He reached down from on high and took hold of me; he drew me out of deep waters. Psalm 18:16, NIV.

Pain cramped Chris's fingers; his teeth chattered from the cold. He couldn't feel his toes—his feet either, for that matter. Chris looked down and discovered he'd lost his left sneaker. How much longer could he hold on? Where had the man gone to for help? The Yukon Territory? He knew there was a ranger station less than a mile away.

When it seemed impossible for him to hold on to the branch a minute longer, the logger burst out of the woods, along with several forest rangers. One of the rangers shouted, "Keep holding on," and pointed to the sky.

Chris looked up. A helicopter! As the copter drew nearer, a man leaned out of the door and dangled a looped rope to Chris. "Loop it around your waist and hold on!" he shouted.

Chris obeyed. He felt himself being lifted out of the water and swinging through open air to a field where paramedics waited to take him to the hospital.

God's people are caught in a raging river more dangerous than Chris's. The angry current of sin tries to sweep us to destruction. Our heavenly Rescuer shouts, "Hold on! I'll save you!"

More certain than the return of Chris's rescuer is that Jesus will keep His promise. In the meantime, hold on!

Hide-and-Seek

If you look for him [God], he will let you find him. 2 Chronicles 15:2, TEV.

laying hide-and-seek with a 3-year-old is different than playing the game with older kids. The object is to be found. When it's your turn to hide, you could find a spot where a little child could never find you. But when playing with little ones, you want to be found. That's what makes it fun.

If the toddler has trouble finding you, you call, "Here, Jarod. I'm over here." And he'll follow the sound of your voice.

If you hide in a closet, you might leave the door open and the toe of your shoe in sight. Success brings shouting, dancing, and laughter.

Searching for God is like an adult playing hide-and-seek with a 3-year-old. God, the adult, could hide someplace in His gigantic universe where I, the toddler, wouldn't stand a chance of ever finding Him. But God wants me to find Him.

That's the adventure God has for you and for me. He isn't hiding where you and I can't find Him. Every page in His Word reveals who He is. From a blade of grass between two slabs of concrete to the mighty redwood forest, I can see His fingerprints. And in the heart of His people, I can hear God speaking to me.

Just stop, look, and listen, and He'll be there.